ADD

AND

ZOMBIES

FEARLESS MEDICATION
MANAGEMENT FOR ADD AND ADHD

Wes Crenshaw, PhD ABPP
Kelsey Daugherty, DNP PMHNP-BC
Foreword by William Dodson, MD

Publisher's Cataloging-in-Publication Data
Names: Crenshaw, Wes. | Daugherty, Kelsey.
Title: ADD and zombies : fearless medication management for ADD and ADHD
    / Wes Crenshaw, Kelsey Daugherty.
Description: Lawrence, KS : Family Psychological Press, 2019. | Includes index. |
    Includes 6 illustrations. | Summary: Guides laypeople and consumers in understanding the evaluation, diagnosis, and pharmacology of attention deficit hyperactivity disorder across the age spectrum so they can lead more informed discussions with their prescriber. It integrates medication and psychotherapy into an evidence-based model of care so that clients can advocate for themselves.
Identifiers: LCCN 2019949736 | ISBN 9780985283384 (hardcover) | ISBN
    9781733462372 (pbk.)
Subjects: LCSH: Attention-deficit hyperactivity disorder--Chemotherapy. | Attention-deficit hyperactivity disorder--Diagnosis. | Attention-deficit hyperactivity disorder--Treatment. | Self-care, Health. | BISAC: MEDICAL / Diagnosis. | MEDICAL / Neurology. | MEDICAL / Pharmacology. | PSYCHOLOGY / Psychopathology / Attention-Deficit Disorder (ADD-ADHD).
Classification: LCC RJ506.H9 C74 2019 | DDC 616.8589--dc23
LC record available at https://lccn.loc.gov/2019949736

Published in the United States of America by

FAMILY
PSYCHOLOGICAL PRESS

Also available on Kindle and in
library binding from Amazon.com

We dedicate this book to our clients. Formal training is important, but well beyond our time spent in classrooms and textbooks, you've taught us everything we know. We hope that by sharing your collective medication management journey with others, we can shed a little light on that path, making it an easier, safer, and more productive journey for those who want to take it.

The vignettes in this book are based on actual clinical cases seen over the last ten years of practice. Identifying details have been disguised in such a way as to meet American Psychological Association Ethical Guideline 4.07 (www.apa.org) for publishing case examples. Where we thought the veil might be thin enough for a client to recognize himself or herself, we asked for and received permission to publish the vignette with the understanding that it contained enough changes to protect confidentiality. The vignettes were selected to represent a broad sample of the medication management cases we commonly see in clinical practice with clients having ADD and ADHD.

CONTENTS

CONTENTS

Acknowledgements

We'd like to thank the staff of Family Psychological Services, LLC for contributing their insights on ADD and ADHD to this book. Additionally, Dr. Wes would like to thank his wife for tolerating the many hours put into this book and his children for allowing themselves to be guinea pigs over the years and for releasing tidbits from their experience to be shared with readers. We also appreciate Peggy Williams who has been a terrific editor for this material. And finally, to Vada Snider and the people of Newton, Kansas we offer a special thanks for hosting us several times on writer's retreats. If you're in Newton some time, don't miss the German Buffet at the Breadbasket. We never do.

Foreword

By virtue of the fact that you are holding this book in your hands, or reading about it online, you or a loved one are considering whether to come face to face with all that it means to take charge of ADD or ADHD. I can understand why you hesitate. It's hard to separate good, reliable information on this topic from the nonsense and intentional disinformation that's so common today. Where should you turn? Who should you believe? If you're like the vast majority of people in your neurological situation, you've tried everything you can think of already to not have to come to this moment. You've tried diets, bribery, taking away toys or privileges, shaming, admonishments to try harder, or simply waiting in the hope that you or your loved one will grow out of it. Nothing has worked for more than a few days at best.

It's a good thing you've opened *ADD and Zombies* right now. It's the companion to Dr. Wes Crenshaw's popular 2014 book *I Always Want To Be Where I'm Not: Successful Living for ADD and ADHD* that masterfully explains what it means to live your life with an ADD-style nervous system. *ADD and Zombies* takes me back thirty years, leaving me to wonder, "Where was this book when I was starting my first medical practice for folks with ADD and ADHD?" At that time there was a growing cottage industry of books describing what it was like to have ADD and all of the obstacles it posed for leading a full and happy life. My response back then was, "OK, I get it! But what do I do about it?" *ADD and Zombies* answers that question. It's all about what to do. It is, in my experience, the best book on medication management currently available to either laypeople or prescribers.

And why is such a book written by a family psychologist and not a physician who prescribes these medications daily? Because Dr. Crenshaw, with the help of Dr. Kelsey Daugherty, PMHNP, has the wonderful ability to explain highly arcane scientific information and jargon in everyday language and logic without dumbing it down. In their descriptions, there is always a genuine respect for the patient's and family's ability to understand this unique way of living and to become a full participant in their own management of ADHD.

Crenshaw and Daugherty recognize two things that are generally lacking in other books on treatment. First, they give more than lip service to the fact that while stimulant medications are dramatically effective, they are insufficient by themselves. Meds need to be paired with therapy. Because one without the other will lead to a disappointing outcome, the authors combine the two in order to obtain not a "good enough" outcome, but an optimal one.

Second, the authors learned what they know in the very best way possible, in the trenches of day-to-day practice. The treatment of ADD is unique in the field of medicine in that it has no textbook. Until *ADD and Zombies,* there was no source to teach you or your clinician how to take a scientific approach to making an accurate diagnosis, choosing and finetuning medication to your particular body and brain, managing side effects, and monitoring the outcome. Successful practitioners have instead taken what little they learned about ADD in their formal training and become astute observers of their own practices, trying to figure out in vivo what worked and what didn't. Hence the name of this book. Prescribers who have not been able to figure this out on their own have produced more than their fair share of zombies.

The authors are the first to acknowledge this; that people have had unpleasant, zombie-inducing experiences with these medications, but equally quick to point out that these shortcomings are not so much in the medications themselves, but rather that many clinicians have never been shown how to use them effectively. Stimulants are among the most effective, safest, well-researched, and potentially tolerable medications in all of psychiatry—if you know what you are doing. Drs. Crenshaw and Daugherty give a master class in how to use them both conceptually and using real-world patient examples that make this sometimes esoteric information accessible to anyone seeking to know what they're getting themselves into and how to do it better.

The zombie outcome is not simply the fault of any given prescriber. It results from a failure of the medical education establishment worldwide. Half of all pediatricians report they do not feel confident in treating ADD and over ninety percent of psychiatrists who treat adults received no training about ADD during their four-year residencies. *ADD and Zombies* gives those professionals the chance to gain mastery right along with you. If they don't jump at this chance—and many will not—you'll find yourself in the awkward position of knowing more than your doctor. Crenshaw and Daugherty know the importance of this and made it the first step of the treatment process in Chapter 5, *Finding the Right Prescriber.*

I am also thankful that Drs. Crenshaw and Daugherty realize that many folks who decide to seek treatment for ADD will feel attacked on many levels. In Chapter 2, *Yes, ADD Does Exist*, the authors prepare you for this with a sort of "self-defense manual" so that you're ready to handle the skewed logic, misinformation, outright stupidity, prejudice, conspiracy theories, lies, shaming, sabotage, obstruction from schools, and just plain mean-spiritedness that you may encounter. You already know who these people are, those who are often in error but never in doubt, those who are eager to jump at any chance to tell anyone that what they're doing to treat this neurological disorder is wrong. Crenshaw and Daugherty have been there before, many times. They can help you through this unpleasant storm to emerge relatively unscathed.

The stated goal of *ADD and Zombies* is very simple: to help you become an educated consumer. But the book ends up doing much, much more than that. It teaches you how to become your own expert, an equal partner in your care or the care of your ADD loved ones. It lays the groundwork for a new type of collaborative doctor-patient relationship that neither you nor most doctors have experienced before. Perhaps most importantly, you will walk with Crenshaw and Daugherty on a journey toward mastery of an area of life that has stumped most people up to this point. It's a wonderful feeling to begin that journey and even more wonderful to arrive.

So now, get started. A new world and a new way of living await you.

William Dodson, MD, Contributor
ADDitude Magazine

Should I Read This Book?

Not I, not anyone else can travel that road for you,
You must travel it for yourself.
It is not far, it is within reach.
Perhaps you have been on it since you were born, and did not know,
Perhaps it is everywhere on water and on land.

— Walt Whitman, "Song of Myself" in *Leaves of Grass*

- *Dr. Wes* -

Taking medication for Attention Deficit Hyperactivity Disorder[1] or any other mental health condition, isn't like taking an antibiotic and waiting for your strep throat to disappear or swallowing an antihistamine and banishing your allergies back into the trees. Getting it right takes a good working relationship between you, your prescriber, your therapist, and your people[2]. We didn't come up with this wild idea on our own. The American Psychological Association notes that effective

---

[1] This is the official and rather baffling diagnostic label from the Diagnostic and Statistical Manual (DSM-5) that yields the acronym ADHD, of which there is an inattentive type, a hyperactive type, and a combined type. However, throughout this book we're going to refer to this condition generically as ADD, because the vast majority of people who have it are not hyperactive. Moreover, most laypeople refer to this condition simply as ADD, and laypeople are the audience for this book. When we are citing another source or talking about the hyperactive type, we will use the term ADHD.

[2] In this book, "your people" can include friends, relatives, coworkers, partners, and anyone else who knows you well and/or with whom you have frequent interplay.

treatment requires "an integrated approach to healthcare delivery" in which mental health providers work with prescribers to determine the best treatment for each patient.[3] The American Psychiatric Association notes, "Psychotherapy is often used in combination with medication to treat mental health conditions... For many people combined medication and psychotherapy treatment is better than either alone[4]." The Centers for Disease Control and Prevention (CDC) agree[5] as does the American Academy of Pediatrics[6].

Thus, in 2013, while writing *I Always Want to Be Where I'm Not: Successful Living with ADD and ADHD*[7], I felt I had to include a chapter about medication management. The problem was that I'd just left my old practice and started a new one, and Kelsey Daugherty, the nurse I planned to hire to do our meds, was still in graduate school at the University of Missouri, Kansas City. This left me, a psychologist, without sufficient credibility to opine much on the subject of medication management. So, despite many years working closely with expert prescribers, I opened Chapter 13 of the first edition of that book by noting,

> *I am not a medical doctor or a psychiatric nurse practitioner (APRN).* I can't prescribe medications, but I am an educated consumer of them. That's what I want you to become, too.

Enhancing your consumer IQ is also the goal for this book, but adding Dr. Kelsey's perspective on the research, theory, and practice of medication management offers readers vastly more practical information than I'm qualified to provide on my own. Kelsey began prescribing part-time at our office, Family Psychological Services, in January 2015 as an APRN while completing her Doctor of Nursing Practice (DNP)[8]. She brings a wealth of the latest knowledge to this volume along with a vibrant style of client interaction. Some of her expertise is shared in

---

[3] www.apa.org/monitor/2012/06/prescribing.aspx

[4] www.psychiatry.org/patients-families/psychotherapy

[5] www.cdc.gov/ncbddd/adhd/guidelines.html

[6] pediatrics.aappublications.org/content/128/5/1007

[7] amazon.com/dp/0985283300/

[8] The Master of Science in Nursing (MSN) is the terminal credential to prescribe in all states that allow independent prescription privilege to advanced nurse practitioners. The DNP is an advanced practice credential requiring additional training in both clinical diagnosis and treatment and research in psychiatric nursing.

her own words, but there's rarely a passage written in my voice that does not reflect her influence. I've learned a lot writing this book with her, so I know how much you can get out of reading it.

We've included in these pages, case vignettes. Some you'll identify with, others you won't, because we've described a broader array of situations than could ever relate to any one person. Likewise, to make this material relatable to the largest number of readers, we often describe "people with ADD" in shorthand as if you're all alike, when we know that's not true. At other times we go to great lengths to point out critical differences between cases.

We imagined three audiences while writing this book. Each will get something a little different from reading it. They are as follows:

People Who Have ADD or Think They Might. Maybe you've been diagnosed with ADD or suspect you should be and are wondering whether medication could help your symptoms. Perhaps you're already on medication but you aren't thrilled with the result. Or, maybe you're satisfied but want to learn more about how to maximize your medication's efficacy[9] and minimize its side effects.

This book is for you. We'll often speak directly to you, just as we might a client in our office. Of course, no matter how fantabulous our advice, it's no substitute for getting your own prescriber. So, if you don't already have one or you'd like to compare your prescriber's model to ours, we'll advise you in Chapter 5 on what characteristics we like to see in an ADD medication practice.

Some books sell gimmicks like "Cure ADD in Five Easy Steps with Exercise and Diet" or "Balance Your Brain with Video Games." We'll critique a few of those alternative perspectives in Chapter 11. You're free to read one of those authors instead, but a lot of books sell because they make change look really fun and simple, when we all know it's not. This book is about doing what's hard—getting a good diagnosis, finding a therapist and prescriber, taking powerful medications the right way and learning to manage their side effects—so life turns out better and easier in the long run. Other authors spend their ink trying to figure any angle they can to deny that ADD exists. That's weird, but we'll discuss it anyhow in Chapter 2 and explain why it matters to you.

---

[9] The ability of your medication produce a desired or intended result.

As a savvy consumer, you might want to research the credentials of anyone handing out advice. As the market has grown, so has the crowd of people claiming to be ADD experts. I've already given you Kelsey's credentials. Here are mine: I hold a PhD in Counseling Psychology from the University of Kansas and I'm Board Certified in Couple and Family Psychology by the American Board of Professional Psychology. I do a lot of media on ADD and write often for *ADDitude* magazine. Just as important, I've spent twenty-eight years and nearly 30,000 hours working face-to-face with clients who have ADD as their primary diagnosis. When I'm not doing that, I'm overseeing nine full time clinicians (and one full time cat) who see clients five days a week. Not all our clients have ADD, but a substantial portion do. In the six years since *I Always Want to Be Where I'm Not* came out, I've spent another five thousand hours with clients and during that time, Kelsey and I have worked constantly to revise and perfect our approach.

This book is a culmination of that effort. We hope it will help you get your medication management on the path to a better tomorrow and hold you steady there.

People Who Love People With ADD. Perhaps your partner, child, roommate, or friend has ADD or ADHD and you want to help improve his or her life, or maybe even save that relationship. You might wonder if medication is really the answer for this person's case or just another marketing ploy by big pharma? You might even question the diagnosis itself. I know how you feel. I've raised two ADHD children of my own and I understand how hard it can be to keep them on a right road and between the white lines (literally and figuratively). As we'll discuss often in this book, there's a love-hate relationship ADD people have with their medication regimen. Helping you and your loved one feel more love and less hate for meds can make all the difference in the world.

This book is also for you. Use it like a reference manual for your ADD loved one to help him or her put all our good medication advice to work on a daily basis. It may not make that task easier, but it can make the time you spend on it more productive and efficient.

Prescribers. Perhaps you're a psychiatrist, primary care doctor, pediatrician, or psychiatric mental health nurse practitioner (PMHNP), and you prescribe medication for ADD and ADHD. You may see more than your share of complicated cases. Perhaps you struggle to sort out your approach to co-occurring disorders, balancing ADD and anxiety, or parsing out depressive from inattentive symptoms. You might worry about stimulant abuse or tolerance building and how to respond to each. Maybe you feel like you're playing medication whack-a-mole, reducing the symptoms for one disorder and making them worse for another.

This book is for you, too. Together, Kelsey and I have spent thousands of hours talking to people with ADD and their families, not just about symptoms and dosages but about the deeper meaning and impact of medication in their lives. There's no substitute for that kind of dialog. If you can't afford the time in your busy practice to build your own database of client experiences, we'll share ours.

Compared to a lot of literature on this topic, you'll find this book an easy read because we wrote it not in the vernacular of medical school, but in the words of the people we see. From our perspective, that's the best language of all to communicate the important concepts of treatment. When people come to see us, they don't really want to talk to a psychologist or doctoral nurse practitioner. They want to talk to people who've learned something about how psychology and medication can change their lives. If you read this book in that same spirit, you'll pick up some tips you can use with your patients tomorrow.

- Dr. Kelsey -

I tell all my new clients that I never meet any strangers at intake, because by the time they get to me, I've gotten to know them through their assigned therapist. Working closely with the same individual, family, or marital therapists who see my clients allows for "real time" updates on their challenges and progress in therapy, offering me a wealth of clinical information upon which to base targeted medical interventions. This is the beauty of the integrative treatment model we practice at our clinic and recommend on every page of this book. Having done it now for several years, I can't imagine practicing any other way, nor can my clients. Many don't realize how unique the experience is.

As a PMHNP, I manage medications for clients from all backgrounds and walks of life, gaining in the process a broad experience and proficiency. The diversity of specialties and know-how among our staff challenges me to develop medication regimens for people who don't all fit into the same box. Quite a few don't fit into any boxes at all, leading us to create unique understandings for each of them, not just pull a label from a book and make it fit their situation. Memorizing a list of ADD symptoms means little if we can't recognize and help our clients gauge the impact and improvement of their symptoms. Making clinical decisions based on words like "typical" or "supposed to" distances us from the people sitting in front of us. Prescribing to a diagnosis devalues our clients and ignores their life experiences which in turn limits clinical outcomes and reduces treatment satisfaction. In this book, we'll explain how to go beyond labels to get deeper into the experience of what it means to have ADD in a variety of contexts.

Being surrounded by therapists also reminds me of the value of dialectal thinking: accepting that two seemingly opposite things can both be true. The complexities of life are vast but the ways in which symptoms impair client functioning are often similar. I wish I had a dollar for every time a client looked at me as if I were clairvoyant when, part-way through the intake session, I say, "I bet there have been times where you got a zero on a homework assignment that you completed on time but didn't turn in," or "I bet you've mastered the art of looking busy while never really getting anything done." I don't have a crystal ball and neither does Wes. We just know what to look for and ask about because, over time, our clients have taught us well.

In these pages, we'll share what we've learned to help you develop a framework for assessing the positive and negative changes that come from medication management. We'll do our best to put into that plain language Wes is so fond of speaking, how unseen activity at the molecular level influences the observable behavior of you and your loved one. Most importantly, we'll help you have a more productive conversation with your prescriber, one that extends well beyond "I just can't seem to focus" or "I need a higher dosage of my stimulant."

Now that you have a pretty good idea of where Wes and I are headed in this book, you can decide if you want to take that journey with us, as many have in our clinical practice.

We genuinely hope you do.

From Zombie to Expert

Tell me and I forget, teach me and I may remember, involve me
and I learn.

— Xun Kuang, Confucian Philosopher

- Dr. Wes -

"I'm really at my wits end with Josh." Jeb shook his head and took a
deep, frustrated breath. "It's hard enough being a single dad raising a
teenage boy without a mom. This whole ADD thing is just getting to
us both."

Susan died when Josh was just six. Until Josh was twelve, his previous
therapist considered his symptoms of inattention and distraction to be
related to the trauma of losing his mom at such an early age. However,
now that Josh was in middle school, that therapist felt she'd done all
she could with play therapy and trauma work. Something else was
wrong. His grades had tanked, he wasn't as mature as his peers, and
his lying was driving away friends and irritating his father to the point
that Jeb had grounded him six out of the last seven weeks. At that
point, the play therapist referred him to our office for an ADD evaluation. He'd been seen by another therapist who found that he easily
met criteria, and he'd begun stimulants about six weeks before this interview. Yet, things weren't off to a great start.

"Dr. Kelsey told me she prescribed you Vyvanse, Josh. You've been
on it for a while now. Have you felt any difference?"

Jeb didn't wait for his son to answer. "Don't even lie, Josh. Don't tell him you've been 'on it' when you've only taken it maybe half the time. The other days you just cheeked the pill."

"You cheek your pill?" I gave him my 'huh?' facial distortion and then a slight smile. "You are aware that cheeking isn't a good way to get Vyvanse into your system, right?"

"Yeah," Josh said. "I mean, no. I don't always cheek it. Sometimes I take it and, yeah, I know that's not right."

"You have to take it every single day," Jeb said. "Or else it won't work and you won't get better."

"Wait a second," I said. "That's not exactly how Vyvanse works. Like all stimulants, it's only in his system for a brief time, maybe eight hours. It's not like an antidepressant where it has to build up a level to be effective. Kind of the opposite, really. The more you take it, the less effective it is."

"Oh, yeah," Jeb said. "I remember Kelsey saying that. But how's it going to work on the days he doesn't take it? It won't, will it?"

"Nope." I turned back to Josh. "Which days do you take it?"

"I don't know. It's kinda random. Like, if I think I'm going to need it that day, then I take it."

"Really?" I asked. "How can you know if you're going to need your stimulant on Monday or Wednesday, but not Thursday? Are you like psychic or something?"

Josh smirked. "I just don't like taking it unless I have to."

"What's not to like?" I already knew his answer. I've heard it many times.

"I don't like how it makes me feel," Josh said. "Like, I take it and it makes me into a zombie."

"You took it yesterday," Jeb said. "I watched you swallow. And then you came home and actually did some homework, and you told me you got an 'A' on your algebra test. Of course, I didn't believe you because you lie so much, so I got on Skyward and I was like, 'Oh my god. He got an 'A.'"

"Is that true?" I asked.

"Sorta. I mean maybe it like, woke me up a little. I don't know. I just take it and all I feel like doing is sitting around reading a book. Like this." Josh raised his hands as if holding an invisible book, leaned forward in a stiff position, and stared blankly into space.

"Right," I said. "We call that studying."

"Me and my friends call it being zombified." Josh dropped his hands and slumped back into the couch. "I don't like it."

I offered a sardonic nod. "So, basically you and your friends associate reading, studying, and getting 'As' with having your brains eaten by roving bands of the undead?"

"That's what I'm talking about," Jeb said. "Even when something is helping him, he refuses any good it can do. He'd rather be jacking around with his friends and getting in trouble and then lying his way out of it instead of doing what he's supposed to be doing in school."

"One of the most important rules at this clinic is that everyone is on the team, and we have to work together. That includes teenagers and even younger kids. You're not just somebody we do stuff to, Josh. You're our client, and we're the servants of your best interests. So, before you give up on meds..." I turned to Jeb. "And before you give up on Josh, I'd like to discuss how we can all get what we want. Okay?"

Like images in a mirror, both gave vacant, skeptical nods.

"Josh," I said. "You want to not feel weird, right?"

"Right. Like I want to be fun and spontaneous. Not all serious."

"But school *is* serious," Jeb said. "And all I want is for you to not end up pulling lumber at Home Depot."

"That's actually my dream job," I said. "At least when I retire. I spend hours in there. But I get your point. I remember you saying that until you finished your degree in night classes, you pulled a lot of lumber."

"Exactly, and I messed up my back. I don't want Josh to make the mistakes I did, partying too much, bombing out of school, and ending up breaking his ass for ten years trying to make up for lost time."

"Josh, would you consider making a deal? Could we divide your time up into serious and fun so that you'd actually mean to do what you were doing. Like, when it's time to have fun, you'd be all-in fun and when it's time to be serious you'd be all-in serious."

"So, wait. Then I'd only take medicine during the serious times?"

"Pretty much." I leaned back in the chair and twirled my glasses by the hinge. "I think I could get Kelsey to go for that. But, Jeb, she'd require you to be giving out the meds and Josh, you'd have to agree not to cheek them, and if you cheated even once, your dad would start putting them in a drink and watching you drink it, because this is like science. We have to know what's really happening to make changes. So, how about it?"

"I'm up for trying anything," Jeb said.

"I'd maybe try that," Josh said. "But I've got one more question. If I've got a track meet, do I still have to take it that day? I don't even feel like running my best when I'm on it."

"In your grade, track meets happen after school, right?"

"Uh huh." Josh nodded.

"Hm. How about we try this? On those days, let's ask Kelsey if you can take half your usual dose in the morning. That won't be so great for school but it will be out of your system by mid-afternoon, so you should have enough impulsive energy for track. I can probably write an accommodation letter so they let you take your tests on track days earlier in the morning when your meds are kicked in or maybe the following Monday morning when your stimulant is its strongest."

"How do we do a partial dose?" Jeb asked. "It's in a capsule."

"That whole dissolving it in a drink thing I mentioned. With Vyvanse, you can create a suspension solution with the contents of the capsules[10]. So, maybe Josh takes half to two-thirds of his normal dose on a short med Friday. You could also do that on weekends if he has homework. He could take a partial dose and work on homework in the morning and then have the rest of the day to himself. And if he doesn't have any school work, maybe he can skip that day. If Kelsey agreed to do your meds that way, would you agree to 100% compliance, Josh?"

---

[10] See Chapter 6

"We could try it," Josh said.

"We don't actually 'try' things here," I said. "We tend to either be willing to do something or say that we are not willing. Are you willing?"

"If we did it like that, then yes, I'd be willing to do it until our next appointment."

"I say, let's try it—or I mean, I'm willing to do my part." Jeb turned to his son. "I want your education to be for you, Josh. I've already been to high school. I don't need to go again. All of what we're doing here is about you. So, if this helps, great."

"You know, Josh," I said. "If when you're on stimulant you learn how to think about thinking and learning—we call that metacognition— then even when you're off of it, you'll have trained your brain to operate that way, and even when you're on short- or off-days, things will go a little better."

"Cool." Josh gave me a thumbs-up.

"You know," I said. "Not only are you on the team, but really you have to be the captain. I just want you to give medication a fair try and see if it doesn't make a positive difference. Less blank-eyed zombie and more thoughtful scholar."

"We'll see." Josh laughed. "But, I think maybe you're taking this a little too far."

Becoming Your Own Expert

Whether you're currently on your own ADD journey or accompanying a loved one on theirs, I understand what you're going through. As a psychologist, I've been down this path many times with many clients. There's no substitute for that kind of real life clinical practice. Except one—being the parent of two ADHD kids. Alex, now sixteen, was diagnosed with ADHD in first grade. His sister, Alyssa, now twenty-three, was diagnosed in second grade. Both have been medicated with stimulants ever since and both have been successful students.

Alex has been able to tell you when he's on too much or too little medication since about second or third grade. He likes being focused so he can keep up with, and at times, exceed his peers. He feels uncomfortable when he has to take a stimulant break (Chapter 9). It's fun to be spontaneous and unguided for a day or two, but he understands the importance of getting things done and without meds much will remain unfinished. That's because, unlike Josh, Alex has grown up experiencing how his brain is supposed to work and expecting it to work that way. Being on medication doesn't feel strange to him. Being off it does.

Alex deals with some side effects. His appetite is so bad that we cut his dosage on weekends to help him eat, supplement his diet with nutritional drinks, and let him eat small meals late in the evening, strategies we'll discuss in Chapter 8. He can seem emotionally flat on stimulants and at times a bit irritable, particularly late in the day. But we all agree the pros outweigh the cons, so the decision is an easy one.

To avoid The Zombie Effect you'll have to become an expert on ADD and how it intersects your life.

That's proven even truer for my daughter, Alyssa. Not only did she graduate from college in 2019 with a major in accounting, a minor in criminal justice, and a 3.93 GPA, she completed a master's degree in accounting in 2020 and is headed for law school in the fall. While stimulant medication doesn't account for all of her success, without it she would never have graduated on time or come this far. She too experiences side effects, including irritability and headaches, but to reach her goal of working as a forensic accountant, Alyssa knows she needs to maintain a consistent medication regimen. Even driving a car is hard for her without stimulants, as she learned recently when she rear-ended another driver while off meds. Oops. Fortunately, I'm also a good mechanic and body man.

Not everyone with ADD or ADHD will have as great a response to stimulants as my kids have had, particularly if they start later in life. But if you want to do as well on medication as the vast majority of the clients Kelsey and I see, you'll have to do more than show up once or twice at your doctor's office, answer a few questions, and drop by the pharmacy. To avoid The Zombie Effect—feeling overmedicated and underwhelmed—you'll have to become an expert on ADD and how it intersects your life. That means setting up and participating in a treatment team, practicing good communication, applying the scientific method, seeing a therapist, and working the program you and your providers devise.

There are several reasons for this. First, when it comes to psychopharmaceuticals, med management is a lot more complicated than you've been led to believe by friends, prescribers, pharmaceutical companies, and popular media. We are, after all, talking about your brain: the three pounds of tissue that make you you. Because your three pounds isn't exactly the same as anyone else's, you're not going to express the effects of medication quite the same way other brains do. Likewise, as a matter of genetic predisposition, your body won't process medication exactly the way other bodies do. Though a good evaluation (Chapter 3) can do a lot to predict which medications will work best for you, there remains a fair amount of trial and error in getting to an optimal regimen (Chapter 7).

Second, after initiating a regimen, we can't tap into your brain and test to see if you're less ADD (or depressed or anxious or anything else) after taking the medication. We rely on you to share your "phenomenological experience[11]" which, in tandem with data from your people, guides every decision point in treatment.

In this book, Kelsey and I will teach you everything we've learned about med management, so you can get started building your personal expertise. As you're reading, please keep these points in mind.

- While Kelsey is a great prescriber of psychopharmaceuticals, she is not *your* prescriber, nor am I your therapist. This book is not a substitute for professional consultation. It's designed to help you carry your end of an intelligent conversation with your treatment team[12]. We've even included citations you might want to look up and diplomatically share with them to improve your treatment plan.

---

[11] What you perceive with your senses, subjectively consider with your mind, and explain to others as your experience.

[12] If you don't yet have a treatment team, we wrote several chapters on how to assemble one.

- Kelsey and I see as clients a fair number of medical professionals and their family members. We've learned that unless a physician is specialized in this area of practice, he or she may not be familiar with these treatment protocols. Many are open to learning and we've taught quite a few. That said, *do not* take this book in, point to a certain paragraph, and say, "Dr. Kelsey and Dr. Wes say you have to do it this way." That's a good way to infuriate any physician or PMHNP. On the other hand, if your prescriber doesn't see you as a key part of the team or isn't interested in your input, you're probably in the wrong office. See Chapter 5.

- Because we organized this book to be accessible to consumers, everything we discuss is reductive—taking complicated stuff and making it seem simpler than it is. When working with your prescriber, be willing to embrace those complications.

- We do not knowingly own any stock in any product we're going to discuss in this book. It's possible that one of the mutual funds that our brokers manage has invested in a pharmaceutical company or two, but we don't keep track of that, so we don't know. Though we've been asked from time to time, neither of us has taken any money or other premiums from pharmaceutical companies to speak about their products nor have we done so for free. Pharmaceutical reps do give us samples and discount cards to help our clients save money or try out various medications before committing their money (Chapter 7), but we're far too rebellious a pair to let things like that influence our recommendations to clients or readers.

If this "becoming an expert" business seems overwhelming right now, notice your anxiety and make a committed decision whether to continue. This book isn't subtitled *Fearless Medication Management for ADD and ADHD* for nothing. But rest assured, the whole thing will become easier as you learn more and gain experience. It happens every day in our office and it can and will happen for you.

Yes, ADD Does Exist

> The good thing about science is that it's true whether or not you believe in it.
>
> — Neil deGrasse Tyson

- Dr. Wes -

"Mom!" Lisa pushed herself to the farthest end of the couch opposite her mother. "Why can't you just accept this? It explains everything I've been struggling with for like, ever. Why I just basically gave up in the spring semester, and I was like, 'Screw school, I don't care.' And why I was headed that way during the fall term, until I—I just was."

Mrs. Wilson looked more uncomfortable than usual, which was saying something. I'd once asked her if she understood the toxic level of anxiety present in her home. She looked back at me and uttered a single word, "Yes."

This made Lisa stand out like a sore thumb, the single ADD person in a family of very anxious people who, no matter how much they might love her, did not understand her. At least that's how I'd come to view her case thus far. Now I was thinking I'd missed something.

"You just didn't buckle down and put forth the needed effort," Mrs. Wilson said. "You need to be more like your sister. Anna may not be the smartest girl in any given class but she knows how to get that 'A' because she puts in the work. And when she comes up a little short, her teachers can see her effort, so they give her a little extra help."

"Well, duh, Mom." Lisa furrowed her brow, pouring all of the intensity she could muster into her five foot frame. "That's kind of the definition of ADD, now isn't it? Not putting forth effort. Coming up shorter than other people. Teachers hating you."

"That's a little harsh," I said. "But I get your frustration."

"When your father and I were young, we just didn't have all these diagnoses and medicines to fall back on. We were expected to do our work, be respectful, and not make excuses for poor performance."

She was probably right. Lisa was the last of six children. When Mrs. Wilson was forty-three, she had been told by her OB/GYN that she was in early menopause. Lisa was born eleven months later.

Mrs. Wilson turned to me. "I just don't understand how you came to this conclusion that Lisa has ADD. You didn't do a brain scan or a genetic test to confirm that. Shouldn't we look further before jumping to any conclusions?"

"Well," I said, choosing my inflection carefully to avoid condescension. "You, Mr. Wilson, Lisa and two roommates all completed the Conners Adult ADHD Rating Scales. I sent email links and you filled them out."

"I remember."

"Do you remember how I scored?" Lisa asked. "I was in like, the bazillionth percentile or something."

"It was actually the ninety-third," I said. "Your mom and dad scored you even higher than you scored herself." I turned back to Mrs. Wilson. "You rated her almost off the chart." I glanced at Lisa. "Can I send her your results?"

"Please do." Lisa folded her arms and looked away.

"We were very exasperated with her at the time. She was on the verge of failing out of sophomore year, and I think that colored our scores— a reverse halo effect, if you will. Besides, I don't see how those tests can measure anything. They're just checklists of opinions."

"Oh my god." Lisa threw herself half over the side of the couch. My office cat, Grace, jumped from her bed on the coffee table and prepared for action.

"Actually, Mrs. Wilson, the tests are norm-referenced and standardized so they compare Lisa to women of her age. The Conners is a widely accepted, valid, and reliable assessment of ADD. But if you want a broader neurological and academic assessment, I can set that up with the University. It's more expensive however, and not a lot more reliable. And, just to be clear, there's no blood or genetic test for ADD. I wish there were. There are brain scans that some clinics provide, but they aren't covered by insurance, they're *really* expensive, and they don't add much to the prediction of ADD beyond what we have here. I can make it happen, but I can't recommend it."

"Why are we even talking about this? I'm an adult and I can make my own decisions and I want to take the effing[13] medicine!"

I addressed Lisa. "We're talking about this because your mother and father have apprised me that if you are put on stimulant medication, they aren't going to pay for further services, and they will ask you to move home and withdraw from college."

Lisa stared at her mom as tears welled up in her eyes. "Why would you do something like that to me?"

"We aren't willing to keep investing in your education if you're not taking advantage of it. And, frankly, neither your father nor I believe in ADD or ADHD or whatever they call it now. We've seen the news, and we know how many young people are misusing and getting addicted to these medications, and we're not going to support you becoming one of them. If you can't make it at the University, you can come home and attend junior college."

"This isn't about me," Lisa wept. "It's about you. You didn't like that therapist your mom made you see back in 1979 or whatever, and you're taking that out on me. Things are different now. People get help."

"I will admit that those experiences made me skeptical of psychiatry, but I think I have good reason. That doctor put me on medicines that made me worse, simply because I didn't obey my parents. And that was even before these big companies started pouring millions of dollars into marketing, trying to convince us that everyone has something wrong with them. Let's remember that my master's degree—"

---

13 Lisa did not, in fact, say "effing," but we've tried to keep this book PG-13.

"Is in business administration, and you took a marketing class, yada yada." Lisa leaned into her mom and pounded out every syllable. "Well, guess what? I'm never going to have a college degree if we don't do something about this. I'll end up like Dad, depending on you to pay my way for the rest of my life. Is that what you want?"

"That's quite unfair, Lisa," Mrs. Wilson huffed. "Your father's strength lies in his art, and you know how hard it is to find a job teaching."

I'd been wondering about Lisa's dad since the day two months ago when Mrs. Wilson brought Lisa in for her intake. When I'd asked about him, his education, and his line of work, Mrs. Wilson said he'd received his bachelor's in the mid-1980s and was now looking to change careers. She clearly didn't want to go further into it, at least with Lisa present. I mentally kicked myself for not digging deeper. ADD is highly heritable[14]. I'd picked up on the anxiety among the other family members, but I'd dropped the ball on ADD.

Mrs. Wilson continued. "I bet half the women in my mother's group at church have kids on some kind of medication. It's a national—"

"Mom! Your attitude is always like 'why pay to be better if you can be miserable for free?'"

"Hold up, you two," I said. "Can we go back to something we discussed in the first interview? Tell me again about Mr. Wilson's education and career path? He did complete a college degree, right?"

Mrs. Wilson grimaced a bit. "He did, but—"

"Yeah, Mom, tell him." Lisa didn't give her a chance to respond. "Dad only finished with a bachelor's in art history because Mom stayed up with him seven nights a week keeping him on task. She literally wrote his senior thesis. Does that sound familiar? Did you rate any items like that on those tests we took, Mom? Like, maybe I'm an apple and the tree isn't very far away?"

"That only proves my point," Mrs. Wilson said. "We've always found a way to cope with your dad's difficulties. I loved him and I still do and I just found the tools we needed to get him through school. Things worked out fine, no medication needed."

---

[14] www.ncbi.nlm.nih.gov/pmc/articles/PMC4071160/

In Chapter 11 of *I Always Want to Be Where I'm Not*, I discuss how anxious people and people with ADD tend to date and mate, how that can work well and/or get difficult in a hurry, and what those couples need to do to survive. Mr. and Mrs. Wilson were beginning to look like a case study.

"I'm not trying to blow this up into a big fight," I said. "But I feel like the stakes are pretty high. I've seen kids—including my own—have great success with a combination of medication and the kind of therapy that you and Mr. Wilson seem to have created on your own over the years, building discipline and finding ways to succeed—"

"She's so exaggerating," Lisa interrupted. "She makes Dad sound like he's doing great, which he is if you only consider his painting. But as far back as I can remember, he's made more money painting houses than canvasses, and he's lost two out of three of his adjunct jobs. The third one closed their program before he could blow it there."

"Those jobs are beneath him." Mrs. Wilson frowned. "He's so talented, and the deans of those schools don't appreciate his style."

"His style? You mean the one where he shows up on Tuesday to teach a class that's scheduled Monday, Wednesday, and Friday?"

"It was his first week. Your dad isn't a calendaring person."

I took a deep breath. "I'm not trying to diagnose anyone I haven't met, but I see where Lisa is headed and I wish you'd hear her out. Lisa loves her dad. She's spoken highly of him. But based on what you're saying, there's evidence that he might have ADD too. You and he are about my age and back in our day two things were different. First, you're right, we didn't recognize ADD as much as we do now. But that's not because it wasn't there. I had friends from high school who were, in retrospect, obviously struggling with it. I still see my closest friend, Rich, regularly, and he's been taking Adderall for fifteen years now. When we were kids we razzed him all the time because he couldn't keep a car on the road. He rolled three wheat trucks, wrecked his pickup five or six times, and he once clipped a high power tower with a combine header. He was smart, so he made it through school and eventually got his master's, but he didn't have an established career until after I was out of my doctoral program in our mid-thirties. Apparently, his dad got diagnosed and did better on stimulants, so Rich went in and started them too. That's just a single anecdote, but we see clients with the same story every week."

"Hmph." Mrs. Wilson looked grim. "I think we can presume that ADD occurs for a small group of people, but surely you'd admit that it's overdiagnosed. I just read a book about that the other day."

"No, actually, I would not. In fact, the whole idea of 'overdiagnosis' is a statistical fallacy. There is a problem of misdiagnosis. That's why we put several sessions into evaluating Lisa, asking questions about her performance in school and social life, and just discussing what's important to her. I was listening to everything both of you said and comparing her to how other young women her age respond to similar questions. What I failed to do was dig further into your family history."

Lisa's eyes seemed glued to my face. "You said two things were different 'back in the day.' What was the other one?"

"As adults, we love to claim that you have it so easy now and we had it so hard. But, when it comes to school, career, and the general pace of life, that's simply not true. You are expected to absorb material in elementary school that we didn't touch until middle school, and in middle school you're doing algebra we didn't see until high school, and in high school, if you're college bound, you're taking AP classes and college courses by the time you're a junior. And even outside of school, you're on information overload due to the internet and social media."

"Yeah." Lisa put her palms on her temples. "And it's so stressful."

"All that takes more brain power, focus, and effort than ever before. We see ADD more clearly because we've improved our knowledge of mental illness *and* our manic world makes people with ADD struggle harder and stand out more clearly."

Mrs. Wilson nodded slightly. "I will admit that some of the work Lisa brought home in high school seemed more difficult than what our oldest child did when he was at the same school in the late 1990s, and even then I thought what he was doing was harder than our homework just twenty years before. I assumed I was just getting older, but you're saying it's a societal change."

"Absolutely. Think of how computers have had to improve over the years to run more complex programs. Brains are a bit like that, except they don't really improve fast enough to keep up. Sure, a medication market has developed to exploit those societal changes. I'm a business person, and I have a bachelor's in political science, sociology, and history. I see where economics and clinical factors intertwine, but even if I were to concede that there's a plot to overdiagnose the world to make big bucks for rich multinational corporations, that has nothing to do with Lisa. She's not a population statistic or a principal of macroeconomics. We have good tools and methods for diagnosis at this clinic, and that never ends. Dr. Kelsey and I will work with Lisa to try different medications and dosages until we get it right and if we find that stimulants aren't helping her, we aren't going to keep giving them to her and she's not going to want to take them."

Mrs. Wilson took a deep, quiet breath and let it out slowly. "I do appreciate that you are trying to approach this scientifically, and Lisa seems to trust you. I'm willing for her to try your suggestions over the next semester and we'll see how it goes. I guess the proof of the pudding is, as they say, in the tasting."

Lisa jumped to the center of the couch and hugged her mother. "Thank you for letting me try this. It's going to make a huge difference. I already know it will."

Lisa knew more than she was letting on. She'd privately confessed to buying Adderall from her roommate at twenty dollars a capsule to get through finals. As unwise as that was (Chapter 10) Lisa had already begun her experiment and the results had been even better grades on her exams than she'd expected. It was too late to rescue her fall GPA, but with Mrs. Wilson's tentative buy-in, we set out to save the spring.

The Big Conspiracy

It's super weird to start out a chapter by proclaiming that ADD, a disorder included in the Diagnostic and Statistical Manual (DSM) since 1968[15] and for which 6.1 million children and teens[16] and untold millions of adults[17] have been diagnosed, is real. We can think of no other mental health condition that has endured such a rousing debate about its very existence. Nobody writes books claiming that depression is a hoax, or bipolar disorder, or schizophrenia. Nobody challenges the authenticity of autism, the diagnostic incidence of which has risen dramatically over the last fifteen years.[18] In the latest version of DSM-5 (2014)[19], some disorders were dropped and others modified to reflect better research, but ADD wasn't even on the list for reconsideration. It's a good bet you don't know which diagnoses were because, other than ADD, mainstream media rarely reports on the debates psychologists and psychiatrists have amongst themselves on how best to conceptualize our clients. Yawn. But everyone knows ADD is "controversial."

Weird indeed, yet here we are.

If you or a loved one have been diagnosed with ADD or are looking to be evaluated, you might think it important to know whether or not it exists. So, let's spend some time debunking a few common ideas from articles and books in the "skeptic press" that blew up in 2014, right after I published *I Always Want to Be Where I'm Not*. If we listed one title, we'd have to list them all, and if we did that we'd have to do a twenty page critique of each. Adding in periodicals and blog posts, we'd end up with a five-hundred page chapter rebutting what amounts to a pile of fluffy nonsense. They've had enough press already, so let's just skim the gist of their arguments.

If you've been diagnosed with ADD, the skeptics are essentially suggesting that you're either a faker or you've been hoodwinked by a vast medical-industrial complex to take expensive medication for a bogus

---

[15] en.wikipedia.org/wiki/History_of_attention_deficit_hyperactivity_disorder

[16] www.cdc.gov/ncbddd/adhd/data.html

[17] There's actually no reliable statistic on the number of adults who have ADD.

[18] www.autismspeaks.org/science-news/cdc-increases-estimate-autisms-prevalence-15-percent-1-59-children

[19] amazon.com/dp/0890425558/

diagnosis. Think *Mad Men*[20], a bunch of clever salespeople using less-than-transparent means to convince you to think things you don't mean to think or do things you don't mean to do. Other doubters take you at your word that you have ADD symptoms, but then propose that if you just lived your life right—got more exercise and sleep, avoided gluten, refined sugar, and red dye, or took certain proprietary dietary supplements—your symptoms would go away. Still others claim that ADD is only a surface manifestations of another "real, underlying" problem, which they purport to correctly diagnose, because you can't have ADD because ADD is not real.

For example, one book claims that if you've been diagnosed with ADD, you may really have bipolar disorder, which to be honest, isn't great news. On average, bipolar is much harder to live with and treat, and the side effects to medicate it are substantial. So, if your prescriber is searching for a diagnosis, root, root, root for ADD every time. And if you don't have bipolar, this same author claims your condition is likely one of nineteen other problems including anxiety, sleep deprivation, depression, allergies, dyslexia, lead poisoning, fetal alcohol syndrome, or perhaps even a vision and hearing deficit, but definitely not ADD. It's the one diagnosis that's not real. Another family therapist, author, and blogger (whose doctorate isn't in any clinical branch of psychology or psychiatry) often posts the best evidence available on ADD and then simply says, "It's not true," sort of like the whole "fake news" cry now used to denigrate anything a politician finds to be in conflict with his or her position on an issue. Wish it away and it's gone.

Scientific evidence from several fields of study in thousands of journal articles over many decades demonstrate that these ideas are without merit. Diet is important, too much sugar is bad for your health, and many disorders do produce ADD-like symptoms. Big pharmaceutical companies are out to make big profits, just like every other company in America, and they love direct-to-consumer marketing. But a good diagnosis has nothing to do with any of this. We don't know how other offices operate, but marketing doesn't influence in the slightest our decisions on how to treat you. People don't come to us to be hoodwinked. They want results and if we don't get results, they quit coming, because, duh. Moreover, a good diagnosis is, by definition, a

---

[20] www.netflix.com/title/70136135

What doesn't exist is evidence that tens of millions of Americans are being misunderstood by careless treaters or swindled by a multilayered conspiracy.

differential diagnosis; so a prescriber should never simply run a checklist of ADD symptoms and send you out the door with a script and a fond farewell. Yes, we see them do it all the time, but that's a clinical problem, not a problem with the diagnosis itself.

What doesn't exist is evidence that tens of millions of Americans with ADD are being misunderstood by careless treaters or swindled by a multilayered conspiracy. What is commonly happening, however, is a rush to judgment in many offices around the country. Sometimes that rush favors ADD and other times it does not. Our goal is to move your thinking from superstition to science and to move the thinking of prescribers from best-guesses to investigation.

If you don't have ADD, you may not understand why all this skepticism is so frustrating to those who do. Think for a moment about your own brain, now and in the past. What troubles has it had? Let's pick a very common and comparatively non-controversial diagnosis that you may have experienced: depression. Perhaps a loved one or cherished pet died. Maybe you lost a job in the great recession or you just come from a family of people who are prone to depression. Regardless, you felt lethargic, irritable, hopeless, disinterested in things you used to like, and maybe even self-harmful. What if someone came along and said "depression does not exist," explaining that what you really need is more exercise or more light or to get over the sadness surrounding your dog's death by getting a new puppy. These things might be empirically true, but is that advice helpful in changing how you think and feel and behave? Are you even able to enact it in your depressed state?

You might wonder why such books sell? They don't, really. Of the top 100 books on Amazon dealing with ADD, the vast majority are designed to help people accept and cope with the disorder. Some offer scientifically based approaches that draw on sound clinical literature. Others offer a combination of folklore, opinion, and/or dietary supplements. Still others offer hope and inspiration including several that recast a debilitating disorder into a lucky break bringing with it unique insight, energy, and courage. Few books sell because they espouse the anti-ADD party line. And why is that? Because debate about ADD doesn't exist, at least in the clinical or scientific community. It's fought instead on the battlefield of politics, emotional reactivity, sensationalism, and ill-informed opinion. Like so much else these days, ADD skeptic books appeal to a core suspicion that we're all being taken for a ride, all of the time, in every way.

I know this because I was once a skeptic. Back in the 1990s, when ADD began to more broadly emerge in the public eye, it really did look like something was up. It seemed a bit too convenient that big pharma, increased prescription drug benefits, and an uptick in diagnoses all fell from heaven at the very same time. Toss in schools supposedly demanding that parents chemically restrain kids, and shortened attention spans due to video games, TV, and the emerging internet, and it seemed pretty obvious that multinational corporations were conspiring to turn us into drug fiends, like the pacified masses in Aldous Huxley's *Brave New World.* Even Bill and Hillary Clinton got in on the anti-ADD bandwagon[21] for about five minutes.

Trained as a family psychologist in the early 1990s, I assigned most child problems to poor parenting, poverty, multigenerational family dysfunction, violence, and a host of other environmental influences. We didn't even think about adult ADD. I was taught to see psychobiological explanations as deterministic[22] and unhelpful in psychotherapy. But, as I moved from graduate school into practice, I began to realize that none of that thinking or intervention made ADD people's symptoms any better until you actually treated their ADD. Those who were treated as we describe in this book, simply dealt better with life problems, even horrible ones like child abuse and outplacement to foster care. Those who weren't, got worse even when their life stressors were comparatively minor. As the years progressed, the more I thought about it and the more clients I saw, the less sense the conspiracy made.

Mythbusting

To make space in your head for a good attitude about ADD diagnosis and treatment, we need to leave behind a few myths drawn from the skeptic literature. Kelsey and I have heard each one many times, some perpetuated by great scholars or well-known commentators. Each

---

[21] www.pbs.org/wgbh/pages/frontline/shows/medicating/readings/brainpolitics.html

[22] Denying or minimizing the ultimate importance of free will.

makes treatment more difficult because it masquerades as sage wisdom when it's really either inaccurate, illogical, irrelevant, or all three.

ADD Is Overdiagnosed

If you deconstruct it, this myth proposes that more people are getting labeled with ADD than could possibly exist in the population. Some really noteworthy people, including many who "believe" in ADD, cling to this one. If you were to do a person-on-the-street interview tomorrow, we're guessing at least 80% of respondents would make this claim.

It's too easy for people to get diagnosed, whether they should be or not. So the issue isn't overdiagnosis. It's misdiagnosis.

And yet, the whole idea of overdiagnosis is based on a logical fallacy. Nobody has any idea how many ADD people really exist in the population, so we can't possibly know whether ADD is overdiagnosed or underdiagnosed. It's anyone's guess and nothing more.

Here's what we do know: a lot of people aren't diagnosed who should be, because they keep showing up on providers' doorsteps, getting evaluated, and benefitting from treatment. Others show up, get evaluated and don't qualify for a diagnosis. If everything is done right, that's exactly how it should be. Unfortunately, all too often, everything is *not* done right. People are getting diagnosed and put on medication who've never been properly evaluated. We see one every week, describing how another professional "eyeballed it" rather than doing any testing or conducting anything approaching a thorough interview. Often, a prescriber spent a few minutes in an exam room hearing the client rattle off a list of symptoms he or she found on the internet, or the prescriber hands the client a quick checklist, often supplied by a pharmaceutical company, before offering up stimulants. That makes it too easy for people to get diagnosed, whether they should be or not. So, as I explained to Mrs. Wilson in the opening vignette, the real issue with ADD isn't overdiagnosis, it's *mis*diagnosis.

If you're not yet convinced, let's pretend for a moment that there really is something called "overdiagnosis" out there in the population; that there are exactly 22.3 million people[23] diagnosed with ADD in America and there should only be 19.2 million. My gosh! That means nearly

---

[23] I just made this up because nobody keeps track of accurate numbers.

three million adults, teens, and children are being incorrectly treated with stimulant medication. Then ask yourself what that has to do with you or your loved one? Is someone else's bad diagnosis any reason to avoid treating your ADD? Or should you just seek a better evaluation and treatment than those three million poor, fictional souls did? Good treatment is never about politics or population statistics. It's about helping you reduce impairment in your life.

Everyone Improves on Stimulants

No, they do not, presuming you're using a clinically informed, evidence-based definition of "improve." As we'll discuss in Chapter 3, stimulant medication sets off a chain of neurohormonal events resulting in an increased availability of mood-modulating neurotransmitters in your brain cells. This helps to influence and improve mood, memory, cognition, and behavior in people with ADD. However, research conducted to compare improvements in cognition among two groups taking stimulant, one with ADD and the other neurotypical, showed improvement in reading comprehension and memory only among the diagnosed group[21]. In short, some people like taking stimulants for their perceived mental boost. Those people are generally kidding themselves, or they are experiencing what we call in the biz "a placebo effect."

Treating ADD Leads to Stimulant Abuse

According to Oxford Treatment Center's well-cited, extensive, and non-sensationalized webpage, stimulant abuse is real.[24] They note:

> ...the increased availability of [stimulant] drugs has resulted in an epidemic of their abuse. In recent years, Adderall abuse and general nonprescription use has risen sharply, especially among young people and athletes.

Wow. That sounds bad. Are we not on the wave of something like the opioid crisis here? No, we are not. Oxford continues:

---

[21] Weyandt, L., White, T., Gudmundsdottir, B., Nitenson, A., Rathkey, E., De Leon, K., & Bjorn, S. (2018). Neurocognitive, Autonomic, and Mood Effects of Adderall: A Pilot Study of Healthy College Students. *Pharmacy*, *6*(3), 58. doi:10.3390/pharmacy6030058

[24] www.oxfordtreatment.com/adderall/

Though it shouldn't be addictive if taken as prescribed for a condition like ADHD or narcolepsy, abusing the drug by taking large doses or crushing the pills to snort them for a euphoric high can and does lead to addiction.

The skeptic press is not as refined as the Oxford Treatment Center in its critique, failing to distinguish between clinical use and addiction, at times even conflating them or proposing that one leads to the other. This could happen, but it doesn't happen very often considering the vast number of people using stimulants.

Besides, any national wave of stimulant abuse has nothing to do with your ADD, unless you've joined the wave. If you have, skip ahead to Chapter 10 right now, read it, pursue the necessary treatment we suggest, and then find a prescriber trained both in the treatment of ADD and addiction.

These Medications Are So New We Can't Be Sure They're Safe for Long-Term Use

The one thing stimulant medication is not, is new. While the exact formulations and methods of delivery have been greatly refined in the last thirty years, the core ingredients are the same as they were back before I was born. Research on stimulants and inattention first began in 1937 when it was discovered by accident that a stimulant medication used to treat severe headaches in children also improved school performance and behavior in several participants. Stimulant-based treatments for ADD were studied continuously thereafter in their individual component forms and combined into various formulations. We see clients in our practice who were diagnosed in the early 1970's and who have been treated on and off with stimulants ever since.

Of course there's a risk with anything you ingest into your body, including a lot of the processed foods most American's eat several times a week. But, there's a substantial risk to not treating ADD as well. Over 350 long-term studies since 1980 have examined the impact childhood treatment has on later functioning in adulthood. Over the course of nine years, data from subjects treated and those untreated were compared on salary, family size, relationships, legal history, driving record, body composition, physical health, mental health treatment, and substance use. Untreated adults had significantly higher rates of emergency room visits, traffic citations, and motor vehicle crashes. The untreated evidenced a forty-six percent higher rate of school expulsion and thirty-five percent higher dropout rate. They were twice as likely to have a substance use disorder in early adulthood, and had significantly higher rates of teen pregnancy, sexually transmitted infection, incarceration, job termination, and divorce[25].

Kids Eventually Grow Out of ADD

The jury's still out on this one. In the 1980s and early 1990s, we believed that ADD was mostly a childhood disorder and only a few people carried it into adulthood. Later, it was thought that people didn't really grow out of it, but instead just exited school in their late teens or early twenties and no longer needed stimulant medication for intense learning. Skeptics held that those who seemed to "grow out" of ADD were errantly diagnosed to begin with.

A body of preliminary research has examined whether the brain scans of young adults diagnosed with ADD as teens are different from those taken during adolescence[26], but as you can imagine, any definitive study is hard to run over the length of time needed to discern such differences. Citing design limitations in the largest imaging study of ADHD to date, Radboud University Nijmegen Medical Centre (2017)[27] notes, "longitudinal studies tracking people with ADHD from childhood to adulthood to see how brain differences change over time will be an important next step in the research." In other words, until we obtain a large sample of teen brain scans and then re-examine them in adulthood, we can't answer this question using that data.

Even if we eventually solve this interesting mystery about who does and doesn't outgrow ADD, the answer will be irrelevant to any child or teen who meets criteria. Worrying about what studies may show us one day about someone else's brain scans won't make your child's life any better today. Treating him or her as we describe in this book, just might.

---

[25] Mariani, J. J., Mariani, J. J., & Levin, F. R. (2007). Treatment Strategies for Co-Occurring ADHD and Substance Use Disorders. *American Journal on Addictions, 16*(s1), 45–56. doi: 10.1080/10550490601082783

[26] link.springer.com/content/pdf/10.1007%2Fs00787-015-0755-8.pdf

[27] www.sciencedaily.com/releases/2017/02/170216105919.htm

I Want to Let My Kids Wait Until They're Old Enough to Decide for Themselves About Medication

Differentiation of child from parent[28] is a critical task of youth. I encourage that process in my own children and in all our clients. As noted in Josh's vignette (Chapter 1), we're true believers in client autonomy and teamwork, even for teens and older children. But, a parent's attitude about taking medication is often the biggest determinant of a child's compliance[29], meaning that the parent has influence that he or she can't simply sidestep. Leaving the choice entirely up to an ADD child, particularly before ninth grade and before the child has come to see the importance of treatment, predicts failure because, as noted, anyone who needs to be on a stimulant will have a love-hate relationship with their meds. Faced with that dilemma, most children will go with the hate and ignore the love, as they might when considering broccoli, cough medicine, or an early bedtime.

You don't let your six-year-old invest your life savings in real estate, because she hasn't enough experience to predict market risks. You don't let your thirteen-year-old have free reign with the liquor cabinet, because he lacks the forethought to protect his future self from today's poor choices. And you wouldn't let your child refuse treatment for an illness like diabetes, rheumatoid arthritis, or Crone's disease, even though all three are quite unpleasant to treat.

Yet, too many parents underestimate the risks and defer to their children's wishes to be med-free until things become intolerable. Frequently, we get college students living away from home for the first time, foundering in the rough seas of freshman or sophomore year, coming in for an evaluation and expressing frustration that their parents knew they had ADD back in sixth grade but didn't press them into treatment. Even when we remind them that their differentiating teenage selves might have been resistant to such pressure, these newly-minted young adults resent parents who did not provide a firm hand of guidance against their shortsighted adolescent judgment.

---

[28] The process by which children form separate personalities, values, and decisional styles from their parents.

[29] Lisa's case at the beginning of this chapter illustrates the opposite condition, where in wanting to take medication, the child is rebelling against parent authority.

If you're an adult with ADD who missed out on treatment as a child, please don't throw up your hands and presume your time has passed. We see new adult clients every week and we know how helpful treatment can be, even after high school graduation. It may be harder for old dogs to learn new tricks[30], but taking action later in the game is a lot better than not taking it at all.

Let's Try Therapy and Coaching Before Doing Meds

This sounds like a very measured approach and it's actually what was originally recommended for teens experiencing depression. We saw the young person for six to eight sessions and tried to address the circumstances leading to his or her sadness. If the teen was still struggling thereafter, we referred to our prescriber and continued with psychotherapy. We still use that protocol at our clinic for such cases, unless we have a good reason to move ahead more quickly, which is about sixty percent of the time.

Here's why that approach doesn't make much sense with ADD. Depression can emerge from many triggers, internal and external, medical and situational, while ADD is a neurological disorder plain and simple. It shows up on brain scans[31]. While there are several differential and co-occurring diagnoses we'll discuss in Chapters 3 and 4, the only treatment for ADD recommended by the American Psychological and American Psychiatric Associations and the American Academy of Pediatrics is an integrated regimen of medication and psychotherapy. Like global warming, this isn't controversial in the scientific community.

Diagnosis. What Is It Good for?

Before you can accept that ADD does exist, you must first accept that it does not. We're not playing mystical existentialist gurus here. ADD does not exist because psychiatric diagnosis does not exist apart from the language we create to describe things we feel and observe. That's also true for physical diagnosis. For example, sphenopalatine

---

[30] In fairness to old dogs, this adage is also a myth. Operant conditioning works just as well for older animals as younger ones.

[31] Jacobson, L. A., Crocetti, D., Dirlikov, B., Slifer, K., Denckla, M. B., Mostofsky, S. H., & Mahone, E. M. (2018). Anomalous Brain Development Is Evident in Preschoolers With Attention-Deficit/Hyperactivity Disorder. *Journal of the International Neuropsychological Society*, *24*(6), 531-539. doi:10.1017/s1355617718000103

ganglioneuralgia doesn't exist either. It's just a name we came up with to describe "brain freeze," when you eat a very cold ice cream and get a brief, painful headache. The inflammation of an appendix seems pretty real to anyone who's felt it, but the name we give it (appendicitis) exists only in our heads and in our textbooks.

The names we give to painful, distracting, irritating, or uncomfortable thoughts and feelings are products of psychology and psychiatry. We can disagree about those names, but the experiences—what we label as symptoms—are real. As generations of medical and psychiatric researchers and practitioners have observed, tested, and revised their understanding of the human body and mind, our ability to apply an agreed upon label to a given set of symptoms has improved. Mostly.

For example, psychologists used to think schizophrenia was more common than it is. We still run into a case, now and then, in which the family psychiatric history includes a relative who was once diagnosed this way and is now symptom free without antipsychotic medication. That can't be, because the diagnosis of schizophrenia requires a progressively deteriorating course. We also thought multiple personality disorder was relatively common in the 1970s. It's now called Dissociative Identity Disorder and we realize it's quite rare. Likewise, the diagnosis of ADD has evolved away from a focus on hyperkinesis to emphasize inattention over hyperactivity. This slight shift means that we can now find more people in that diagnostic category since we are no longer watching only for little boys "running around as if driven by a motor." They are, in fact, a small fraction of people with ADD, not the exemplar of it.

What has not changed in psychodiagnosis is symptom presentation, which is the real basis for any medication regimen. Some clients present with feelings of sadness. Some have problems with reality testing. Some have too much energy, others not enough. Some focus into their inner worlds rather than on what's happening around them. Some are energetically goal oriented, while others are enthusiastically all over the place. Some are too careful for their own enjoyment of life, overestimating the risk of a few specific things or the world in general. Others are impulsive, wholly disinterested in risk until they've gotten themselves face-to-face with it or worse. Some are always on edge, short tempered with others or even violent. Some convert their worries into behaviors or physical symptoms they cannot control. Others have thoughts that intrude into their minds and won't go away no matter how much they try to ignore them. Some can't sleep enough, others can't sleep at all, and still others sleep all the time. Some can't understand other people's motives and intentions, constantly miscuing on how to respond. Some appear to have an aversion to the truth. Others can't conceal anything from friends or family out of a misplaced sense of guilt and shame. Some are so conscientious that they lie awake at night worrying about what they said or did and how it might offend those close to them. Others thoughtlessly offend family and friends by being inconsistent, not showing up on time, failing their commitments or obligations. The list extends for several pages.

You label others for these symptoms. The inconsistent people you call unreliable or flakey. The untruthful ones you call liars. The sleepy or low energy ones you call lazy. The internalizing ones, you call daydreamers. The careful ones you call worriers. The irritable and irritating ones you call a whole host of expletives usually related to unsavory body parts. The impulsive ones you call careless, and so on.

Kelsey and I label people too. We call them names like Major Depressive Disorder Recurrent or Generalized Anxiety Disorder or Adjustment Disorder with Anxiety and Depression or Attention Deficit Hyperactivity Disorder, Inattentive Type. But when we *Diagnosis has as much to do with economics as it does treatment.* do it, our labels carry consequences. We're creating a condition in our clients' medical history that may stay with them forever. So, we take our labels very seriously.

We'll let you in on a little secret if you promise not to tell the American Psychiatric Association, publisher of the DSM-5. Psychiatric diagnosis has as much to do with economics as it does treatment. Kelsey and I sound very precise when we tell you that you have Major Depressive Disorder, Recurrent, Moderate. But if you were to pass through the drive-thru at our office[32] and hand us a slip of paper with that label written upon it, we'd know very little about how to treat you. It's not like a throat infection. You could hand a note to your doctor at her

---

[32] Just kidding. Thankfully, insurance reimburse hasn't gotten so bad that we need a drive-thru. Yet.

drive-thru saying you have a throat infection, and she would hand you a Z-Pack.

Even within a specific category like Major Depression, there are many flavors and influences. Does your depression come back at predictable times of the year or in response to certain triggers, like loss or disappointment or other external factors? That's called exogenous depression. Or is it always part of your experience, persisting even when things are going well? We call that endogenous. Does it present as agitated in which you feel irritable and on edge or lethargic where you never want to get out of bed? Does it have a tinge of grandiosity, like Abraham Lincoln who wrote twenty years before the civil war, "I am now the most miserable man living. If what I feel were equally distributed to the whole human family, there would not be one cheerful face on the earth... I must die or be better, it appears to me[33]?" These are all questions we must answer because each suggests a different intervention medically and in psychotherapy. If you want to compare this to a treatment for a physical problem, think of it like oncology where the kind of cancer you have and where it's located dictates whether it will be treated with surgery, and/or chemotherapy, and/or radiation. And if you ask three oncologists, you'll often get three different answers because every situation and patient is different.

Generally speaking, ADD isn't quite as complicated to diagnosis as depression and anxiety, because it doesn't have as many flavors; though some authors, like Daniel Amen, MD, beg to differ[34]. The majority of the cases we treat in children, teens, and adults are categorized as ADHD, Inattentive Type, though we also see a fair number of combined (Hyperactive and Inattentive Types). There is some debate over whether an ADHD, Hyperactive Type really exists because without the core element of inattention, hyperactivity is more likely to reflect a mood disorder, probably of the manic type. Kelsey and I have rarely seen anyone of any age with this version of ADD, and the ones we think we might have seen, spawn endless arguments in our office.

Before you let us, or anyone else, call you names that exist only in a book called DSM-5 and represent clusters of symptoms you describe for us using imperfect language, you should commit to memory the

---

[33] housedivided.dickinson.edu/sites/lincoln/letter-to-john-stuart-january-23-1841/

[34] amazon.com/dp/0425269973/

following four laws[35] that should guide any diagnosis: symptom presentation over labels, deviation from the norm, impairment, and medical necessity. Each is described below.

Symptom Presentation Over Labels

Here's another secret you shouldn't tell any mental health provider who swears an allegiance to DSM-5: Kelsey and I kind of wish diagnosis would go away. If we have to call you names, we'd rather call you "That guy who has an agitated depression who responds well to lamotrigine" or "The college student who can't finish any project she starts, has poor time management, can't get herself to class, procrastinates everything 'til the night before and then pulls an all-nighter, and never cracks a textbook." Or maybe, "That nice, overly polite girl who worries about everything from what people think of her to whether she'll get into a good college and she's only in seventh grade." This is because diagnoses don't make your life difficult. Symptoms do. If we addressed your sadness or worries or inability to hold a thought, nobody would care what name we called you, would they?

Unfortunately, two entities in the world of medicine do care a lot about diagnosis—your insurance company and your prescriber's licensure board[36]—and they're going to keep caring until hell freezes over because diagnosis serves a different purpose for them than it does the rest of us. The only way your prescriber can bill your insurance for seeing you and you can get your prescription costs covered, is if the prescriber calls you the right name. Each diagnosis has a specific code used to determine if it's covered. No diagnosis, no payment. It's that simple. And even if you forgo insurance and pay cash, under the medical model used by psychiatrists and PMHNPs, treatment and medication can only be ordered when a diagnosis is present, just as with diabetes, the flu, or a broken leg.

Those of us who see diagnosis as a figment of our clinical imaginations find these discrete labels confining. A good example is autism.

---

[35] As far as I know, these aren't really published anywhere as "laws," but we're going to use that term as one might in a physics text—principals that underlie the discipline of diagnosis and which are essential to its correct application.

[36] Your therapist's licensure board is probably less interested in the medical model of treatment requiring diagnosis. When psychologists, counselors, and clinical social workers provide treatment to relieve a client's symptoms on a cash basis, they do not need to provide a diagnosis.

Increasingly, and especially among our ADD clients, we've come to see what we term "a sliver of autism" (Chapter 4). There's not enough there to really give the diagnosis of Autism Spectrum Disorder, but without taking those symptoms into account, it's harder to understand the client. There are also clients who are what we term, "ADD leaners," people who are impacted by ADD symptoms but don't have enough of them to make the diagnosis stick, or whose symptoms are so mitigated by anxiety that they remain beneath the clinical threshold. When we've gone out on a limb and treated these folks, despite the lack of a clean diagnosis, many have gotten better. One nearly dropped out as a freshman before beginning treatment. Recently she graduated from a doctoral program in physical therapy. She barely met the criteria for ADD and anxiety, which really made no difference in the end. What mattered was that we treated her problems and not her label. Others, have sent us back to the drawing board to find a new solution, but the point is that we focused on symptoms and dealt with labels.

Superfans of diagnosis (yeah, they exist) argue that without a universal psychiatric language, we can't communicate easily with other providers. But, Kelsey and I question whether "easy" communication is the same as "good" communication. Shortening a person's story of mental health difficulty to "Bipolar II Disorder" not only diminishes our understanding of their situation and limits their treatment, it diminishes their humanity. Instead, in our office, we use diagnoses to begin a discussion of our clients (and bill insurance), but we never end with it.

Deviation

Another whacky thing we hear quite often in the skeptic press is that "everyone has ADD," as if these symptoms are really just a natural part of the greater human condition. Don't we all procrastinate at times or lose things or forget an appointment or mess up our schedules? People who are clearly not diagnosable often exclaim, "Oh my gosh, I left my phone at the office. I'm so ADD!" These glib attributions violate our second law of diagnosis, deviation from the norm.

Unfortunately, this term "normal" has become synonymous with "good" and abnormal with "bad," which is a misnomer. To illustrate, heavy alcohol consumption in college is certainly the norm, but it is not good. Having a consistently cheery disposition and hopeful outlook is not normal, but it is correlated to good mental health.

In clinical practice, "normal" simply means falling within the sixty-eight percent center area of the bell curve[37]. For something to be considered a disorder, the symptom presence and severity must fall out in the tails of the normal curve, beyond "one standard deviation," which places them above or below the sixty-eight percent center of the "normal" population. If you are "two standard deviations" above or below, you're outside ninety-five percent of the population on the symptoms in questions. Three standard deviations and you're in the ninety-ninth percentile. Remember the Conners instrument I mentioned earlier? That's exactly how it distinguishes people who have ADD from the neurotypicals who do not.

So, by definition, not everyone can have ADD because if everyone had it, nobody would. ADD would be normal and having laser-focused, great attention would be a superpower held by only a few. Claiming otherwise is pretty demeaning to people who really do have ADD. Maybe you're just making excuses for something we all share and that we just handle better than you do, which is kind of what the skeptic press is going for in this argument.

When it comes to children, another popular adage is that "kids are being diagnosed with ADD just for being kids!" always written with an exclamation mark or two. Again, we'll forgo citations to avoid adding fuel to that strange fire, but you won't have any trouble finding commentators—even prescribers and psychologists—claiming that the real problem for kids today isn't ADD but bad parenting, not enough gym classes, attempts to control the natural exuberance of normal children, poor eating habits, and so on. There's a whole lot wrong with this supposition, but suffice it to say that based on the law of deviation, a *good* diagnosis for ADD requires the child to be significantly different from his or her peers on the variables related to ADD.

As noted, the other misattribution made by nearly every skeptic article, is that the best indicator of ADD is hyperactivity. Since inattention drives all forms of ADD, we can't presume that external observation of behavior will give any indication of internal focus or attention span, particularly for older children and teens. This is why ADHD is such a bad brand for a disorder that doesn't usually present with the "H."

---

[37] en.wikipedia.org/wiki/Normal_distribution

Impairment

Our third law of diagnosis has to do with how ADD impacts the person being assessed. To be diagnosed, ADD has to cause problems. Instead, more than one popular book has, in recent years, lifted up ADD as kind of mystical altered state, adding energy, creativity, and unique insight to one's life. All one must do, the authors claim, is tap into this resource to find your hidden strengths. Yes, there really are aspects of ADD that can be useful to its owner, but that's also true of anxiety, depression, bipolar disorder, autism and many other mental illnesses as noted by Kay Redfield Jamison in her book *Exuberance* (2004)[38].

A diagnosis is not simply a quirk or different way of viewing the world. It is, by definition, an impairment.

But a diagnosis is not simply a quirk or different way of viewing the world. It is, by definition, an impairment. You cannot have ADD or any mental health condition, and not suffer from having it, except when it's well treated and even that can be a battle. If you say, "I have ADD but I don't take medicine and it doesn't really affect me," then my friend, you don't have ADD. If you say, "I have ADD and it's really helpful in my life," you're either on a really good stimulant or you don't have ADD.

Understanding impairment will be vital while reading this book and talking to your prescriber, because even more than symptom reduction, our goal is to reduce the extent to which your diagnosis screws up your daily functioning. If you take a stimulant and you still notice that you're procrastinating and acting on impulse, but those issues now have less impact on your life, you and your prescriber are making progress. We do have cases where a person with ADD has such a remarkable response to stimulant medication that it's hard to believe they're the same person who could barely finish a project, a chore, or even a sentence, two weeks before. But most clients will still struggle to overcome impairment even while taking medication. I wrote *I Always Want to Be Where I'm Not* to help you fight that battle.

---

[38] amazon.com/dp/0375701486/

Medical Necessity

The final law of diagnosis is mostly relevant to insurance reimbursement, but as such, it impacts treatment more than it should. You probably don't know this, but for you to get your broken leg set in a cast and paid for by insurance, someone has to certify that setting your leg is medically necessary. Don't worry, it's accepted medical practice to set broken legs, so you're not going to be sent home from the urgent care office with a note saying "Goodbye and good luck" pinned to your shirt. At least I hope not. However, let's say the doctor wants to go further and put a pin in your leg to improve the healing process. That might exceed the standard of practice for setting broken legs, so the insurance company could deem it unnecessary until the doctor provides specific reasons why it won't set correctly without the pin. The doctor can go ahead and put in the pin without justifying it, but the insurance company may deny the charges related to that procedure, leaving you with a big bill. There are a bazillion examples of this and the more intense or complex the procedure, the more rigorously the doctor has to justify medical necessity.

This happens because insurance companies weren't built to trust their members or contracted providers. Every day, their corporate executives rise and shine, look in the mirror, think about doctors, patients, and hospitals and repeat this mantra: "waste, fraud, and abuse." They see us as a vast mob conspiring to rip them off, and they're especially distrustful of mental health providers. They can see the x-ray of your broken leg and ask one of their contract doctors or nurses to review it. To show medical necessity for psychiatric diagnosis, however, the provider must attest to and document each of our "laws of diagnosis" and write a treatment plan reflecting how to remediate them using a recognized procedure. The provider must also demonstrate "amenability," that the client is freely seeking treatment and is open to what is being recommended. The provider must attest that the client is likely to benefit from the treatment or, if the client is already being seen, would become (more) impaired and symptomatic if it were discontinued.

And why do you care about this? Because medical necessity is the key to unlocking services for you or your loved one. We're not proposing you learn to game the system to get a diagnosis so you can grab those stims and run. But without understanding the threshold of medical necessity, many clients and their families minimize symptoms and impairment in what we call a "halo effect." This is most common among parents who down-score their son's or daughter's testing because they "don't want to label" him or her, when in fact they are coming in for exactly that purpose.

In other cases, partners feel sorry for the client and don't want to speak ill of him or her. Sometimes both partners have symptoms of ADD and neither is ready to admit it, so they tend to cover for each other. This can happen even when the couple is on the verge of breaking up due to ADD-related conflict. Most peculiar are people who come in saying, "I don't want a diagnosis on my health record," but who still want medication. How many ways could that go wrong for somebody's medical license?

If you just want psychoeducation or coaching or an assessment of your situation, and you're willing to pay cash, it's not unethical for a therapist to see you without labeling you "ADHD" and putting that in your permanent health record. But if you want to pursue medication or psychotherapy and get it paid for, a diagnosis is going to happen and medical necessity must be established.

Diathesis-Stress Model

Since we're geeking out on labels in textbooks written about symptoms of the mind, it's worth discussing our personal favorite framework of psychopathology. The diathesis-stress model is designed to resolve the age-old nature-nurture debate with regard to mental health by describing psychological problems as "the result of an interaction between a predispositional vulnerability and a stress caused by life experiences"[39]. Your "diathesis" (predisposition) includes genetic, psychological, biological, or situational factors that create your core vulnerability or invulnerability to symptoms of depression, ADD, anxiety, etc. This interacts with your life experience (stress) to either raise or lower your susceptibility to mental illness. The more stressful the life events you experience, the more likely you'll be to have symptoms outside the norm and which impair your functioning.

People who exit early childhood with low predisposition are less prone to mental breakdown regardless of life circumstances. In other words, it will take a lot of bad things piling up to express mental illness and

---

[39] en.wikipedia.org/wiki/Diathesis–stress_model

when you do, you're more likely than people with high predispositions to bounce back. We think of the imaginary space between one's core disposition and their point of breakdown as one's "level of compensation." For example, a client born to a very anxious parent who then parents that client anxiously in the first few years of life will likely have a high diathesis for anxiety. To get up and function in the world, this person must pack a lot of compensatory skills into the small space between their predisposition and their threshold of breakdown. It's like having a very small fuel tank on your car. You're always refilling it because you're always about to run out of gas. If we throw in some variables in childhood like poverty, violence, parental substance abuse, etc., we increase the need and diminish the capacity for compensation. Then, when life's stressors roll in, the tank runs low pretty fast and you "decompensate."

Conversely, a child born to conscientious, but "low-expressed emotion" parents and raised in a calm, authoritative environment is likely to exit childhood with a low predisposition, particularly if the parents also encourage the child to take healthy risks to stretch their resilience. This person will have a large compensatory tank and much less need to draw on it, given their resilience to stress. It might take exposure to combat or the violent loss of a parent or other loved one for this person to decompensate, and recovery would be quicker and less fraught.

The diathesis-stress model offers a multivariate explanation for why one person becomes depressed and another does not when faced with the same circumstances. For example, imagine two twins from the Jones family which has a multigenerational history of depression. The first child is exposed to peer bullying and poor teaching in his fourth-grade class and decompensates into depression. The second experiences a positive social network of peers and a vibrant, highly engaged teacher in his fourth grade class—factors we refer to as "protective." Each child's diathesis is about the same but their circumstances either help or hinder compensation. Consider a fourth-grader from the Smith family down the street. The Smiths have no history of depression. Their son is in the same class as the Jones boy, with the bullies and a poor teacher. He comes out of the experience weary, frustrated, but comparatively unscathed. These stressors have less impact on his overall mental health.

Kelsey and I apply the diathesis-stress model to ADD, too, but with a very different spin. Most people who are eventually diagnosed with ADD will have as their primary diathesis a genetic predisposition to the disorder. This is because ADD is highly heritable and not at all correlated with environment, as Larsson, Chang, D'Onofrio, and Lichtenstein (2014)[40] found in their study of the records of nearly 60,000 twins. They write of their research:

> The best-fitting model revealed a high heritability of ADHD (0.88; 95% CI, 0.83–0.92) for the entire sample. Shared environmental effects, on the other hand, were non-significant and of minimal importance. The heritability of ADHD in adults was also substantial (0.72; 95% CI, 0.56–0.84).

While it's possible through head injury, emotional trauma, or other insult, for a child or adult to become symptomatic, such cases are far less common than those presenting with a first-order relative with symptoms of ADD or a symptomatic relative one generation back.

The Larsson et al. findings also refute ADD skeptics who claim environmental underpinnings for ADD or argue that we're exaggerating the behavior of rambunctious kids. ADD clients of all ages come from great homes, terrible homes, expensive homes, and homes reliant on food stamps. They attend private schools in the wealthiest suburbs of Kansas City and districts that barely retain state accreditation. At the post-secondary level we treat ADD clients as undergraduates, graduate students, and quite a few who are tenured professors.

With all that emphasis on diathesis, you might wonder what role stress even plays in the presentation of ADD. Some take studies like Larsson et al. to mean "none at all" and are particularly defensive of parents, reassuring them, as one author did twenty years ago, that "it's nobody's fault[41]" when a child has ADD. This takes the diathesis side of the equation too far. Parents don't cause ADD, but good, authoritative parenting can mitigate the extent to which it impairs their child. An effective, positive, parent-child relationship is a protective factor that buffers the child against the effects of ADD by providing adaptive

---

[40] www.ncbi.nlm.nih.gov/pmc/articles/PMC4071160/

[41] amazon.com/dp/0812929217/

outlets to deal with the academic, social, and developmental impairments caused by the symptoms.

Conversely, errant parenting stresses ADD children in myriad ways, thereby increasing their impairment. Mrs. Wilson's handling of Lisa is a good example. Failing to seek treatment or, worse, shaming children for needing it enhances the effects of an ADD diathesis. Other ways include maintaining an unstructured home, failing

Failing to seek treatment or, worse, shaming children for needing it enhances the effects of an ADD diathesis.

to hold children accountable for their actions, hovering over them, criticizing rather than guiding them, and quite commonly, asking them to do as you say and not as you do. No other non-genetic factor impacts an ADD child's outcomes more than parenting.

As you're adding all this up, you may discover a paradox in the diathesis-stress model that goes like this: If ADD is highly heritable and effective, structured parenting is essential to mitigate its effects, aren't the people doing the parenting likely also to have ADD, thus making it hard for them to structure their kids more effectively than they do themselves? Yikes. That sounds like one of those irritating logic puzzles on my daughter's LSAT. But yes, we encounter this quite frequently and it plays out in several ways. As I discussed earlier and illustrated in the vignette, we've found that ADD people tend to mate with people who lean to the anxious side. Moderately anxious parents tend to be conscientious and highly concerned about their children's wellbeing. So, even if their children pick up the ADD diathesis from one parent, the other often provides a balance in raising their kids.

Occasionally, an ADD person marries another ADD person and has a house full of ADD kids. It's difficult to describe the multi-layered interaction of diathesis and stress in these families. Suffice it to say that if you encounter one you will never question the validity of this model.

Caring Too Much or Too Little

Now that we've given you a mini grad school lesson in diagnosis, let's back it down a notch and discuss an easier, more intuitive way to understand ADD by imagining it on a continuum with anxiety. In our model, we think of people with ADD as not caring enough about the many details of life and anxious people as caring too much. Of course, based on that bell curve we discussed earlier, most people fall in be-tween and well short of either diagnosis. However, under this model everyone will either lean toward ADD (we call them the "carefree" types) or toward anxiety (the "careful" types).

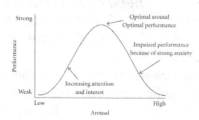

Figure 1: Curvilinear Relationship Between Anxiety and Productivity

Research shows that anxiety has a curvilinear relationship to produc-tivity, as illustrated in Figure 1[42]. You'll perform best when you have just the right amount of anxiety, caring enough to put forth good effort. If you care too much and get stressed, you'll function poorly. Care too little, and you won't try hard enough. You've undoubtedly experienced each of these conditions at different points in your life.

In the language of impairment, how far you lean at a given moment determines whether this is just an interesting part of your personality or an actual problem requiring diagnosis and treatment. In the language of deviation from the norm, we're saying that the "leaners" are still within the center sixty-eight percent of the normal distribution, with the careful people falling just below the mean of ADD and the carefree people above it.

While this "caring model" isn't perfect, and it hasn't been empirically validated as we describe it, it can help you practice metacognition—thinking about your thinking—or help you understand your partner, child, boss, etc. Readers of *I Always Want to Be Where I'm Not*, report it to be a helpful mindset. So, let's look further at how ADD people and anxious people differ, as we'll come back to this construct several times throughout this book with regard to how it impacts medication man-agement.

People with ADD

In describing clients as not caring enough about the many details of life, we aren't implying that they don't care morally—as if they don't

---

[42] en.wikipedia.org/wiki/Yerkes–Dodson_law. Citation includes the above diagram. Note that although it looks like a normal distribution curve it is not. The line shows a curvilinear relationship between arousal (anxiety) and performance, not the distribution around a mean. Ah, the joy of statistics!

worry about the environment or they ignore the rights and welfare of others. Maybe they do, maybe they don't. Instead, we're using the term "caring" to mean taking seriously all the important but largely boring details one encounters in life, rather than ignoring or avoiding them. Unfortunately, in their frustration, people tend to label not caring with words like lazy, thoughtless, impulsive, irresponsible, reckless, haphazard, rash, hasty and lackadaisical in response to an ADD person's lack of intent, incomplete projects, lost assignments, blown-off commitments, and other relationship shortcomings.

ADD-leaners seem carefree, but generally care enough to get business done. They're the creative spirits we all know and enjoy. They're fun at parties, interesting, and spontaneous. They have fresh ideas, keep several projects going at a time, finish their most interesting work, pursue their strongest ideas, and foster their best relationships. They easily drop plans, relationships, or obligations that aren't working, and get over problems and regrets more quickly than anxious folks. They plan well, though not as easily or as thoroughly as anxious people.

When they decompensate, folks with ADD, and to a lesser extent, ADD-leaners, become overwhelmed and disorganized in thought and behavior, feeling an urge to cut and run when life throws too much complexity their way or, paradoxically, when they get stuck in something really difficult or boring that they can't get out of.

Anxious People

Anxious folks live their lives on the other tail of the distribution, caring more than is helpful to get the job done. They're so focused on what concerns them that they notice every minute detail of themselves and their environment, taking in more information than they can possibly use. They can't get their minds off what *might* happen, no matter how unlikely, so they overplan everything. Regardless of how skilled or talented they are, anxious people feel inadequate to meet other people's demands, not because they ever let themselves fall short, but because they fear they will. They need things to be orderly and predictable to feel safe and at peace. They may at times experience intrusive ideas (thoughts they can't get out of their heads). In extreme cases they may even develop obsessions and compulsions as a way to compensate for their anxiety.

Back toward the middle of the distribution, we find anxious-leaners who are far less intense. They're seen as conscientious, thoughtful, intentional, and precise. Employers and parents love them because they strive to please. They win favor from teachers, friends, and dating partners, who find them attentive, authentic, and considerate.

When anxious folks and anxious-leaners decompensate, perhaps in response to a traumatic or untoward incident, they usually go to their strength, concentrating effort and trying even harder. That sounds great and it can work, but when things fall apart, it pays to step back and calmly consider a new or different approach. That can be hard for anxious folks who are naturally attracted to structure and predictability, especially for those further out on the tail of the distribution who warrant an actual anxiety diagnosis.

It would be really nice if this whole caring business were as black and white as I just made it sound, and it is for most people. They lean either anxious or ADD. But about twenty-five percent of people diagnosed with ADD also have a diagnosable anxiety disorder, and quite a few of the leaners lean both ways. Let's look at how caring works for them.

Anxious-ADD People

Having both anxiety and ADD blows up our beautiful normal distribution and metaphorical continuum, because we're asking you to think of someone as being on both ends of the same spectrum, which is impossible in such a model. Nor can we think of that person as lying right on the mean, because the large number of folks who live there are reasonably balanced between careful and carefree. We need a new model for the anxious-ADD folks. Ideally, it would illustrate anxiety as protective for ADD and vice versa, such that anxiety would press ADD people to care more than they otherwise would and ADD would help anxious people to lighten up and approach certain situations with less fear and greater spontaneity. That would be neat!

Ah, if only it all worked out so nicely. In real life, ADD people with anxious leanings really will tend to get farther in school, at work, and in life than their ADD-only peers, because anxiety gives them a kind of built-in stimulant. They may neglect what they're supposed to focus on, but then, they get upset about neglecting it and get back on task. That energy may come at the last minute, but the work gets done.

However, just as the curvilinear model predicts, the more anxious an ADD person is, the more tortured they feel, at the mercy of their brains dragging them back and forth from not caring enough to caring too much to feeling overwhelmed to giving up to shaming themselves for failed effort. They second-guess themselves constantly and lack confidence in their abilities and decisions, even when others see them as quite competent. They often say, "I hate myself," or at least, "I hate my brain." And they're especially prone to depression. Getting them to make a decision is like pulling teeth because they're so afraid of making the wrong one, as they feel they have many times before.

Hydraulics and Zombies

Dealing so often with the interplay of ADD and anxiety, we've come up with what we call our "hydraulic[43] rule" of medication management. Simply put, if you have correctly diagnosed ADD and little or no anxiety, the point of medication is to raise your anxiety just enough so that you pay attention to necessary details, tolerate boredom, follow through on whatever needs to be done, practice metacognition of thought, behavior, and emotion, manage time, encode and remember written or auditory material, keep commitments, and so on.

One way the Zombie Effect appears is when ADD clients are medicated in such a way as to make them too anxious[44] to accomplish the tasks at hand. You kind of march through life, eyes forward, focused on only one goal, hopefully an intended one, unable to disconnect and shift in a way that enhances performance. Everything seems too important and everyone sees you as too serious. In contrast, our goal in the art and science of medicating ADD is to get you to the top of the curvilinear relationship between anxiety and performance, caring not too much and not too little. That's easier said than done of course, which is why this book isn't ending just yet. We'll return to how ADD and anxiety intermingle in Chapter 6 and discuss how to treat them in tandem.

---

[43] Don't worry. All you need to know about hydraulics to get this analogy is that when you put pressure on one end of a hydraulic system it, by design, pushes out the other end.

[44] This sometimes presents instead as too serious.

Having reached the end of this chapter, you may worry that we're trying to make you into more of an ADD expert than you wanted to be, and you're probably right. So, before we move on, consider that the skeptics are right about one thing: ADD is serious. Having a diagnosis attached to your medical record for the rest of your life is serious. Taking a powerful stimulant is serious. Combining several medications to treat the co-occurring psychiatric conditions we'll discuss in Chapter 4 is especially serious. We try to be entertaining in this book, using conversational language and funny zombies doing tricks and, here and there, a picture of my cat. But that's because our topic is serious and any levity we can bring is typically welcomed by our clients and, we think, also our readers.

And yet, in the popular press surrounding ADD, we find a country familiarly divided firmly into camps of true believers and haters, serving only to trivialize the entire matter. The true ADD believers read my book or several others and decide, "Oh my gosh, that's me. All my problems can be solved if I just give myself over to the ADD bandwagon." The haters show up in protest, for reasons we don't quite understand, from many positions and factions, all of them convinced that when DSM-6 comes, ADHD should be rebranded "BS."

If you're reading this book, we presume you're leaning toward the true believers camp. Just know that Kelsey and I didn't write it to encourage anyone to "believe" in medication management for ADD, a condition which is no more faith-based than diabetes or kidney stones. ADD doesn't care if you believe in it or not. It doesn't matter what name you make up for it. It's going to exist one way or the other.

So, at the end of the day, all our expert-making is intended to help you think critically about what's going on with you and about diagnosis in general, and then take the action you deem appropriate. We want you to understand how complicated concepts go together in complicated ways and how we can make them more understandable without diluting or dumbing down what it takes to get you into the best-fit treatment possible.

And with that in mind, let's examine how ADD evaluation should really be done, instead of how it often is.

Brain Journey

Simply put, diagnosis wields immense power. It can provide us access to vital medical technology or shame us, reveal a path toward less pain or get us locked up. It opens doors and slams them shut.

— Eli Clare, *Brilliant Imperfection: Grappling with Cure*

- Dr. Wes -

"I guess I don't understand why you need all this information." Dan fidgeted with his sweatshirt zipper and scraped the side of his thumb with the nail of his index finger. "I don't mind giving you whatever helps, but I didn't think we'd have to go into so much depth just to get me a prescription for Ritalin or whatever. My buddy at work, Todd, just went to his primary care doc and she gave him a prescription."

"You can go to your primary care doc if you want," I said. "That's not what we recommend, but people do it all the time."

"Well, he's the one who told me to come here. I don't think he's as excited about ADD as Todd's doc is."

"Do you know why?" I asked.

"Not exactly. Afraid of getting sued or something?"

"Probably not." I chuckled. "I do know Dr. Jackson. He's a good guy and very careful about controlled substances. He isn't one of those ADD skeptics, but he does think people don't get a proper diagnosis before taking stimulants and, based on experience, we'd agree."

Dan nodded hesitantly. "That's kind of what it sounded like, but also, I felt like he didn't trust me or something. I'm not trying to be a drug addict or dealer. I just got this big promotion from coder to management, and I've never had so much to learn before, and to be honest I was never great in school. But, I'm not trying to do anything wrong."

"I get it," I said. "Please don't assume Dr. Jackson or I are worried that you're pulling something on us. We just aren't interested in contributing to the misdiagnosis or overtreatment of ADD. Stimulants can be life changing, but they really aren't all that much fun to take, so you only want to use them if you really need them. Figuring that out is what we'll start working on today."

"Jackson also said something about you guys doing my prescriptions, at least for a while, until we can get it right. Do you do that?"

"I don't. I'm a psychologist. But my doctoral nurse practitioner does." I gestured toward the door. "You passed her office on the way in. We all work closely here to get the best outcomes."

"And he wanted me to see you for therapy," Dan said. "Is that really necessary? I don't feel like I need to lay on a couch."

"It's necessary if you want to be seen here. Therapy, I mean. You can lay on the couch if you want, or just sit on it, or whatever. What matters is that you agree to our way of doing things. It's taken many years to develop this program and we have a lot of demand, so we don't compromise on evaluation or treatment. If you meet criteria for ADD and you're impaired enough to take medication, there's a lot you need to learn in order to get the most out of it. It's like getting physical therapy after surgery. You get the medical procedure and then you have to learn and do some exercises to make it work."

"Does your cat ever sit on people's laps?" Dan nodded toward Grace, lying on the coffee table.

"Sure. But she chooses when and who. Do you like cats?"

"Is that like, part of the evaluation?" Dan smiled for the first time, but just a bit. I wasn't sure if he was kidding.

"Yes," I said. "It's always the first question Grace asks."

Dan opened up a wide grin. "I have two. They kind of help me calm down when I pet them. That sounds dumb, but it's true. I wish I could have one at my office, like you do."

"This should kickstart your relationship." I tossed Dan the small bag of cat treats I keep on my desk. Grace sprang into action, following the treats to his lap.

He laughed and opened the bag as Grace kneaded his leg. He fed her one treat and then another as she settled in. His demeanor shifted as he stroked her fur.

"The other reason we want you to do at least a few months of therapy is because we need to see how the medication is affecting you. We start the evaluation today, but it really continues until you're ready for discharge. Among other things, we'll talk a lot about how you're integrating meds into your life."

Dan scratched under Grace's chin. "And do I see the nurse practitioner over all that time too?"

"Yes. More often at first, less so later on. She'll follow up on issues related to the medicine, like sleep patterns, appetite, mood, and so on. I'll examine the psychosocial issues, like how you're doing at work and whatever aspects of your life ADD makes hard. For example, are you married or in a relationship?"

"Relationship," Dan said. "Her name is Janie."

"What does Janie think of this whole ADD thing?"

He sighed. "Honestly, she's really wanting me to get treatment. Her brother has ADD, and Janie says it really messed up their whole family. She's been bugging me about it for a while, but until I got the promotion I didn't really think it was affecting me that much."

"Would Janie come in?"

"Uh. Maybe. I mean, yeah. I know she would. Why?"

I made a quick note on my laptop: Janie's name and that she'd be a good resource. "It's helpful during the evaluation, and later in treatment, to have input from people who care about you. Do you trust her judgment?"

"Yeah. She's great. But sometimes she gets frustrated with me. I'm forgetful, and I probably play too many video games, and she's really neat and I'm not."

"You live together?"

"Not anymore." Dan glanced down at Grace and began petting her gently, but with greater intensity. "The dishes, laundry, vacuuming, the bathroom situation, it was just too much for her. I guess I live like a fourteen-year-old single guy even if I'm not living alone, so after six months, she got another apartment in her old building. I miss her being there, but I understand."

"But you're still dating?" I made a few more notes.

"Yeah. She invites me over and things go better that way."

"So, you're not big on cleaning." I chuckled. "And what about overall organization at work, at home, in your car?"

"Bad," Dan said. "Everywhere. Janie says it looks like I live in my car. We take hers when we go out. Hers looks like she just got it from the showroom."

"How do you deal with all that chaos?" I gestured toward my head. "I mean you've kept this job for several years and they want to promote you, so you must have a system."

"Yeah. I'm a computer guy. I have a notes app on my computer that links to my phone, and I basically do what you're doing right now, write everything down that I need to remember. I also have a to-do list, and I can synchronize my personal and company calendars."

"Impressive," I said. "Do you remember to feed those programs?"

He glanced up at the ceiling and let out an exasperated laugh. "You've done this before, huh?"

"I have. Let me guess. You have all these neat systems and gadgets in place, but then you forget to actually use them consistently. Sometimes you legit forget, other times you just can't get up the energy it would take over ten seconds to put the event into your phone. Other times you get on every one of those apps and lay out a beautiful agenda of everything you need to get done—"

"And then it sits there mocking me, because I do maybe half of them and feel bad for not doing the other half. One time I put our anniversary on my calendar so I'd be sure to remember it, but then, because it fell on a Sunday this year, I forgot to look at the calendar until Monday morning when I was checking to see what I'd scheduled for work that day. I was really ashamed. Janie took it in stride, but I know it hurt her, like she's not important enough for me to just check my effing calendar when that's not true at all. It just looks that way from my behavior."

We're always interested in whether a client presents with a childhood history of ADD, but that's harder to measure without reading a school record that few clients can access. If we rely on a previous diagnosis, we may blindly adopt someone else's poor evaluation process. If we accept the absence of a diagnosis, we could miss a great many cases of inattentive type ADD. Occasionally, a client will bring in a childhood evaluation, but usually we're left to ask general questions about every grade from elementary through college.

Dan recalled that he'd done well until about third grade and then began having difficulties keeping up. He even texted his mom from the session to refresh his memory. God bless texting. His mom recalled his early elementary teachers saying that Dan was a nice boy, but a bit developmentally delayed. They reassured her though, confident he'd catch up. But by fourth grade the school was considering holding him back in order to let him gain some maturity. Thankfully, Dan's parents feared he would later drop out as a nineteen-year-old senior[45], so they passed on that idea. By middle school, they'd hired a tutor and Dan's grades improved. However, in high school, despite two or three hours of homework each evening and tutoring, Dan only managed a 2.6 GPA. His parents weren't ecstatic, but they felt he was trying his best. Thereafter, he went to a junior college that offered tremendous support services for students with learning difficulties. After graduating, Dan worked a couple years in information technology before

---

[45] Retention (holding kids back a grade) is rarely practiced now in the United States because the graduation rate of retained kids was found to be much lower than for kids who struggled like Dan, but who were not retained.

completing his bachelor's at a well-known for-profit trade school. He wondered aloud if he'd basically bought a diploma, but that paper landed him a good job in the IT department of the University, where he'd now worked his way up to head a team of six programmers.

I clicked a few boxes on my computer. "If I were to ask you how well you concentrate or pay attention to things that aren't very interesting, what would you say?"

"It's hard. Even when it's important to me, like Janie or a program at work, I lose interest or get distracted from what I should be doing. I always find a way to get back on task, but it takes me extra time to get done what other people do easily. Weirdly, that's why I'm getting the promotion. They say I'm the hardest working guy in the office. What they don't know is that I'm just constantly playing catch up."

"Is it hard for you to give close attention to details?"

Dan nodded. "Definitely. And when that happens, I make these stupid, careless mistakes. Even with gaming, I'll drift off into thinking about work and mess up and get killed. And gaming is something I really like to do. So, imagine what happens with something boring."

"Yikes," I said. "I bet that's a real struggle." I clicked a bit more. "Until Grace got on your lap, you seemed kind of restless and fidgety." I demonstrated the same fidgets I'd seen Dan make early in the session.

"Yeah," he said. "If I don't have anything to do with my hands, I'll pick my fingers or nails or do anything to just be in motion. I try to either pet my cats or play a video game. I can't really sit down and just watch a movie without something else to do."

"Are you impulsive? Like, do you tend to act first and think later?"

"That's complicated. If I were to just do what my gut tells me to do, I'd be impulsive. But there's this little voice in my head telling me 'no, that's not right,' like I'm my own mom or something. But when it comes to something like throwing my used McDonalds bag in the back seat and not in the trashcan, I guess I am impulsive. So it varies."

"Do you or Janie find that you have rapid mood swings?"

"I wouldn't call them mood swings." Dan's brow furrowed. "Maybe a little, but not like manic or depressed or anything. I just don't have much frustration tolerance. I have to count to ten a lot, I guess."

"Like a short fuse?"

"Janie would say so. My family was kind of high strung. Nice, never abusive or anything, but just loud. So, I may not be a great judge of what's normal when it comes to temper. But yeah, I think that's me."

"Does Janie ever complain that you aren't listening to her? Not like, 'you don't value my opinion,' but like you're literally not listening or you need her to repeat things."

Dan looked toward the window and touched the corner of his eye. "All the time. And that's not how I was raised. My parents taught me to respect women. When Janie says that, I feel like an asshole. Like I'm letting down my mom."

"That is painful, Dan. I appreciate how much you recognize that it hurts others when you're not connecting to them."

"Doesn't make it better. I guess I never realized this stuff was tied in to ADD. But when I hear you ask these questions, I can see how it would be. I just thought I was...not this."

"I understand," I said gently. "You said you start a lot of projects. Do you eventually finish them?"

"Only if they're really important or interesting. It's almost like I have to scare myself to do it. Like I tell myself, 'your gonna lose your job, Dan,' and I'll sort of psych myself out...usually at the last minute. Procrastinating actually seems to help. Isn't that weird?"

"Not for folks with ADD," I said. "Is it hard to feel good about yourself or that you're able to do things as well as other people do them?"

"Yes," Dan said emphatically. "I hate that. I am always second guessing myself and thinking 'you're so stupid. How did you miss that?'"

"Hm. This is kind of a touchy one," I said. "So, whether you actually get addicted or not, do you gravitate toward addictive behaviors?"

Dan nodded. "That's Janie's biggest complaint, that I can't walk away from gaming. I'll play from like seven in the evening to two-thirty in the morning, and then I have to get up for work and I'll keep hitting snooze and then I'm late, and no matter how much I know it's hurting me, I just keep doing it. The only way I survive at work is by staying 'til six-thirty or later, and then I get home and I just have to play but now I only have eight hours so I'm up 'til three-thirty. I get my entire sleep cycle screwed up during the week and the weekends are worse."

"How about caffeine or nicotine? How much of those stimulants do you use?"

Dan gave a puzzled look. "I never thought of those as stimulants. I mean I know they are, but when you put it like that—I don't smoke, but I drink coffee all morning and a sports drink at lunch. I actually have a caffeine powder I use when I go to the gym, but to be honest, I sometimes use it at work, too."

"Does it keep you up at night?" I asked.

"Not really, no. I can drink a pot of coffee and go right to bed."

I chuckled. "Poor man's Ritalin. However, that's not super healthy, and if we find you have ADD and you go on meds, you'll have to talk to Kelsey about dropping way down on other stims. On top of medication, caffeine can cause problems, especially at that level. Speaking of which, have you ever borrowed anyone's Vyvanse or Adderall, or any other stimulant for any reason? Don't worry, it's confidential."

"Nope," he said. "I'm pretty much a caffeine guy. No pills. Yet."

"Do you find that you have trouble understanding or following through on instructions at work or at home?"

"That's a mixed one," Dan said. "Like if I'm building something, I actually like looking over the plans and seeing how it goes together. But if I'm learning a new software package, I kind of just wing it. I figure 'there's always undo.'"

"And if the boss calls you in, are you able to follow her directives?"

"I take copious notes on my computer or even sometimes, I'll secretly record her and then play it back later to be sure I'm really getting what she wants me to do. Geeze, I sound really pathetic here."

"Not at all," I said. "That's a good workaround, but I think you should do your recording thing out in the open, so you aren't seen as a spy or something. Do you find that you tend to avoid tasks and activities that require a lot of mental effort over a long period of time?"

"I'd love to do a crossword puzzle in *The New York Times*, and I'm pretty good with words, but I just can't. I get frustrated and give up.

But I can sit for hours figuring out a new video game. At work, it all depends on what I'm doing. If I have an interesting coding puzzle, I'll stay there 'til eight or nine o'clock, until I make it run. But if I have to read a book that requires real thought, like a computer science or engineering book, I literally fall asleep."

"Dan, do you have any relatives who you think might have any of the symptoms we've discussed today?"

"I think maybe my mom," he said. "She's always been a fun person, always on the go. We had these big backyard parties at our house where all the neighbors came over. But Mom didn't finish high school. She married my dad at nineteen. He was a truck driver and she worked at the diner, and I think they dated for like a week, and then he had a load to take to Vegas. She quit her job without notice, and they went there and got married by one of those Elvis impersonators. Not even kidding. They'd tell that story like it was so funny and carefree, and now that I'm older and look back, I'm like 'hey guys, what were you thinking?' Dad is actually a pretty serious guy. He owns six trucks now, and he's retired from driving. He was so in love with her, I think he just liked her crazy energy. She never worked again. Before I was in school, we just road the truck with him, and when she had to stay home and put me in kindergarten, Dad says she was never the same. Like she felt tied down. It makes me feel bad, really. But they had my brother later on, so I guess she liked being a mom."

"Tell me about your brother. What's he like?"

"I think he takes after Dad. He did better in school, went to a real college and played football for them. Graduated with a business degree. He wasn't a great student, but school was never as hard for him as it was for me."

I finished up the notes on my laptop and turned back to Dan. Grace yawned, stood up and stretched. She senses when a session is about to end and gets ready to jump down and walk the client out to the lobby. No, really. My cat does this five or six times a day.

"I think there's a real good chance you have ADD, Dan, but I'm going to ask you to take a test and have Janie take one too. It's called the Conners Adult ADHD Rating Scales. I'll send you some email links and you can forward one on to her. Is there anyone else who knows you well enough to fill one out?"

"I actually see my brother a lot. We're pretty close. Would he do?"

"Does he know you from, like, an academic or work perspective?"

"No," Dan said. "Not so much. But my boss might be willing. She's been really vested in my career and has a degree in educational administration, so she knows about stuff like this. Do you think it would hurt me at work, though if someone thinks I have ADD?"

"It's up to you and what you feel comfortable sharing, but you're protected by the Americans with Disabilities Act, so if you're asking someone to fill out a test about ADD to help you get treatment, they can certainly refuse, but they can't do anything to demote you or change your pay. It's a violation of federal law."

"I think it will be fine, then." Grace leapt to the floor as Dan stood up. "You know, this hasn't been too bad, really. I kind of like talking about this stuff, getting it off my chest. I was pretty leery of coming in, but I feel like maybe this is the start of something that could help."

"I'm glad too, Dan. If I had a buck for every person in his late twenties or older, who's had a good experience getting treatment for ADD, you and I could retire."

Dan laughed. "And you have a really nice cat too. Does she live here?"

"Yep. She'll be happy to see you the next time you come in. I'll bill you for these tests and send the links tonight. Get them done and then come back and see me in two weeks. I have the same time open."

You Are Not a Diagnosis

Do you know what an IQ really is? It's how smart you are, right? Wrong. It's what the IQ test measures. You're given the Weschler test appropriate for your age group by someone like me who is qualified to give it, or you take one of two short versions of the Stanford-Binet online[46]. And when you're done, you get an IQ score. Nothing more and nothing less. These tests tap into certain discrete areas of thinking associated with variables socially defined as educationally advantageous, like verbal language or quantitative reasoning or processing speed. As psychologists, we've studied what it takes to do well in school, the military, and in the workforce and written the test to match that. Unfortunately, this simple concept of IQ has taken on a whole life of its own in popular culture.

As Daphne Martschenko (2017)[47] points out, the history of IQ testing is checkered and controversial. Yet, when you see that little score with a mean of 100 and a standard deviation of 15, you're pretty sure you know how smart you are. We've even made up different names over the years, like "genius" or "mentally handicapped," to go along with those scores. These are names we call the thing the test measures.

As we discussed in Chapter 2, it's the same with any psychological diagnosis. Yet, too often Kelsey and I hear that "Lisa is ADD" or "Tressa (Chapter 4) is depressed, bipolar, and ADD, and by the way, she's also a little autistic." Without proper context, these labels can become who you are, rather than a set of symptoms that describe your struggles in life.

Without proper context, these labels can become who you are, rather than a set of symptoms that describe your struggles in life.

Even Kelsey and I practice this cognitive distortion[48] in the pages of this book by referring to "anxious people" or "ADD people," because it's too awkward to write a book with hundreds of references to "people who have been clinically assessed and have been found to have sufficient symptoms as to be classified under the diagnostic category of ADHD." Just remember in consuming this chapter, that words are magic, and it's a very short distance from describing someone as an "ADD person" to objectifying him or her. It's doubly bad when that person is you or your spouse or your child. So, let's proceed onward, with caution.

---

[46] stanfordbinettest.com. We're not recommending this, just noting it's here.

[47] www.businessinsider.com/iq-tests-dark-history-finally-being-used-for-good-2017-10

[48] Ideas and beliefs we make up in our heads to counter reality and favor our private logic.

Getting to Know You

Even when practiced well, psychodiagnosis is an imprecise and arcane science, but it is, nonetheless, a science. Any art involved comes from intellectual intuition, or what Malcom Gladwell describes in *Blink* as the ability of an expert to be "able to act intelligently and instinctively in the moment [which] is possible only after a long and rigorous course of education and experience.[49]"

While most, but not all, physical disorders allow for direct observation of pathology, most psychiatric conditions are inferred from the verbal report of clients and, preferably, those who know them. Like any communication, a psychiatric interview involves a sender and a receiver trying to understand each other. That's why doing an interview with a client who is not a speaker of the evaluator's native language lies between difficult and impossible. It can even be dangerous. It's not easy, but a good medical specialist can figure out what's wrong with many patients, absent good communication, by running tests of bodily fluids, ultrasounds, x-rays, etc. There are advanced technologies for psychodiagnosis, but nothing has replaced a good face to face diagnostic conversation, and we're betting that nothing ever will.

That's why it pays to go into your evaluation with an understanding of what's helpful. You don't want to sound too eager or well read. The prescriber may take this as a sign that you're trying to get unnecessary medication. But you do want to bring with you all the information you can and to be ready to field questions. Just as important, you want to come out of that interview (or series of interviews) knowing that your evaluator is doing his or her job well. We'd like to say that's a given, but it's not, which brings us to the five steps you'll need to take to get a good diagnosis.

Step 1: Seek a Highly Qualified Professional

It seems logical to start your search for evaluation at your primary care physician's (PCP's) office. Trust me, it's not. As Dr. Dodson pointed out in the Foreword, most, but not all, pediatricians and PCPs lack adequate skills and instrumentation to make a good diagnosis of ADD. He or she might (or might not) ask you to fill out The Vanderbilt

---

[49] amazon.com/dp/0316010669/

Assessment Scale[50] which is nothing more than a checklist of symptoms from DSM-5 without reference to any norm group[51], all in about twenty minutes. They may not say it overtly, but when the most reputable skeptics complain that ADD is overdiagnosed and overtreated, they're usually pointing the finger at the minimalist protocols used by PCPs. If your goal is to get on meds as fast as you can, the PCP path will probably get you there. However, the more of this book that you read, the less satisfied you'll be with that approach.

Instead, look for a psychologist or other mental health provider who specializes part of his or her practice in the assessment and treatment of ADD. You might try asking your physician for a referral, but you'll often do better searching the internet yourself. *Psychology Today* has a pretty good national directory[52] that will come up at the top of any Google search in your community. Our office is on it. You might also check out the directories compiled by *ADDitude* magazine[53] and CHADD[54] which can at least narrow your search to self-proclaimed specialists in ADD. Just remember, each of these listings is a paid advertisement, so click through to each provider's website to vet his or her training and experience.

As you begin to contact providers, ask each for their diagnostic and treatment procedures for ADD, because you'll prefer someone you can continue to see after the diagnosis is made. It may take some time to figure all this out. At our clinic I screen every intake request—between twenty-five and thirty-two a week—and interact by email with prospective clients to be sure we're all on the same page of music. For example, we won't admit anyone who is just looking for an evaluation. We're so sold on the model we describe in this book, that we forgo the substantial revenue stream we could get by just evaluating people, handing them a report of our findings, and sending them back to their physician or therapist. We only want to see clients seeking evaluation

---

[50] www.nichq.org/sites/default/files/resource-file/ NICHQ_Vanderbilt_Assessment_Scales.pdf

[51] Meaning the Vanderbilt cannot assess the rule of deviation from the norm we discussed in Chapter 2.

[52] www.psychologytoday.com/us/therapists

[53] directory.additudemag.com

[54] chadd.org/professional-directory/

with a plan to pursue treatment and medication management if they do qualify for diagnosis[55].

Some therapists will do a brief phone screening, but don't be discouraged if those you contact prefer not to. We find that having clinical staff return phone calls takes time away from client care, but we do answer questions over email about our procedures for anyone expressing an interest in treatment. If you don't get any response from a provider, you may be learning something about their style.

Many providers, including our office, have a HIPAA compliant online form that you're asked to complete before they will agree to see you or your loved one. We know these forms are super boring, but we encourage you to provide more information on them than you think anyone would need. Nothing is more aggravating than to have the prospective client write in the concern box: "I have ADD" or worse, leave the box blank. And yes, that happens five days a week despite a prompt that says "give a detailed explanation." A richer answer gives the provider a better sense of what's going on. Here's a great one, drawn from a recent intake request, but disguised:

> I'm having a bad time in my first year of college. I do good writing papers, but I'm terrible on tests. Even on papers, I wait to the last minute and then stay up all night. I play video games rather than do my homework or study for the exams, and my parents won't continue me next year at the university if I don't get at least a 2.5 GPA. My girlfriend thinks I have ADD. I asked at the health center and they recommended I come to you for testing and maybe some tips on how to cope with it. I don't know if I want to be on medication, but if you recommend it, I'm open to trying. I need help!

Isn't this a compelling paragraph? Don't you want to help this young person? We did. It's clear how much he or she[56] is struggling and how earnest the person is. It's actually a plus that the applicant mentions reluctance about medication. Some people write something like, "I really need to get on a medication for my ADD or else I'll lose my job

---

[55] We do indeed evaluate some new clients and find they do not need treatment for ADD.

[56] Yes, the person mentioned a girlfriend, but don't assume anything. We see many clients who are dating same-sex partners.

[scholarship, spouse, etc.]." While he or she could also be acting in earnest, the tight focus on medication throws a flag for us. People do come in feigning (or wishful thinking) a diagnosis just to get performance enhancing stimulants. As we'll discuss in Chapter 10, that's a really dumb idea. Given the love-hate relationship noted earlier, nobody should *want* to be on these medications. They should only need to be. In that spirit, it's better to say something like, "If I do come up as ADD, I'd like to find out if medication, therapy, or both would be useful in managing my condition." It's good also to believe that.

Since the publication of *I Always Want to Be Where I'm Not*, the demand for our services has exceeded our capacity, even with eight   therapists and Kelsey in the office. When trying to refer people to other providers, we've learned how frustrating the search can be to find someone who fits this model and takes your health insurance and is close to your home or office and so on. Because it's hard, we actually get requests from all over the world for video consultation. We love hearing from readers, but we don't provide clinical services that way and we don't recommend you elect that method either[57].

There are plenty of providers out there ready to serve you. The real question is which ones can actually pull it off?

There are plenty of providers out there ready to serve you. The real question is which ones can actually pull it off? Sometimes you'll run into more than one who can't, before finding one who can. Of this we propose the old axiom, "If at first you don't succeed, try, try again." Far too many people in need, give up.

Step 2: Psychiatric Interview

Before administering a standardized test, the evaluator should visit with you for at least an hour and sometimes two or more, depending on how complicated your situation appears to be. In more difficult cases, the evaluation really never ends, with half our treatment time spent monitoring and re-evaluating, trying to rethink what's going on as you improve, decline, grow, encounter new stressors and so on.

---

[57] We do offer short term video consultation to help you get or confirm a good diagnosis and access and utilize services, but we don't do therapy or prescribe over video.

Every evaluator has a style for conducting ADD assessments, but unless you're about six years old, he or she will want to investigate how you've gotten this far without treatment. Some of that conversation may seem cagy, almost like the evaluator doesn't believe you. There are two reasons for this. First, nobody wants to incorrectly diagnose someone who is just drug seeking. Second, the evaluator needs to understand your level of impairment by examining how much ADD messes with your daily functioning. In the parlance of this book, you might just be an ADD-leaner and stimulant medication might be an overtreatment. The evaluator can only solve that puzzle by thoroughly examining the diagnostic issues discussed throughout this book.

Step 3: ADD Testing

For psychologists, it's kind of shocking to learn that not every evaluator uses a valid and reliable testing instrument that compares you with a standardized sample of people your age and gender to measure how you deviate from the norm group. Yet, it's unusual for anyone to come to our office with a good testing profile, even if they've been previously evaluated and treated. That not only makes diagnosis less robust, it makes it hard to get educational or work accommodations should the need arise.

We use the Conners-3 instrument for children and the Conners Adult ADHD Rating Scales (CAARS) for adults administered through a secure online interface[58], so respondents can complete it anywhere in the world as long as they have email and internet access. The Barkley Scales[59] are also good, valid, and reliable and operate similarly.

Testing for ADD is unusual in that it includes not only your responses, but those from at least two observers who know you well. For pre-college students, that usually means a parent and an educator, though finding a knowledgeable and willing teacher is much harder once you leave middle school. By college, you'll have to rely on a roommate and/or best friend, unless you go to a very small school with a low teacher-to-student ratio. Typically a parent still serves as the other observer, unless you've been away from home for several years. If your parents are divorced, each should complete separate forms. If they're

---

[58] Multi-Health Systems Inc. www.mhs.com

[59] www.guilford.com/cgi-bin/cartscript.cgi?page=pr/barkley19.htm

married and on good terms, we usually let them fill out the form together. If the testing profiles come back with one minority report—either high or low scores—it may be wise to get another observer.

If you're an adult who did not attend or has already graduated from college, you may have an even harder time finding observers, especially if you tend to be introverted. Longer-term romantic partners, friends you've known for several years, and occasionally, employers, supervisors, or other workmates can be good resources. Once in a great while, we'll have a client who can't identify any valid observer, but does have a history that looks positive for ADD. In those cases, we'll use the self-report form of the CAARS and, if the client is above the clinical threshold and other data match, do a trial run of medication. But we always prefer a multipoint evaluation.

You will need two and sometimes three sessions to complete the interview and go over the testing. These should be covered in part by insurance, presuming your policy has mental health benefits[60] and you've met your deductible if you have one (Chapter 7). The total cost for the Conners or Barkley test should not exceed $200 with two observers, and it may be less. The evaluator may or may not attempt to bill the testing to insurance and your company may or may not pay.

Step 4: Rule Out Alternative Hypotheses

Some conditions produce symptoms that are similar to but are not ADD. The process of discerning these is referred to as "differential diagnosis" because we're comparing two (or three or four) possible conditions and selecting one. In this section, we'll briefly review the most common culprits that lead to misdiagnosis. In Chapter 4, we'll go back and review many of the same conditions, instead, as co-occurring disorders alongside ADD. Yep. It just keeps getting more complicated.

Poor Sleep. Sleep and ADD can interact in so many ways, it's difficult to keep them all sorted out. Determining what's what can greatly impact your initial evaluation and ongoing treatment. Bad sleep can come from poor sleep hygiene[61] or a disorder like sleep apnea or primary

---

[60] Most states require some mental health coverage but some don't and others allow companies to push all mental health services to deductible. We consider this reprehensible.

[61] Not keeping a well-regulated sleep-wake cycle in which you get seven to ten hours of sleep per night at roughly the same time.

insomnia, any one of which can yield symptoms of inattention and poor concentration. Research shows, without dissent, that good sleep is necessary to stabilize minds already caught up in emotional and cognitive storms[62], and bad sleep is a key element in stirring up those storms to begin with[63].

This idea has been taken a bit too far by the ADD skeptics, as illustrated in a 2017 article in the *Chicago Tribune*[64] citing a theory the author called "provocative and controversial," that ADD is just another kind of sleep disorder. William Pelham (and just about everyone else) disagrees. He's cited in the article as an ADD researcher who directs the Center for Children and Families at Florida International University. He notes that only a handful of children, out of thousands he's studied, may have been misdiagnosed with ADD due to a sleep problem. This matches our clinical experience.

Still, sleep must be examined in any good evaluation of ADD. Other than carefully charting your sleep and wake times and how often you were awakened at night, one of the best indicators of bad sleep is the afternoon nap. Likewise, if you need to pull over to snooze while on a drive of more than an hour, you've got a sleep problem. Here are some additional clues drawn from questionnaires given at sleep clinics, including some pretty serious ones, which I've marked (!) to indicate the need for immediate medical attention. Like, put this book down and call the sleep clinic right now. They include:

- feeling drowsy during the day beyond what others notice;
- feeling unrefreshed or tired in the morning;
- experiencing lapses in time or blackouts (!);
- performing poorly in school or work because of sleepiness;
- falling asleep while reading, watching TV, riding as a passenger in a car for an hour, watching a movie in a theater, lying down, or sitting and talking with someone;
- falling asleep after eating lunch (without alcohol);

---

[62] www.medicaldaily.com/how-much-sleep-do-you-need-national-sleep-foundation-revises-recommended-hours-shut-320602

[63] www.newsweek.com/not-sleeping-enough-go-crazy-mental-health-681203

[64] www.chicagotribune.com/lifestyles/health/ct-adhd-sleep-disorder-20170921-story.html

- dozing off while sitting in traffic for a few minutes (!);
- falling asleep while driving (!!!).

If these issues are present, your evaluator may want you to do a sleep study to help resolve the mystery of sleep versus ADD. We've done this several times and come up with valuable results, even if it's just to rule out a sleep disorder. Generally, any prescriber can get this set up for you at a local sleep clinic, but you'll want to ask around. Some clinics seem very concentrated on breathing, which is great if you have apnea. Others are more broadly focused, which is what you want.

Of course, the insurance company gets its say, and it may ask you to do an in-home test kit instead of a lab-based study. This might *sound* great. I mean, who really wants to snooze in a sleep lab? But it's not a good idea, because the home kit is limited in what it can assess, and for our purposes, we need a broad evaluation. If you are assigned a home sleep study, you'll pick it up from a medical supply retailer and follow its instructions over the number of nights recommended by the sleep physician. Sometimes this will do the job, but often it won't, at which time the insurance company should authorize the lab study.

You'll arrive at the clinic just before bedtime and fill out questionnaires. Then the tech will hook you up to a bunch of sensors that measure just about every function you can imagine from oxygen levels to eye movement. It's pretty impressive, but also cumbersome, so it takes a little patience to tolerate. That's not always easy for an ADD person who also has sleep issues, so the weird nature of the lab itself may make good data collection tricky. If you have breathing issues consistent with apnea, the tech will wake you up midway through the night and apply a CPAP machine that basically pressurizes your airways to keep them open. This serves as both a test and demonstration of that technology. You'll leave the lab about 5:00 a.m., head home, and make an appointment with your sleep or primary care physician to look at the results. If you can't get to sleep in the lab, the doctor will consider various strategies to get the observation done. It can get quite involved, but usually, it's not.

If there are no abnormalities in the sleep profile but getting or staying asleep remains a problem, work with your therapist and prescriber as we describe in Chapter 8. As you modify each variable, examine whether sleep improves, gets worse, or is no different. A Fitbit or smartphone app like Sleep Cycle can be helpful in gauging how much deep and light sleep you're getting or how much you're lying awake. Just remember, these apps are better at showing that your sleep is bad than confirming that it's good.

If you can't get results with any of these sleep tricks, the best guess is ADD-related insomnia and it's time to talk to your prescriber about medication. The psychopharmacology of sleep is a tricky business, particularly amongst the ADD crowd, as multiple variables come into play. In Chapter 6, Kelsey will share ideas for how we've approached this problem in our clinic with a broad array of clients.

Bipolar Disorder (BiD). We've seen scores of clients with mood disorders, most often Bipolar II or Disruptive Mood Dysregulation Disorder (DMDD) in teens. Some are obvious and respond predictably to treatment. In other cases, we begin by thinking the client has ADD only to realize that BiD was the best-fit diagnosis. Less often we start with BiD and end up with ADD. Quite often, we find ourselves treating both (Chapter 4). This is because the symptoms of ADD and BiD are so similar that they can be easily mistaken for one another, especially when hyperactivity is present. Both may present with inattention, excessive energy, poor judgment, impulsivity, hyperkinesis, disconnected thought, irritability, mood dysregulation, sleep problems, racing and/or jumbled thoughts, and so on. Here are the telltale signs we use to make the distinction:

- **Broader and more severe changes in mood.** Some people with ADD have significant mood fluctuations, often the result of boredom, sleep deprivation, a stressful situation, or heavy demands on executive functioning. However, you'll know a real manic or hypomanic[65] episode when you see one by the severity and suddenness of the mood fluctuation. The person becomes extremely irritable or inappropriately elated without any inciting event. These mood states may last for hours, days, or even weeks. A person having a manic episode feels irritable, regardless of what's going on.

- **Inflated self-esteem and grandiosity.** While this varies greatly among people with ADD, they generally aren't known

---

[65] A less intense but still impairing elevation of mood.

for having high self-esteem or self-efficacy. In fact, the Conners tests actually include a measure of self-concept. When people with bipolar disorder experience mania, their sense of themselves may become grandiose or narcissistic, asserting that their skills or rights or potentials are superior to others. Occasionally, this reaches the point of a delusion, like believing one is talking directly to God or has insight into the minds of other people or animals or aliens or even politicians. People with ADD may sometimes come across as narcissistic, but this will typically present as "defensive" or "compensatory" narcissism, meaning they are trying to make up for a negative self-perception by making themselves seem better than others in some regard. That's very different from a person experiencing mania who believes wholeheartedly in his or her grandiosity.

- **Increased, revved-up energy.** Manic energy can be exhilarating, highly goal focused, and at times scary, uncontrolled, and uncontained. People with the hyperactive form of ADD can certainly feel excited and energetic, but rarely as intensely as someone having a manic episode. Also, that kind of energy is rarely goal oriented, except during periods of hyperfocus in which the ADD person strives obsessively to finish something, lest he or she lose focus and never get it back.

- **Impulsive or self-destructive behaviors.** People with ADD are no strangers to impulsivity. In Chapter 2 of *I Always Want to Be Where I'm Not*, I discuss the critical task of living with ADD as thinking before you act, moment to moment, every day. Without that kind of mindfulness, it's easy to head down an unwise or dangerous path. For people with bipolar disorder, impulse control is even harder, because during a manic phase they have even more energy to make stuff happen. Hypersexuality, substance abuse, reckless driving, criminal behavior, and relational disputes, all of which are problematic for ADD people, reach extreme levels for people who have BiD. However, for most bipolar people, these periods of poor judgment and impulse control come only during manic phases, whereas people with ADD face low-grade impulsivity on a daily basis.

- **Psychotic process.** I've seen a lot of misperception and misguided reasoning among people with ADD, but I've never seen psychosis. However, among those with correctly diagnosed BiD, disordered thinking can emerge during manic phases, including thought intrusions, delusions, and in the worst case scenario, hallucinations.

Depression. In a few cases, clients present with such a substantial degree of depression that they find themselves preoccupied, easily distracted, unable to concentrate, avoidant of tasks that require mental energy, low on self-esteem, unable to start or finish projects, and so on. In short, they have all the symptoms of ADD but are, in fact, just really depressed.

Doing this kind of detective work takes time, which is why it's not going to happen in a primary care doc's office nor even in a single psychiatric intake.

The secret to teasing this out is to go back into the client's history and ask the client and family what was observed in grade school, middle school, high school, college, etc. If the client has always shown these symptoms, it's more likely ADD, with any depression resulting from the many difficulties that disorder creates for those who have it (Chapter 4). If the client has acquired depressive symptoms later in life and had no significant struggles before onset, depression is a good guess with the ADD symptoms emerging from the mood disorder.

Doing this kind of detective work takes time, which is why it's not going to happen in a primary care doc's office nor even in a single psychiatric intake. In fact, we often see clients who've been seen elsewhere, usually by a PCP, and given an antidepressant when upon further examination, the client has ADD.

Trauma.[66] It's hard to pick the most difficult differential diagnosis to discern from ADD, but a good guess would be the several conditions resulting from trauma, particularly Post-Traumatic Stress Disorder

---

[66] This section was coauthored by Jordan Mayfield, LSCSW, a trauma-informed therapist on staff at Family Psychological Services (www.fpskansas.com) who is available to consult on cases of ADHD and trauma via video conferencing.

(PTSD)[67]. While a traumatic event can come at any age, children are particularly susceptible to the kinds of mental insult that later emerge as ADD-like symptoms, so it's worth taking a moment to look at how trauma impacts children's brains in a way that's surprisingly similar to ADD. So closely can these conditions mimic each other, that the skeptic press has, at times, proposed that trauma explains far more cases of ADD than could ever be plausible. And yet, to properly diagnose you, your evaluator must consider any history of trauma and differentiate its results from legit ADD. Even seasoned professionals struggle with this, in part because misconceptions about both conditions abound; and far too often therapists and prescribers get caught up in their own pet theories while failing to look beyond what they think is obvious (see "The Wisdom of Uncertainty" in Chapter 4).

ADD is typically present from birth, though the symptoms may not present until later in childhood. Those symptoms may go unnoticed until much later in life, but if you really have ADD, the condition can retrospectively be traced back to one's earliest years. In contrast, PTSD results from a traumatic event or series of events in a child or adult's environment which cause changes in the brain leading to physiological, cognitive, and emotional changes in how one processes stressful incidents and worries. It leaves afflicted clients feeling chronically unsafe, which in turn causes them to excrete much higher than normal amounts of the stress hormone cortisol. They respond more easily and often to the fight/flight part of their brain called the amygdala, becoming so consumed with their own safety that they cannot pay attention to and be present in their daily lives.

Despite their different origins, trauma disorders and ADD may both include symptoms of inattention, impulse control, lack of focus, insomnia, distractibility, impulsivity, irritability, poor memory and concentration, anxiety, sensitivity to sensory stimuli, depression, low self-esteem, and propensity toward addiction. While the exact presentation may change as children age into adulthood, neither condition is likely to vanish entirely, and the symptoms of either disorder may remain steady or even increase as the adult encounters new, stressful

---

[67] This condition is often up-diagnosed (given to cases that don't merit such a severe label) because providers don't realize other diagnoses may better suit the client's response to the traumatic event. For example, sometimes based on symptoms, trauma is better conceptualized as a severe adjustment disorder.

situations. This leaves many trauma survivors struggling well beyond childhood with symptoms that can look a lot like ADD.

Knowing this, we can speculate that trauma might "cause" ADD symptoms, particularly in children, because once traumatized, the client may eventually meet the criteria for ADD when they did not start out that way in early childhood. Trauma essentially rewires and impacts the development of a growing brain, stunting the growth of areas that deal with emotional regulation, impulse control, and self-awareness, which is exactly how ADD develops but for different reasons. The difference lies in the reason for that impact or what we call "etiology."

To clarify diagnosis, we must try to go back and assess the client's functioning prior to a known trauma. If the client had no such symptoms before the incident, the case for trauma is strong. This is easier to do for adults, because they have a whole social network of friends and family that knew them before the incident. It's harder for children, because they have no such history and in some cases, may not even have disclosed the trauma, or it has become so integrated into their lives that they don't realize its impact until much later in life. This is most common in children from homes in which there is child abuse, domestic violence, or high-conflict divorce.

Substance Abuse. Some of you aren't going to like this, but substance abuse, including those cultural faves marijuana and alcohol, can generate ADD-like symptoms. We're not talking about recreational use. We're talking the heavy, frequent use that's common these days, particularly among young adults and teens.

Marijuana is so revered now that any critique, even of heavy use, is looked upon and dismissed by its many avid fans like a belief in evil fairies. We're not getting into that debate in this book. We're just saying that when you're asking to be evaluated for ADD, but you're also drinking heavily or smoking a boatload of weed every week, you're more likely to get a referral for a substance abuse evaluation than a trip to the prescriber's office. We'll return to this in Chapter 10, but for now just remember that for any professional to accurately assess you, the effects of substance abuse must be ruled out and you won't find many prescribers willing to chase drug abuse with stimulants. Some won't even continue the conversation after they realize you're drinking or getting high every day.

Step 5: Get a Referral for Treatment

Once your evaluator has a good working diagnosis and has established sufficient impairment to warrant medical necessity for treatment, he or she will probably refer you for medication. If your evaluator plans to continue as your therapist, we hope that person has an integrative treatment relationship with a psychiatrist or psychiatric nurse practitioner in the same practice or, failing that, someone nearby. In reality, however, we know this isn't common (Chapter 5).

Your evaluator should also suggest some form of cognitive and behavioral therapy in his or her office or elsewhere to help get your show on the road. Of these, we prefer Acceptance and Commitment Therapy (ACT), a change in stance since publication of *I Always Want to Be Where I'm Not* and a model that will be included in its next revision. At our clinic, therapy ranges from a few sessions to learn the thirteen principles outlined in that book to long-term treatment intended to apply them to a successful life. We've seen some ADD clients for three months, others on and off for over ten years, and the majority somewhere in between. Many go away for months or years and then come back as life happens to get fresh ideas on how to organize themselves around it.

Buyer Beware

Here are a few consumer tips as you go out into the medical-industrial complex, trying to get your money's worth. They will not be well received by some in the ADD community, but they are well-reasoned and based on both practice standards and clinical experience.

Big Ticket Assessment

Some psychologists go overboard and want to give a whole battery of tests for IQ, achievement, and/or neurology. That might be interesting and, in some complicated cases, necessary; but it will get expensive in a hurry, and health insurance rarely covers that cost. If, during the clinical interview, you disclose a history of head injury, neurological impairment, seizure, or learning disability, and your testing for those conditions isn't up to date, a psychologist may want to test or retest you. Head injury can cause ADD-like symptoms that medication can help or hurt, depending on where the injury is located. Stimulants and other medications can also induce seizures. If there's no indication of any of these conditions, there's little reason to pay for a full neurological workup.

If there's no indication of head injury, neurological impairment, seizure, or learning disability, there's little reason to pay for a full neurological workup.

If you really do want to get a full psychological evaluation, the most inexpensive way is through a local university that has a graduate program in clinical psychology. We recently had one done to get a better picture of my son's learning strengths and weaknesses at the University of Kansas Psychology Clinic and the cost was just $400. That's a great deal—only about twenty percent of what it would cost if we did it in our office. Testing at a university is conducted by grad students, but they're up to date and eager to please[68].

If you feel you need a neurological evaluation, remember to keep reasonable expectations. A couple years ago we referred a late teen, whose diagnosis we just couldn't figure out, to a neurologist for further assessment. We'd been fairly successfully treating the girl for ADD, anxiety, and depression, but she had what we refer to as "swiss cheese" memory. She expressed great consternation about not remembering things and feeling like she was in a cognitive fog. It wasn't exactly the Zombie Effect. More like she felt "not as sharp" as she thought she should be. We ran genetic testing, churned her meds three or four times, and sent her for a sleep study that came up negative. Eventually we even sent her for transcranial magnetic stimulation (TMS). Nothing seemed to work, so we sent her first to a neuropsychologist and later to a neurologist. One of the least productive meetings I've ever attended was with the neurologist who confirmed the neuropsychologist's finding that nothing was wrong with her. He suggested that what we needed to do was treat her more aggressively for ADD, anxiety, and depression. Errr.

---

[68] We do not recommend this as a treatment referral for folks with ADD. Unless the client has a very simple and straightforward case, the need for specialization is just too great.

There may be occasions when this level of evaluation is medically necessary, but in the vast majority of ADD cases, the main takeaway from a full-tilt assessment is a large bill.

Even Bigger Ticket Assessment. A few clinics around the country evaluate ADD using Single Photon Emission Computed Tomography (SPECT) scans and Quantitative Electroencephalography (qEEG). While these sound like something Scotty would use to beam you up, they're really high-tech measures of brain wave activity.

The problem with each can be understood using a simple cost-benefit analysis. A single SPECT scan costs at least a thousand dollars and insurance generally won't cover it because it adds little to the prediction of ADD and is thus deemed to be "not medically necessary[69]." Most ADD experts still consider SPECT scanning overkill at best, and at worst, inaccurate and unproven in diagnosing or treating ADD. In fact, the American Academy of Pediatrics doesn't recommend *any* lab tests for ADD. As famous as this research is in the popular press, most notably that of Daniel Amen, MD, it hasn't been peer reviewed and replicated by the scientific community.

It's a similar story for qEEG, which is used to investigate various neurological conditions including ADD. Yet, it too is expensive and largely unnecessary. Even the FDA, which approved qEEG nearly seventeen years ago, admits it's only intended to be used in conjunction with the same kind of diagnostic interview and standardized testing we described in this chapter.[70] The American Psychiatric Association, the American Neurological Association, and most experts on ADD state that qEEG isn't reliable enough to diagnose any psychiatric disorder.

-Dr Kelsey-

Genetic Testing. Since ADD tends to run in families, and since genetic research is becoming more advanced all the time, wouldn't it be prudent to look for an ADD diagnosis there as we do with say, Cystic Fibrosis? Not yet. Research on ADD from 1992 to 2008 focused heavily on neuroimaging, twin studies, family studies, and case-control

---

[69] www.additudemag.com/adhd/article/783.html

[70] healthland.time.com/2013/07/16/reading-the-brain-fda-approves-first-scan-for-diagnosing-adhd/

studies[71] all designed to establish whether ADD was hereditary and how it impacted the structure of the brain. Good findings come to those who wait. A decade of research indicates a ninety-two percent rate of heritability in identical twins with ADD regardless of differences in reading capabilities or IQ[72]. Wow. This research eventually expanded to include the identification of twelve specific genes that greatly influence biological processes like mediating the transportation and reuptake of dopamine (Chapter 6). A key area of the brain to which this dopamine is transported is the caudate nucleus. Located right in the middle of the brain, it's one of the structures that aids reward processing. When dopamine regulation is inefficient, yielding too much or too little dopamine, as it is for people with ADD, this reward center functions inconsistently. Unconscious memory starts to lag, inhibitions drop, and motor functions changes. This not only underlies the "how and why" of ADD, it plays a major role in controlling how our bodies regulate movement and our ability to learn and remember.

One study looked at the genome[73] of 1,156 ethnically homogenous but unrelated children. One of the many characteristics recorded in each participant's genome was the presence of variations in the observed patterns of gene sequences, or genotypes. While there is no "ADD gene," there are many genes that influence the possible expression of ADD symptoms. One is the COMT gene which provides a couple of enzymes in our body that form an instruction manual for how to conduct signals from cell to cell and break down other chemical messengers. One of the chemicals that is signaled and directed by this gene's functioning is (you guessed it) dopamine. These enzymes carry out these instructions in the part of the brain responsible for executive functions such as planning, impulse control, short-term memory, and abstract thinking. The presence of a COMT variation appeared significantly more often in participants known to have ADD, suggesting that

---

[71] A type of retrospective observational study used to determine if an exposure is associated with an outcome, in this case having a genetic link to a diagnosed first-order relative like a parent or sibling and leading to an outcome of ADD.

[72] Levy F, H. D. (1997). Attention-deficit hyperactivity disorder: a category or a continuum? Genetic analysis of a large-scale twin study. Journal of American Academy of Child and Adolescent Psychiatry, 36(6), 737-44.

[73] The complete set of DNA and genes.

dopamine signaling and transportation varies at the genetic level in people so diagnosed.

Genetics research provides important methods and technologies for studying the differences between those with and without ADD at the chromosomal level, allowing us to improve our understanding of the neurobiological conditions and their treatments. But these tests haven't evolved to the point where they can confirm or refute an ADD diagnosis through objective assessment. Because we cannot be certain if or when genes will express their traits and cause a disorder, we haven't a clear roadmap for a given diagnosis. That's why genetic testing results are given as probabilities of expression.

If you or your loved one are impaired to the point that you're considering genetic testing for ADD, do you really need a geneticist to confirm the presence of a duplicated section on one of your forty-six chromosomes before you decide to seek treatment? Precision is a wonderful thing in clinical practice, but when it comes to ADD, genetic testing offers little to add to the accuracy of diagnosis

Someday, the big ticket technologies we've discussed above might evolve to the point that they prove efficient and effective for diagnosing ADD, particularly in complicated cases that can't be understood with simpler, less expensive methods. That will be a fine day indeed. Here and now, most folks with ADD will do just fine using the evaluation methods we recommended earlier in this chapter.

What Else Could Go Wrong?

The definition of genius is taking the complex and making it simple.

— (probably) Albert Einstein

- Dr. Wes -

"I'm really struggling, Dr. Wes." Tressa hunched forward over her paper notebook and then back again in a subtly fraught rocking motion. "My meds just aren't working anymore, and I feel like I can't go to school tomorrow."

"I share your frustration." I shook my head involuntarily before realizing how that probably looked to the girl, and then decided to just go with it. "Since the first day you showed up in my parking lot, we've been trying to pin down a good working diagnosis for you."

"Well I'm sick of it. I wrote it all down in here." She patted the notebook. "I don't see how I can keep on like this. I'm so depressed, and I can't focus, and I just don't even want to get up every day."

"Right. Let's remember that wanting is different than—"

"Willingness. I know all that. I know I'm not going to want to do any of this, but I'm going to have to choose whether to do it anyhow because it's important and, yeah, so I guess I'm willing to go, but I just don't want to feel like this!"

Spending time with Tressa was like playing a game of chess in which your opponent finds a way to keep you in perpetual check. I kept playing, but whenever I found the path of progress, she found a way to corner me again.

We had every tidbit of data on Tressa that we could ever want. I'd known her since she was born, sixteen years ago. I'd treated her mom, Jennifer, for post-partum depression and then, upon discovering that Jenn had an underlying bipolar disorder and ADHD, I'd treated her successfully for ten years thereafter. I'd seen Jenn through bouts of debilitating, even suicidal, depression, helped her deal with her marital and family-of-origin difficulties, and guided her through various disappointments in business, all of which pressed her back and forth between compensation and decompensation. We'd addressed a painful history of trauma in late adolescence and helped her learn to embrace the many conflicting roles of adulthood. At times over the years, to avoid hospitalization, Jenn would come and sit in my waiting room so I could see her for a few minutes between sessions. My previous nurse practitioner had worked well with Jenn, and after an extensive, well-reasoned, period of trial and error, we eventually got her stabilized on Lamictal, Concerta, and Abilify. Jenn transferred with me to my new practice, and Kelsey began seeing her in 2014. Despite countless life stressors and a very high diathesis for multiple symptoms, Jenn became a testament to a good team executing a well-integrated treatment of medication and psychotherapy.

Given her mom's history, it surprised no one when Tressa began exhibiting symptoms in early adolescence. However, even I, a guy known for seeing difficult teens, was taken aback by how intense Tressa was. When Jennifer brought her to her first appointment late in middle school, Tressa wouldn't even get out of the car. She wasn't trying to be oppositional, she just seemed terrified, as she sat in my parking lot, doors closed and windows rolled up. Eventually, we were able to get her into the office for about fifteen minutes, just enough time to give her my pitch, which consisted mostly of, "I have a cat."

She didn't return for six months.

But she did return, and slowly we began to develop a tense, at times combative, and at other times gentle and caring relationship. But it was never easy. She felt everything too deeply, cared way too much, had intrusive thoughts and fears, was irritable and quick to anger, then embarrassed and sorry she'd said whatever she'd said or done whatever she'd done, even if nobody else noticed, and she hated it when nobody noticed. She was irritating and irritable, living in a constant state of fear that she might be exactly so. Sometimes, she would work hard at something she liked, other times she seemed to have little will or motivation.

A tall, pretty girl, Tressa could have been a model, yet she had body and gender dysphoria. She was awkward and socially hesitant, yet she could go on stage and perform a rockin' guitar solo with her band. I'd seen her do it. She exuded confidence and strength on stage, then went home and locked herself in her room, refusing to go to band practice for a week. Her lack of psychological integrity was so great that she couldn't hold onto goals, values, or even a sense of self for more than a day or two.

In the language of Chapter 2, Tressa had a broad range of symptoms that were well outside the norm for girls her age. Given her mom's history and that of her extended family, one could conceptualize this as anxiety (we tried and failed) or just as easily, the early signs of bipolar disorder (closer but not quite). Many diagnosticians would see Tressa as being in the early throes of borderline personality disorder and leave it at that. While that diagnosis should not be given to a teen due to a lack of full personality development before the early twenties, many add it implicitly to their internal notes.

Interestingly, ADD was the last thing Kelsey and I thought Tressa had. We'd chased that theory early on, but her Conners testing—completed by both parents, a teacher, and Tressa—came back *below* the 50th percentile. We presumed she'd picked up her father's genetics which leaned to the anxious side. Whatever label you gave her, Tressa was severely impaired by her symptoms, so Kelsey and I eventually decided to go against our testing on this one rare occasion and try stimulant medication along with her regimen of mood stabilizers.

Even as we were trying to get a foothold in the case, Tressa simply stopped going to her freshman year of high school and begged her parents to let her do online school. In our experience virtual and home schooling is a terrible idea for kids with mental health problems. These programs require far more internal discipline than does regular school and for Tressa, and most of the kids who attempt this method, self-regulation is in short supply. In Tressa's case, it ended badly, and she emerged from that semester with very few credits.

In the middle of all this, I began training in Acceptance and Commitment Therapy (ACT, pronounced like the word "act," not spelled out, A-C-T). Dissatisfied with standard cognitive techniques that seemed to bore and irritate most clients and particularly teens, I took a workshop at the American Psychological Association convention entitled "ACT in the Treatment of ADHD." I was immediately hooked and began more intensive training with some of the key figures in that area of study, including Stephen Hayes, Kelly Wilson, and Robyn Walser, all clinical psychologists.

Since this is a book on medication, I'll save the ACT treatise for a future revision of *I Always Want to Be Where I'm Not*, but the short version is that rather than try and help Tressa feel better, we changed our focus to helping her *do* better, accepting the uncomfortable and painful feelings and thoughts her symptoms brought, "defusing" them from her behavior and helping her to choose how she wanted to respond. When she started her sophomore year, she was encouraged to hate every minute of it, to really notice and be aware of that hate, to let it flow freely throughout her consciousness, and whenever she felt the need to cry or pound her fist or express her displeasure, to do so freely (but politely), all while getting up, riding to school, going through the door, sitting in class, and so on. This was jarring for both Tressa and Jenn, as both heard me implying that Tressa's desire to feel better was hopeless and that she would always be impaired. However, as you might predict, as Tressa began doing better, she began to feel just enough better to keep trudging forward—though it was still trudging.

"How about we pause a moment to take stock, Tressa," I said. "A year ago you wouldn't leave the house. You got into a perpetual thing where all you did was avoid anxiety, which is about the worst advice therapists have ever given kids. Then you came to see me and we changed up the approach and, between therapy and meds, you only missed four days of school last semester. You've kicked ass."

A pout crossed Tressa's face and her eyes glistened.

"What?" I asked with a dry tone. "I'm telling you that you're someone I admire for putting forth such an effort against the most difficult feelings and thoughts. And this upsets you?"

She began to cry. "It shouldn't be a celebration when someone just does something everyone else can do easily. I'm just going to school."

"And you're back in the band and you showed your art at a local gallery and we actually made a little bit of progress on gender dysphoria. You can see your progress as no big thing, but I'm going to continue to see it as heroic. You got up and did what needed to be done. Mostly."

"I know." She pulled a tissue from the box on the end table near the couch. "But that's when my meds were working, and now I just can't feel them anymore."

"I've said this before, Tressa, but I'm going to say it again. Medication will never be some kind of magic pixie dust. Vyvanse isn't a pep pill. Cymbalta and Lamictal don't make anyone happy. You have to get up and organize your life to generate joy and meaning and curiosity. Seroquel will only help you sleep if you decide to value sleep more than staying up and doing homework or surfing the web. Ativan is fine once in a while, but it's easy to just keep wanting to take it to prevent yourself from feeling anything and that's just another kind of avoidance."

"So, what am I supposed to do?" She flopped back against the sofa. Grace raised an eye and then settled back to her catnap. "How do I live like this?"

"We both know you have a lot of genetic crap to overcome and a big part of that is getting you through the next few years with as little impairment as possible so that when you're older you'll have gotten from your teen years what you need as an adult."

"I know that too." She went after yet another tissue. "That's why I go to school. It's not because I like it."

"Yes, and you go because not going actually adds to your sense of craziness. There you are, alone in your room, looking out the window, messing with the internet. As difficult as it is to go to, say, band practice, it's what we call 'behavioral activation.' It's therapeutic, whether you feel like doing it or not and there's no medication Kelsey can give you that's going to make you better if you're not putting the medicine to the right use."

"God." Tressa's countenance shifted from sad to wistful. "I just want it to be over."

"Meaning?" I intentionally arched my brow.

"No, not that. Not my life. I just want all the fear and bad focus and lack of energy to be gone. You don't know what it's like."

"No, I don't." I leaned in toward her. "But I do know that I've been down this path before and Kelsey and I will keep at it with you until we get it right, just as long as you keep working with us. Every time I see you and every time Kelsey sees you, we think about your case, discuss it, and try and fix something."

"Why is it taking so long? It didn't take that long with Sophie. I sent her to see you, and you had her figured out in like three weeks. She's all in love with her Adderall. Adderall just made me crazier."

"You answered your own question. I'm not going to talk about Sophie in particular, but let's just say that your case isn't real straightforward. You don't have just one thing or even two. There's no neat little box to put you in."

"Wouldn't that be great if there were? I could just be anxious, or ADD, or bipolar. I envy those people. I have to be a bunch of things that don't even play well together. Who would even want to live in here?" She tapped her head.

"I understand, Tressa. But just know that no matter how difficult or complicated or frustrating this gets, we will never ever give up on you."

And we have not.

- Dr. Kelsey -

In the last chapter, we discussed how some conditions can be mistaken for ADD. In this one, we take a different tack, examining what diagnoses may occur alongside ADD, interweaving to form a sum that is usually greater than its parts. There are no better examples on my caseload than Tressa and Jenn and no better argument for working closely with a prescriber and therapist to find a path through a jungle of competing psychological influences.

Looking back, I think that early on I got distracted in her case by what seemed to be treatment-resistant depression[74], rather than realizing that was only one part of the larger puzzle. Tressa ruminated obsessively at her perceived inabilities. The several strategies she used to temporarily quell her discomfort—like not going to school—did nothing to lower her depression and instead opened the door for further self-loathing. Going to school felt bad. Not going to school felt bad. Tressa just felt bad.

When we started kicking around the idea of a stimulant trial, the case was nearing a point of crisis. Jennifer had been treated successfully for sixteen years for ADD, so it was logical to consider that diagnosis. But that fantastic norm-referenced, reliable, and valid testing instrument we fawned over in Chapter 3 didn't bear it out. My psychiatric interview and Wes' diagnostic evaluation showed Tressa's performance and engagement in her daily life to be distracted, avoidant, and full of projects she never finished. Yet, she didn't quite meet the symptoms for ADD, even if she certainly met the impairment criteria.

Finally, everyone—her mom, dad, Wes, Tressa, and I—agreed that, given her mother's history, we had to try a different approach: a controlled experiment. If we didn't, Tressa's fall semester in a new school might end up like her entire sophomore year at the old one. While the risks were not insubstantial, they were outweighed by her distress and inability to function.

After a few initial trials using the same medications Jennifer had found effective, we eventually found a better fit with Vyvanse[75]. It wasn't the miracle Tressa had hoped for[76], but it did reduce her propensity to collapse in a heap when she fell behind or became so disorganized that she gave up trying to make the next right decision. With Vyvanse, she

---

[74] The term "treatment-resistant depression" is commonly used to describe major depressive episodes that have not satisfactorily responded to at least two trials of antidepressant as a single therapy.

[75] As noted earlier, when we mention brand name medications, we have no financial relationship with the companies that produce them.

[76] We'll discuss managing expectations many times over the remainder of this book.

started reporting change in how she managed tough emotions, and this in turn changed how she interacted with the world.

Still, we had a long way to go. While Tressa had made it to school most days that semester, she continued to battle mood instability. We hypothesized this as a side effect of stimulants (Chapter 8) before realizing that she was actually more mood stable while on them. Jennifer had always fought anxiety and an agitated depression that leaned into the bipolar II realm. As Tressa's condition seemed increasingly parallel to her mom's (and several relatives up that family tree), we modified our medication regimen to fit that model. Again, no miracles, but as we added medications, we saw improvement.

Depending on how you slice it, this was either a great triumph over mental illness or a scary walk down the oft-debated path of overmedicating a teenager. As a team, we've done all that slicing, second guessing ourselves about forty times, and still coming to the conclusion that for a few rare teens this is not only the best path, it is probably the only one. Area hospitals, psychiatric residential treatment facilities (PRTFs), and intensive outpatient programs (IOPs) are full of teens like Tressa. Yet, she has never been hospitalized nor even been taken to the emergency room, nor has she made an attempt on her own life. We did enroll her in Dialectical Behavior Therapy (DBT) and at times saw her more frequently than other clients. But she remains in large part her own young woman, free of psychiatric restriction.

Tressa's case is, of course, more complicated than average, and we include it specifically to illustrate the difficulty of treating multiple diagnoses even with an ideal team. If you or your child (or both of you) are going to get the full benefit from any treatment, co-occurring diagnoses need to be identified and factored into the equation. In this chapter, we'll usually discuss less complicated cases to make our diagnostic points clearer. Please remember that such simplification stretches diagnostics in the opposite direction of what we saw with Tressa, making co-occurring conditions appear more straightforward to detect and treat than they really are.

Bad Sleep

- Dr. Wes -

In the last chapter, we discussed how bad sleep can mimic ADD and cited a *Chicago Tribune* article that went so far as to propose that ADD was a kind of sleep disorder. Unfortunately, none of the researchers cited in that piece mentioned the inverse and more common ways sleep and ADD collide. There are several, and it's critical to your treatment to figure out which one applies to you.

ADD-Related Insomnia (ARI)

In order to discuss this problem with ease, we had to invent a name for it. That seems odd, because poor sleep is widely recognized as a symptom of bipolar disorder, anxiety, and depression, yet it's not formally acknowledged in tandem with ADD. Not everyone with ADD will have it of course, but when ARI does appear, it seems to do so at the onset of puberty, then continue through young adulthood, and often, well beyond. As our made-up name implies, correctly identified ARI isn't really a co-occurring disorder, but a product of the condition itself. While teens and young adults are notorious for poor sleep, ARI is very different in that the client doesn't simply avoid sleep, he or she can't get it despite good effort. When asked, clients describe their minds running a mile a minute on fifty things during the day and that this does not shutdown conveniently at 9:30 p.m. each night. For some ADD clients, any quiet time outside their body makes for an extra loud time inside their head, which is exactly how ARI is experienced.

Delayed Sleep Phase Syndrome

This isn't a product of ARI, but of the poor sleep hygiene that so many folks with ADD love to hate or maybe hate to love. These clients state with great certainty that they are "just not morning people" and that all their superpowers of attention and focus and achievement only kick in late in the day, such that they must stay up until midnight or 2:00 a.m., or maybe all night, to do all the things that need to be done. The preference for these individuals to function as night owls makes sense when you consider that children, adolescents, and adults with ADD have a late onset of melatonin as compared to their neurotypical peers[77]. This can greatly improve with initiation of stimulant medication, which tends to get people up and going in the morning much the

---

[77] Veen, M. M. V., Kooij, J. S., Boonstra, A. M., Gordijn, M. C., & Someren, E. J. V. (2010). Delayed Circadian Rhythm in Adults with Attention-Deficit/Hyperactivity Disorder and Chronic Sleep-Onset Insomnia. *Biological Psychiatry, 67*(11), 1091–1096. doi: 10.1016/j.biopsych.2009.12.032

way a magnum dose of espresso does for most of us. However, any gains are lost if the client refuses to get into a healthy sleep-wake cycle. In a worst case scenario, we find clients going against Kelsey's explicit instructions, misusing their medication late in the day to take full advantage of their late-set circadian clocks (Chapter 10). That brings us quite nicely to a co-occurring sleep disorder that is the product of ADD treatment itself.

Stimulant Related Sleep Disruption

As if things weren't complicated enough, stimulant medication is well known to cause disrupted sleep. Compared to other medications, stimulants wash out of your system pretty quickly, but for some people it's not quick enough to avoid carrying over into the nighttime hours. This is really where different medication designs come into play. A close working relationship with a prescriber can help you learn which stimulant to use and when and how to use it, because the last thing we need is to fix one problem (ADD) and create another one (chronic insomnia). We'll return to this problem as a known side effect in Chapter 8. For now, just understand that if you're being evaluated while on a medication, a key element of understanding the ADD-sleep puzzle is determining which came first, the chicken of unusual sleep or the egg of ADD.

Anxiety
- *Dr. Kelsey* -

In Chapter 2, we proposed that ADD and anxiety can be thought of on a continuum in which people with anxiety care too much and people with ADD care too little. Folks who lean so far toward the anxious side as to be diagnosable, experience some or all of the following:

- **Excessive and/or unrealistic worry.** Generally, these worries will be broad, difficult to control, present more often than not, and occur across a number of places and/or activities. While they can be specific to, say, social situations, flying, or certain stimulus like snakes, specific phobias tend not to interact with ADD in the same way that more generalized, free-floating anxiety does.

- **Motor tensions.** These include restlessness, tiredness, shakiness, or muscle tension, particularly clenching problems like irritable bowel, tooth grinding, temporomandibular joint (TMJ) pain, or the kind of "knots" a massage therapist will detect across certain areas (or all) of your body.

- **Autonomic hyperactivity.** This isn't the kind of hyperactivity we think of with ADHD, where one is "driven by a motor." Anxious hyperactivity may include heart palpitations, shortness of breath, dry mouth, trouble swallowing as well as those on the lower end of your digestive track like nausea, diarrhea, or constipation.

- **Hypervigilance.** You may not know how to define it, but if you've had it, you'll recognize hypervigilance. It's the feeling of being "on edge," unable to concentrate or make decisions. It can also include trouble falling or staying asleep (unrelated to primary insomnia) and irritability, which you'll notice within yourself or which will be pointed out by others. These symptoms will appear or get worse as your stress increases.

When symptoms of both ADD and anxiety present together, treatment gets convoluted in a hurry.

- **Intrusive Ideation.** These are, quite simply, ideas you can't get out of your head. They range from annoying preoccupations to obsessions. Most people with anxiety will have some intrusive thoughts, though most fall on the less severe end of the spectrum.

When symptoms of both ADD and anxiety present together, treatment gets convoluted in a hurry. However, before you and your evaluator can validate them as separate diagnoses, you must first stop and consider if both are present and if they are, which one might be driving the other. This is important because, even though there are only three possible diagnostic combinations for ADD and anxiety, each requires a different approach to medication management. This creates more trial and error than any of us would like because there's no other way to know how the two intersect in a given client.

Anxious-ADD. In this presentation, the client should be diagnosed with both ADD and anxiety. In our clinical experience, this is the most common scenario when a client is showing symptoms of both conditions. I usually try to manage the anxiety first with an SSRI[78] or SNRI[79], because leading with stimulants can push the client's anxiety over that curve we discussed in Chapter 2 to an unproductive level where he or she "cares too much." Very rarely does that reach the point of inducing anxiety attacks, but usually it comes in the form of unremitting jitters, feeling "wired," or brief bouts of obsessive or compulsive behavior. If that doesn't go away in two or three days in a person we've presumed to have only ADD, we switch to this dual diagnosis.

ADD Primary. In this condition, a formal diagnosis of anxiety is not warranted. Instead, the client's primary diagnosis should be ADD with accompanying anxiety symptoms secondary to that. This is the second-most common mixed condition. Because the symptoms are the same, it can be hard to differentiate this from the first scenario, even after a good diagnostic evaluation. The quickest way to find out is to initiate stimulant medication. If the client's anxiety drops to a subclinical level, we've nailed it. If it goes up or remains the same, and the ADD symptoms are mitigated, we go back to the ADD-anxious conceptualization and add an SSRI or SNRI. Because we prefer to be cautious with people's anxiety, especially students in the middle of an academic semester, I'll often start such clients on a stimulant along with an SSRI or SNRI as a precaution. Then, after three to six months, we re-evaluate the need for anxiety management. If the SSRI/SNRI can be reduced without triggering anxiety, this is the best conceptualization, and we taper the client off the additional medication.

Anxiety Primary. This is the differential diagnosis discussed in Chapter 3 in which the client's anxiety is actually causing ADD symptoms. It's the least common scenario in our experience, but it does appear in people who have really bad endogenous anxiety, histories of trauma, and/or anxiety in their family tree. These clients care so much that they become preoccupied, distracted, and unable to get anything done. An experienced evaluator may hypothesize this condition, but it's tough to prove without a medication trial. If an SSRI, or more likely an SNRI,

---

[78] A selective serotonin reuptake inhibitor (like Lexapro, Prozac, Zoloft, etc.) that is used to treat moderate anxiety.

[79] A serotonin norepinephrine reuptake inhibitor (like Effexor, Cymbalta, Pristiq, etc.) that is used to treat moderate anxiety and can also help with depression and focus in tandem with stimulant medication when treating mixed conditions.

reduces both the client's anxiety and ADD symptoms, this is the best conceptualization. If we suspect this, as we did at one point with Tressa, the last thing we try is a stimulant because the chances of blowing up the anxiety are too great. That doesn't mean we never give it a shot, because some people still have ADD symptoms even after their anxiety is in check (moving us back to the ADD-anxious hypothesis). It means we get there slowly and add the stimulant when the client is otherwise stable; and we're prepared to back out if we see a debilitating increase in anxiety symptoms.

Depression

For many folks who come to our office, depression and ADD go hand in hand. The harbingers of a depressive episode are as follows:

- **A persistent, sad, or irritable mood.** When it co-occurs with ADD, depression tends to be more endogenous than related to external circumstance. While one can have a brief depressive episode related to life difficulties alongside ADD, we usually label this as an adjustment disorder with depressed mood and do not expect it to last more than three to six months[80].

- **Loss of interest in previously enjoyed activities.** This is different and must be distinguished from the ADD tendency to move from one interesting thing to the next or to give up on a project when it becomes boring. For a depressed person, if it happens at all, shifting focus to a new activity is unlikely to generate new and sustained pleasure or satisfaction.

- **Significant changes in appetite and/or body weight.** While people with ADD often have weight fluctuations, these tend to be related to dysregulated eating or inconsistent stimulant use. Folks who are actually depressed lose their willingness to eat, which if one is on stimulants, is the only tool available to maintain body weight (Chapter 8). Conversely, some depressed people overeat as a way to comfort themselves and

---

[80] This presumes the upsetting situation does not go away. In some cases, clients are in a long-term state of adjustment to an upsetting situation that just keeps chugging along. Examples include an abusive relationship, the chronic illness of a parent, or a perpetually troubled marriage.

regulate mood. Those with ADD find it harder to cognitively override that tendency or distract themselves from binging.

- **Disruption in sleep patterns.** As noted earlier, people with ADD may also have ADD-related chronic insomnia. For depressed people, poor sleep will instead come in waves that closely follow their mood fluctuations. Those with agitated depression will tend toward insomnia and those with low-energy presentations usually sleep too much. When depression co-occurs with ADD and the symptoms include insomnia, long-term sleep and mood patterns must be examined and compared with any changes that come into play after stimulant use versus emerging in tandem with other depressive symptoms.

- **Low energy and poor concentration.** Failure to persist is a defining characteristic among people with ADD who may become easily fatigued in situations where their mental energy is overtaxed or which they find boring. However, this tends to be a long-term pattern in ADD, whereas depressed people will generally experience increasing and decreasing symptoms over time. The exception is dysthymia, a long-term unremitting depression.

- **Feelings of worthlessness, inappropriate guilt, and/or recurrent thoughts of death and suicide.** This symptom set forms a critical distinction between people who have only ADD and those who also have depression. Typically, ADD-only clients have less intensive and less frequent feelings of self-harm. Those with co-occurring depression, are more prone to self-harm ideations and behaviors.

As with anxiety, there are three ways depression and ADD can present together. While you may think we're splitting hairs in these categories, as you work with a skilled prescriber to conceptualize and treat your own case, you'll see why. Each presentation alters how we intervene with both therapy and medication.

ADD Leads Depression

Most often we find ADD driving a client's depression. Wes often reassures his new clients by saying, "If you have ADD and you're not depressed, you don't really understand your situation very well." Few argue the point. Despite some feel-good books asking you to look at

ADD as a gift, most folks would prefer to wrap this one up well before next Christmas and give it away as a white-elephant.

Untreated ADD may have already impacted your self-esteem, self-efficacy, ability to relate to others, and general sense of well-being.

If we apply a stimulant and therapy and your depressive symptoms remit, this hypothesis is retained and additional treatment for depression may not be necessary. There's a catch, however. Unless you are very young—before middle school age— untreated ADD may have already impacted your self-esteem, self-efficacy, ability to relate to others, and general sense of well-being. While writing this chapter, we did an intake on a very sweet fifteen-year-old girl named Kayla, who presented with depression and anxiety to the point that she was feeling a lot like Tressa: hating school, wanting to lay around the house, but courageously choosing to act according to her values, dragging herself to school every day where she was always miserable. Kayla's grades dipped to near failing in the fall semester of her freshman year but she pulled herself up to all As by spring break. And yet she was still sad, worried, and hopeless, unimpressed by her own remarkable comeback. Asked about the root of her depression and anxiety, the articulate girl choked up. "I just have really high standards for myself and everyone else and I just think I'm never going to get there. So I get overwhelmed and just hate myself."

Spoken like a true depressed person. She even admitted thoughts of self-harm, though she assured me she had no intent or plan; these were scary ideations. I asked Kayla if she felt her anxiety was pressing her toward depression, as is often the case among highly self-conscious kids. She nodded through her sad affect. "I'm just trying so hard. I do nothing but study and then I do okay but other days I just don't care. I completely gave up last fall. Then I realized that I needed to care."

"Is there anything else that brings you down?" I asked.

"Well." She hesitated and bit her lip. "I love my little brother, but you know, he has autism and ADD and sometimes they kind of forget about me because he has so many issues."

"Wait, what?" I said. "When you and your mom were in here, I asked you about mental health issues in the family. She didn't mention this."

"Right," Kayla said. "That was kind of weird. He's only my half-brother so I think she thought you meant, like my dad or something."

The light came on. I brought Kayla's mom back in and asked if anyone had ever considered ADD as a diagnosis in Kayla. Nobody had, but both immediately saw the connection. I finished the intake and asked Wes to send out testing on her. She scored well into the clinical range and we started her on stimulants.

It usually takes a while to correct all the life issues that come with years spent living with ADD; so even if focus and concentration are improved, the other baggage—school failure, financial problems, relational difficulties—remain depressing enough to warrant treatment of both disorders. That's the route we took in Kayla's case. Her sadness and worry were so great, and she'd been so adamant in asking her mom to get her in to see us due to her suicidal thoughts, that I didn't feel we had time to risk being wrong. So we began Kayla's treatment as if ADD were a secondary condition using an SNRI alongside stimulants.

I saw Kayla last week and she's a whole new girl. We'll see if that holds during the fall semester, but it was an auspicious start. Given this improvement, we now suspect that the real conceptualization for Kayla is ADD leading depression, and believe that she may eventually discontinue antidepressants as she responds to an improvement in her ability to take on the world.

Depression Leads ADD

It was possible that my interest in Kayla's sibling and his ADD would prove unwarranted. He was only her half-brother so their genetic connection was less than if they'd been full first-order relatives. Upon further inquiry, I also learned that her step-father had significant mental health issues that had warranted treatment and which had included ADD in a cluster of several diagnoses. Her brother's diagnosis might reflect that and not any commonality of genetics through her mom. If that were true, it would have been reasonable to hypothesize that Kayla's depression was actually leading her ADD as a differential diagnosis. We were really making an educated guess. If we discontinued her stimulant, as we would routinely do to allow her a break (Chapter 9) and her concentration, focus, and motivation continued unabated, we might decide not to continue treating the ADD symptoms as her depression had resolved, and with it, her ADD.

Unfortunately, we don't find depression leading ADD very often, and we don't expect that will be Kayla's final conceptualization. We typically see it only among clients with the most debilitating symptoms. For a handful of these clients, depression management will do the trick, usually with an SNRI like Effexor or Cymbalta. For many more like Kayla, just addressing the depression won't be enough without ancillary treatment for ADD.

Some prescribers imagine this scenario as one in which stimulant medication simply helps clients overcome symptoms of low energy and depressive outlook, without any need for an additional diagnosis, that stimulants might be an ancillary treatment for depression. That could happen, but in practice we don't add stimulants for anyone we don't see as also having ADD. Too many complications and not enough gain. Thus, when stimulants work, we presume we've tapped into an underlying ADD, not that we're pepping up a deeply dysphoric client.

ADD Coexists With Depression

In this condition, we see the two diagnoses as separate. We usually come upon this when we are first successful in treating depressive symptoms in a client who presents with that complaint, as Kayla did, but only later realize that the client is still struggling in school, relationships, or career. They feel better, but they just aren't doing any better in areas of life reflective of ADD.

Understanding depression and ADD as equals, rather than one leading the other, is important in deciding how to manage your meds. For example, if we know that you're prone to bouts of depression, wholly apart from how your ADD symptoms impact you, we can learn not to overrespond when you experience a dip in mood as your ADD medication reaches a tolerance point. We can take note of the calendar, realize you're ready for a stimulant break and understand your irritability as the result of the diminished impact of stimulants. We can also predict that, due to your co-occurring depression, you may have a more severe mood dip while taking that break than someone who does not have freestanding depression.

Conversely, we might decide not to boost your stimulants above your therapeutic dose to avoid negatively impacting your mood state and make your depression worse. In a few cases, we might simply have to give up treating the ADD because of complications with chronic depression. However, because the normal interplay between stimulants, SNRIs, depression, and ADD is pretty good, when we see adverse side effects when adding stimulants to a depressed client's regimen, we quickly start to consider a different co-occurring diagnosis. We'll examine it next.

Bipolar Disorder

Bipolar disorder (BiD) may be the most commonly misdiagnosed condition we see, especially among clients presenting with ADD symptoms and those with a history of depression that has responded poorly to treatment. Myriad accounts of bipolar disorder have been written elsewhere, so we won't try and do it justice here. We just want you to understand how BiD can present alongside ADD and how that increases the delicacy of any medication intervention your prescriber might attempt.

This turns out to be pretty important information, as the pool of folks with co-occurring ADD and BiD is vast. As Harvard Medical School psychologist Roberto Olivardia notes:

> Approximately 10 million people in the United States have [bipolar disorder]. Research studies show that about 70 percent of people with the condition also have ADHD, and that 20 percent of people with ADHD will develop Bipolar Disorder[81].

Seeing those numbers astounded even Wes and I, but we were not surprised at Olivardia's next proposal:

> The tragedy is that, when [these two] disorders co-occur, the diagnoses are often missed. It can take up to 17 years for patients to receive a diagnosis of BiD. As with any co-occurring disorder, it is important to receive the right diagnosis as early as possible to treat the condition effectively.... Since the comorbidity rates are high, any time someone is diagnosed with one, the presence of the other should always be looked for.

We see this all the time: clients evaluated by primary care physicians or by mental health providers without sufficient experience or training,

---

[81] www.additude.com/bipolar-disorder-adhd-puzzle/

clinicians handing out one diagnosis or the other, missing the larger picture and compromising treatment. Or, conversely, primary care providers hesitant to start anyone with a history of bipolar disorder on a stimulant for ADD, no matter their current stability, for fear of exacerbating a stimulant-induced-psychosis. So, as with all things ADD, we suggest you become the expert on your symptoms and potential diagnoses rather than relying on anyone, even a professional, to do it for you.

As its name suggests, bipolar disorder can present as a fluctuation between extremes of mania and depression, but it can also present as primarily manic or primarily depressed. Assessing impairment can be particularly tricky, since BiD is one of the few mental health conditions that can range from pretty helpful to catastrophically disastrous, particularly when it is primarily manic. Mania can provide immense mental energy to fuel creativity and imagination. It can drive people to achievements that others consider impossible and insights that everyone else has missed. Wikipedia has an extensive, well-documented list of famous people who have revealed their own BiD diagnoses.[82] In his book, *A First-Rate Madness*, professor of psychiatry Nassir Ghaemi ponders how bipolar disorder may have both troubled and energized a dozen historical figures, including Franklin Roosevelt, Adolph Hitler, and Abraham Lincoln.

For many people however, bipolar disorder isn't about making great art or creating amazing inventions. It's about dangerous highs and/or deathly lows. People with BiD are far more likely to commit suicide than people with correctly diagnosed unipolar depression, because their lows tend to be more agitated than their unipolar peers. That brings us to our next point.

Manic Depression: The Case of Mr. Lincoln

- Dr. Wes -

Though it is based on historical speculation, a good illustration of primarily depressed bipolar disorder may be found in Abraham Lincoln. Most psychiatric historians, including author Joshua Wolf Shenk[83], recognize that Lincoln was depressed or in a state of "melancholy" as it

---

[82] en.wikipedia.org/wiki/List_of_people_with_bipolar_disorder

[83] amazon.com/dp/0618551166/

was called back then. While you might imagine being president during the civil war to be pretty depressing for anyone, Lincoln's history of mood instability dates back to at least young adulthood and is summarized by Shenk in *The Atlantic,* where he writes:

> In January of 1841 Lincoln submitted himself to the care of a medical doctor, spending several hours a day with Dr. Anson Henry, whom he called "necessary to my existence." Although few details of the treatment are extant, he probably went through what a prominent physician of the time called "the desolating tortures of officious medication." When he emerged, on January 20, he was "reduced and emaciated in appearance," wrote a young lawyer in town named James Conkling. On January 23, Lincoln wrote to his law partner in Washington: "I am now the most miserable man living. If what I feel were equally distributed to the whole human family, there would not be one cheerful face on the earth. Whether I shall ever be better I can not tell; I awfully forebode I shall not. To remain as I am is impossible; I must die or be better, it appears to me."[84]

Yikes. That's some dark prose. Shenk also describes how Mr. Lincoln likely wrote and published a poem in an 1838 issue of the *Sangamo Journal,* under the title "The Suicide's Soliloquy." Let's just say that the poem was not mistitled. In other passages, Shenk describes friends and family having to keep sharp objects away from Lincoln and the man himself at times worrying about carrying a pocketknife, lest he do himself harm.

If Mr. Lincoln were to present this way at our clinic in 2020, we would not treat him for depression. We would start with a hypothesis of bipolar, primarily depressed. He was an ambitious fellow. He taught himself law. He ran for Congress and eventually the presidency. As anyone who has read his speeches knows, he was immensely creative, able to come up with just the right words at just the right time to say things we all still remember. These are not the marks of a depressed person. Even his supposition that he was "the most miserable man living"

---

[84] www.theatlantic.com/magazine/archive/2005/10/lincolns-great-depression/304247/

echoes manic grandiosity. At minimum, his depression was constantly agitated. When we see that presentation, we think bipolar disorder.

A 2000 study by the National Depressive and Manic-Depressive Association (DMDA)[85] found that sixty-nine percent of patients with bipolar disorder are misdiagnosed initially and more than a third remained so for at least ten years[86]. Because manic phases of bipolar are easily observed, most of these diagnostic errors happen when people with depressive bipolar disorder are misunderstood as having unipolar depression.

So, how does Abraham Lincoln fit into a book about ADD and Zombies? Because he's a good analog for clients like Tressa who are rarely manic in the "bouncing off the walls" sense and yet are not simply depressed. They do not respond well to SSRIs like Lexapro or Celexa, often becoming more agitated and dysphoric instead of calmer and less depressed. They go through ruminative cycles, and like Lincoln, may even become a bit grandiose in their assessment of how bad things are. They are "manically depressed" in the truest sense. Though one could not see Lincoln as having ADD by any stretch of the diagnostic imagination, we've seen quite a few folks with ADD who also have this "Abraham Lincoln" type of BiD.

Bipolar-ADD Treatment

Whether it comes in a manic, mixed, or depressed presentation, the impact of BiD on the medication of ADD is unparalleled by any other co-occurring disorder. There are about fifty ways to fail with this treatment and about two to succeed.

I was having lunch at the American Psychological Association with a psychologist friend who asked about my specializations. Among them, I mentioned that our office treated a lot of teens and young adults with ADD and bipolar disorder. The friend almost choked on his appetizer and asked, "How do you keep your license?"

---

[85] psycnet.apa.org/record/2003-02267-010

[86] It's worth noting however, that in the twenty years since that study, greater attention to bipolar disorder has led to the same concerns about overdiagnosis that we discussed earlier in this book with regard to ADD. Again, the problem isn't overdiagnosis, it's poor diagnosis.

He reacted that way because treating ADD-BiD with any kind of stimulant has the potential to trigger a manic episode. Where a spike in anxiety with administration of a stimulant can usually be tolerated and quickly rectified, triggering mania can create all manner of trouble for the client. So, here's how I answered my colleague's question,

Where a spike in anxiety with administration of a stimulant can usually be tolerated and quickly rectified, triggering mania can create all manner of trouble for the client.

which will sound pretty familiar at this point in the book: We practice very tightly integrated medication management and psychotherapy. If we didn't, none of us would be willing to work with this population. So, if you have ADD-bipolar, it's imperative that you find an actual treatment team instead of winging it with a therapist in one office and maybe your primary care doc or psychiatrist across town.

The other key to success is found in the voice of you and your people. The coordination of stimulants and mood stabilizers is an ongoing and complex process requiring careful trial and error, well beyond even the most delicate ADD-only medication regimen. If ever we needed to hear your comments on the three pounds of tissue between your ears, and get the opinion of those who love you, it's in this situation. And these discussions won't come once or twice. Treating ADD-bipolar involves keeping up with the changes in personality, emotional state, and brain chemistry that come with any mood disorder. Staying in harmony with those tides or, to the extent possible, ahead of them will be a critical job for you, your therapist, your prescriber, and your people. Working with that model over the years, we've had few treatment failures and plenty of successes. And we both still have our licenses.

- Dr. Kelsey -

Wes is right. I've spent many hours playing phone tag with all kinds of medical specialists, and in the end, the level of collaboration between any two offices can never match what happens within one. That will never be as important as it is in treating ADD and BiD. Bipolar clients with a co-occurring diagnosis of ADD typically have a worse course of illness compared to those who do not, including more recurrent mood episodes, increased prevalence of anxiety and substance use disorders, poorer psychosocial functioning, and increased instances of legal problems[87].

Think of the use of mood stabilizers in treating BiD as you would those bumper-rails you pull up along the gutters in a bowling alley. The bowling ball is your mood. The rails still allow the ball to drift left and right down the lane but they prevent it from slipping outside the field of play. A mood-unstable BiD client is prone to irritability, depression, anxiety, mania or all of the above, often in response to triggers incongruent to the emotional response. Why? Dopamine transport hyperdrive. As we've discussed, dopamine is central to executive functioning. But too much of a good thing can be a bad thing. Starting a client with an unstable mood on a stimulant risks anything from irritability to psychosis, so regulating dopamine activity is essential before introducing a stimulant which, itself, increases the brain's access to dopamine. In Chapter 6, I'll address more specifically how we get that done with medication.

Autism
- Dr. Wes -

The official DSM-5 diagnosis for this set of symptoms is Autism Spectrum Disorder (ASD). According to NIMH, ASD is

> A developmental disorder that affects communication and behavior. Although autism can be diagnosed at any age, it is said to be a "developmental disorder" because symptoms generally appear in the first two years of life[88].

For once, DSM's branding is spot on because ASD really does exist across a wide range of types and severities. Like bipolar disorder, ASD ranges from kind of interesting and helpful to profoundly debilitating. Many on the high functioning side are gifted and talented, with a tendency to look at things differently than anyone else. That end of the spectrum has caught the public's imagination in movies and TV shows like *The Good Doctor, Billions, The Big Bang Theory,* or my personal favorite, *Temple Grandin.* Some people with ASD can learn information in unusual detail and remember it for long periods of time. Some can

[87] Sadek, J. (2016). ADHD and Bipolar Disorder. *Clinician's Guide to Adult ADHD Comorbidities.* 55-60. Doi: 10.1007/978-3-319-39794-8_6

[88] www.nimh.nih.gov/health/topics/autism-spectrum-disorders-asd/index.shtml

memorize visual and auditory material better than neurotypical peers. Many are adept at math, science, music, or art. Some can solve problems that others don't even see. I've even known a few clients who take pride in "identifying" as ASD, though I would not, myself, encourage anyone to call a DSM-5 diagnosis an identity.

On the other end of the ASD spectrum, clients lack the capacity to care for themselves, hold a job outside a sheltered environment, or for some, even communicate. While we agree ASD is a useful way to understand clients, it can be difficult to describe its symptoms in a way that includes everyone on such a wide spectrum. Regardless of level of impairment, DSM-5 defines all persons with ASD as having:

- difficulty with communication and interaction with others;

- restricted interests and repetitive behaviors; and

- a series of personal and interpersonal symptoms that limit the ability to function in school, work, and other areas of life.

Specific characteristics found in people with ASD include some, but not necessarily all, of the following:

- minimal eye contact with a tendency to look away from people;

- appearing to lack enjoyment of objects or activities by pointing out or showing them to others;

- in younger children, failing or being slow to respond to someone calling the child's name or to other verbal attempts to gain attention;

- difficulty maintaining a fluid, back and forth conversation;

- talking at length (for some, one might say endlessly) about a favorite subject without noticing that others are not interested or without giving others a chance to engage;

- facial expressions, movements, and/or hand gestures that do not match what is being said or that do not fit accepted social interplay with whomever they are engaged with;

- an unusual vocal tone ranging from sing-song to flat and robotic, and/or difficulty modulating volume despite cues from others;

- trouble understanding or taking another person's point of view or understanding or predicting the actions of other's despite adequate or superior intellect;

- repeating certain, often unusual behaviors; in extreme cases, this can include *echolalia* where the person repeats the words of others as if they were his or her own;

- intense interest (sometimes fixation) on certain topics, such as numbers, details, or facts, going well beyond being an aficionado;

- excess focus on something like moving objects or parts of objects simply for the sake of engaging with them, not because that engagement serves a purpose;

- getting upset by minor changes in routine or setting that is outside developmental norms or social customs;

- being more (or sometimes less) sensitive than others to sensory input, such as light, noise, clothing, or temperature;

- sleep problems; and/or

- mood instability, irritability, and emotional overresponse, typically referred to as "meltdowns" or "breakdowns."

The exact cause of ASD has been the subject of broad (and at times, wild) speculation, including the wholly disproven idea that vaccines are linked to ASD. All we really know about its etiology comes from correlational studies which suggest one is more likely to end up on the spectrum if one has:

- a sibling with ASD;

- an older parent, most notably an older father (yep, my daughter is an example);

- certain genetic conditions like Down syndrome, fragile X syndrome, and Rett syndrome; and/or

- a very low weight at birth.

And that's about it, which isn't very much nor very useful. Far clearer is the fact that over the last decade, the rate of autism has gone up dramatically. The Autism and Developmental Disabilities Monitoring (ADDM) Network estimates that the prevalence of ASD has increased from about one in 150 children during the survey period 2000–2002 to one in sixty-eight during 2010–2012. In the most recent study, published in 2014, prevalence varied widely by state, but the aggregate found one in fifty-nine children to be diagnosed with ASD, meaning that since the 2000-2002 count, the incidence has risen 150%[89]. So, where did all these autistic folks come from? Doesn't a doubling in prevalence constitute an epidemic? Perhaps we have a national health crisis on our hands? Or is it just another conspiracy?

Despite what you may have read in the ASD alarmist press (which apparently doesn't hang out much with the ADD skeptic press) the answer is "nope, no epidemic." Folks with ASD have always been there, but only recently have we thought it important to notice them[90].

> *Once we began to think of autism as a spectrum, we started seeing many more folks with low-key versions of it.*

Once we began to think of autism as a spectrum, we started seeing many more folks with low-key versions of it. I would further argue, in the vernacular of this book, that there are ASD-leaners who do not meet the criteria for the disorder, but who nonetheless have a few notable symptoms. At our clinic, we see them often and traditionally refer to them as having a "sliver of autism."

As you read over the above lists, did you notice how many characteristics also appear among folks with ADD? This is because, unlike some of the other disorders in this chapter and despite the skeptic's contrary view, ASD is rarely a differential diagnosis to ADD. It's nearly always co-occurring. There are even those who believe that high functioning autism and ADD are so intertwined that they belong on the same spectrum[91]. As with most theories that propose to explain away ADD, this one takes the commonality between the two and stretches it beyond reason. While most people with ASD show many symptoms of ADD, most people with ADD have few if any symptoms unique to ASD.

It is, therefore, odd how long it took psychiatry to accept that these two diagnoses could coexist. As recently as DSM-IV TR (the immediate predecessor to DSM-5), we were directed not give a child with ASD an additional diagnosis of ADD, even as most research suggested

---

[89] www.cdc.gov/mmwr/volumes/67/ss/ss6706a1.htm?s_cid=ss6706a1_w

[90] www.scientificamerican.com/article/the-real-reasons-autism-rates-are-up-in-the-u-s/

[91] www.spectrumnews.org/features/deep-dive/decoding-overlap-autism-adhd/

exactly the opposite to be true[92]. Today, with DSM-5 reversing this long held assertion, we understand that not only is co-occurrence possible, it's pretty common[93] with estimates ranging from 37% in some studies to as high as 85% in others. From a clinical standpoint, in our office we initially presume that anyone who has ASD also has ADD, and we take an especially close look at our ADD kids to see who may also have at least a sliver of autism.

Autism-ADD Treatment

Unfortunately, accepting this high level of co-occurrence hasn't made ASD-ADD any easier to treat. There aren't any medicines for ASD. In the higher functioning end of the spectrum, treatment is all about learning the rules of social convention and doing a lot of radical acceptance and cognitive override to follow them. Some folks with ASD have significant mood fluctuation, to the point that they look almost manic at times. They may have frequent emotional breakdowns as external stimuli overwhelm them. Some providers mistake this for anxiety. However, standard medications that help anxiety often won't quell this kind of mood instability. Instead, such clients may do better being treated with mood stabilizers, almost as if they were actually bipolar.

Not surprisingly, when it comes to stimulant use, this tendency toward dysregulation can be almost as problematic for the ASD crowd as it is for folks with BiD. Stimulants can so irritate ASD clients that at one point it was recommended prescribers forgo using them[94]. However, in many of the cases we've treated, the combination of stimulants and mood stabilizers has had a dramatic impact on the quality of the client's life at home, work, and school.

While a stimulant won't directly help ASD-ADD folks be more socially adroit or disengaged with their interior worlds, it can help them learn the rules and pay attention to the details that underlie them, and that can make a huge difference. One of our most difficult teens was so diagnosed and yet, with consistent medication she managed to attend a major eastern college far from her Midwest home and do well there. It wasn't a picnic, but she made it.

---

[92] www.ncbi.nlm.nih.gov/pmc/articles/PMC3422050/

[93] www.frontiersin.org/articles/10.3389/fnhum.2014.00268/full

[94] www.ncbi.nlm.nih.gov/pubmed/16919137

Trauma[95]

In Chapter 3 we discussed how trauma might generate ADD symptoms, particularly in children. The reverse is unlikely, however, because ADD cannot create the symptoms of PTSD without a history of trauma. People with ADD, particularly younger ones, are more prone to high-risk behavior, relational problems, and addiction, leaving them more open to potential traumatic events. ADD children can be more difficult to manage, raising their risk of abuse from a caregiver. But these examples are secondary social effects of the disorder and not the kind of direct, physical impact trauma has on brain functioning. Additionally, people with ADD diathesis may be less resilient and more prone to impairment than their neurotypical peers, so when they face the stress of trauma, they experience its worst effects.

Some people who've been traumatized also have ADD. And when they do, each condition worsens the impact of the other.

While teasing out the differences and overlap of these two conditions can be confusing, we know with certainty that they co-occur. Some people who've been traumatized also have ADD. And when they do, each condition worsens the impact of the other. Thus, an assessment for trauma and related disorders is essential in a broad psychosocial assessment of clients presenting with ADD. If you're not having that conversation with your provider, and you're concerned about how trauma may have impacted you, it's time to discuss it. As your treatment process unfolds, the differences and intersections of these conditions may become clearer.

I've worked with a number of clients who presented with PTSD and, after we had reprocessed and contextualized the traumas, the clients still struggled with classic symptoms of ADD. In such cases, it makes sense to go back and do a thorough examination of family history and conduct ADD testing. In most cases, the traumas date back to childhood, so it's hard to parse out which came first, the ADD symptoms or the inciting event. Moreover, in cases of familial child abuse, particularly those that end up in the foster care system, it's difficult to know

---

[95] This section was coauthored by Jordan Mayfield, LSCSW, a trauma-informed therapist on staff at Family Psychological Services (www.fpskansas.com) who is available to consult on cases of ADHD and trauma via video conferencing.

what role genetic predisposition may have played in creating ADD diathesis and what role the many stressors of growing up in an abusive home or living in foster care may have invoked.

PTSD Treatment

- Dr. Kelsey -

Since no medication can go back and undo a traumatic event, psychotherapy is typically the most effective treatment for PTSD. However, in complex cases that also include many symptoms of ADD, we've come to believe that, in the absence of evidence to the contrary, it's best to assume the worst. If we see symptoms, we presume there's a disorder behind them. That goes double if we see a family predisposition for ADD.

Thus, we would tend to treat ADD and any co-occurring trauma symptoms while also working in therapy on the trauma. Failing to do this gums up the entire process because clients have a much harder time responding to therapy if they're fighting the effects of ADD. Treating that side of the equation allows them to be more active in and present for their trauma treatment. On the other hand, if ADD is not actually present and a client with PTSD is prescribed a stimulant, it could well make him or her more anxious and hypervigilant, so I'm always monitoring these cases carefully and staying in close contact with the therapist.

It's especially important for clients with PTSD and ADD to be diligent with stimulants as ADD quite often exacerbates symptoms of PTSD, leaving the client more tired, scattered, impulsive, and reactive. As a prescriber, I can foresee a negative cascade of events when stimulants are absent, and I want my clients to foresee them too, rather than experiencing them firsthand. This also makes necessary stimulant breaks (Chapter 9) particularly dicey and emotionally painful.

Personality Disorders

- Dr. Wes -

We can't do justice in this book to the complex and controversial diagnostic category of personality disorders (PDs). Volumes have been written on the topic, countless theories proffered, and numerous treatments developed. Thus, distilling the core aspects of what you need to know in this section is wildly reductive. If you want to learn more, you'll have no trouble finding resources.

The key difference between PDs and every other co-occurring diagnosis is that they are conceptualized as "ego syntonic," meaning clients experience the symptoms as being in harmony with their identity and less in need of change. Most disorders, like ADD, anxiety, depression, etc., are seen as "ego dystonic," meaning the client feels the symptoms are out of sync with who they are and who they want to become. While ASD is often experienced by those who have it as ego-syntonic, usually at some point, higher functioning clients begin to understand and become distressed about how they intersect with the rest of the world. That can happen with personality disorders, but it usually comes in response to some external stressor—like loss of family or social support or a run in with the law—making the symptoms more difficult to tolerate or rationalize as "just how I am." This idea of a psychiatric diagnosis interwoven into one's personality is a pretty heavy concept, which is why this category is often debated and its treatment highly specialized.

The concept of a disordered personality harkens back to an era of psychoanalytic psychiatry that is now seen by most professionals as passé. In this section, Kelsey and I won't weigh in on the validity or usefulness of this diagnostic category. We're just saying that it exists, that providers still give and treat many of the PD diagnoses, and that the symptom overlap with ADD is so great that it confuses and vexes even trained and experienced prescribers as to what is differential and what is co-occurring.

And if that doesn't get you interested in knowing more, consider this: the political structure and professional belief system around personality disorders are so powerful that they may actually impact your diagnosis and treatment more than the symptoms you bring into a provider's office. And nobody will tell you that. If your diagnostician "believes" in PD in general or has a special attachment to one of the PD diagnoses, he or she may see you this way and ignore critical aspects of your ADD or miss it entirely.

Conversely, if the diagnostician doubts this entire construct of personality he or she may *over*estimate the impact ADD has on your life and underestimate the need for additional treatment to address these core personality issues. Most importantly, once you've been diagnosed with a PD, providers will look at you and treat you differently than your ADD-only peers. That might be good or it might not be. It all comes down to how well the provider really sees *you* and not the diagnosis they imagine you to be.

While there are ten personality disorders recognized by DSM-5, only two—Antisocial Personality Disorder and Borderline Personality Disorder—are immediately relevant to our discussion of co-occurring diagnoses. Others could co-occur with ADD, but that's far less common. We'll go over those and then I'll close with an alternative hypothesis as to how ADD and PD may be conceptualized in tandem. That bit of conjecture won't change what happens once the diagnoses are given, but my hypothesis offers some reflection on the value of early intervention and prevention.

Antisocial Personality Disorder (ASPD)

In discussing Antisocial Personality Disorder we return again to DSM-5's weird branding. Most laypeople presume the term "antisocial" has something to do with not liking to be around people. There is a PD for that, but it's called Avoidant Personality Disorder and we rarely see it in treatment because those who have it are, as the name implies, well beyond introverted. That has nothing to do with being antisocial.

As soon as I tell you what ASPD used to be called in its less politically correct days, you'll immediately recognize it. The first edition of the DSM (1952) listed something called "sociopathic personality disturbance," describing those who had it as "...ill primarily in terms of society and of conformity with the prevailing milieu, and not only in terms of personal discomfort and relations with other individuals." One of the subcategories or "reactions" was described as "antisocial," meaning the person was always in trouble, failed to learn from even very negative consequences, had no loyalty to anyone or anything, was callous to the rights and welfare of others, lacked responsibility, and tended to rationalize his or her objectionable behavior.[96] In DSM-II (1968) "antisocial personality" became listed as one of ten personality disorders with features similar to those in the original DSM. It also described a separate "dyssocial personality type" for people deemed dishonest and for those involved in lower-level crimes: con artists, gambling cheats,

---

[96] en.wikipedia.org/wiki/Antisocial_personality_disorder

prostitutes, and drug dealers. In this context, "antisocial" means working against society and social convention, not retreating from it.

DSM-III (1980) formally changed the diagnostic label to Antisocial Personality Disorder which was continued through DSM-IIIr (1987), two editions of DSM-IV (1994, 2000), and into DSM-5 (2013). In this most recent manual, ASPD is said to describe a pervasive pattern of disregard for and violation of the rights of others, occurring since the age of fifteen, as indicated by three or more of the following:

- failure to conform to social norms with respect to lawful behaviors (e.g., repeatedly performing acts that are grounds for arrest);

- deception (e.g., repeatedly lying, use of aliases, or conning others for personal profit or pleasure);

- impulsivity or failure to plan ahead;

- irritability and aggressiveness (e.g., repeated physical fights or assaults);

- reckless disregard for safety of self or others;

- consistent irresponsibility (e.g., repeated failure to sustain consistent work behavior or honor financial obligations);

- lack of remorse, (e.g., being indifferent to or rationalizing having hurt, mistreated, or stolen from another).

This diagnosis cannot be given to anyone under eighteen because the very idea of a personality disorder requires that a personality already be formed and it's been decided in the hallowed halls of psychiatry that this cannot happen before age eighteen[97]. Psychopathic behavior in children and teens is diagnosed as either Oppositional Defiant Disorder or, for severe cases, as a Conduct Disorder.

Why should you care about psychopathy and the personality disorder misbranded to diagnosis it? First, consider the overlap between the above-cited ASPD symptoms and the criteria for ADD (impulsivity,

---

[97] Yes, this is controversial. On one hand, eighteen is pretty young when we know that adult brains are not yet finished developing until age twenty-five. On the other hand, evidence of sociopathy is often seen before age eighteen. This is conceptually true of all personality disorders, but it is especially emphasized with ASPD. Feel free to do some research and form your own opinions. We can argue it six ways to Sunday.

poor planning, recklessness, inconsistency). Then note how many symptoms appear as secondary features among ADD folks you known, including non-conformity, rule breaking, lying to avoid embarrassment, irritability, disregard for others, irresponsibility in friendship, work, finance, school, etc., and avoidance of personal responsibility.

In fact, in *I Always Want to Be Where I'm Not,* I wrote several chapters on these very attributes. In Chapter 8 (Responsibility), I discussed the vexing case of Leandra, a young adult with correctly-diagnosed ADD who got involved with two guys at the same, one of whom was a gang member and who, predictably, stabbed her other partner in the leg after catching them together. No matter how convincingly I made my argument, Leandra refused to see her culpability for the incident, rationalizing her role as an innocent bystander because she did not herself stab the guy. In the years hence, this has remained standard operating procedure for Leandra and it hasn't turned out well. One of the questions proffered in her vignette was whether she was a psychopath. Based on many years of experience with this young woman, I find she not only meets three of the criteria listed above, she has at one time or another, met all seven. And yet, there is no doubt that Leandra has ADD, and when she has been treated effectively for it, she has gotten into less trouble and been more successful. She's not the only one. Between twenty-five and forty percent of people currently incarcerated in the United States are thought to have ADD[98]. Some percentage of these folks also have ASPD[99].

In an attempt to consider psychopathic traits in children, DSM-III (1980) identified four subtypes of conduct disorders (essentially juvenile ASPD): undersocialized-aggressive, undersocialized-nonaggressive, socialized-aggressive, and socialized-nonaggressive. The undersocialized children were thought to lack empathy and affection and to engage in inappropriate social relationships, which the authors considered more characteristic of psychopathy. The authors used the word "undersocialized" to avoid the negative connotations of what

---

[98] add.org/undiagnosed-adult-adhd-a-high-cost-for-society/

[99] You might think every criminal would qualify for ASPD, but that's not the case. In fact, a significant and controversial cottage industry has grown up around determining which incarcerated individuals are psychopaths and thus unlikely to be rehabilitated and which are not and might wisely be paroled. Episode 436 of *This American Life* (www.thisamerican-life.org/436/the-psychopath-test) addresses this topic in an interesting and entertaining fashion.

they really meant (sociopathy), but it quickly became misinterpreted to mean that the child was not well socialized by parents or lacked a peer group. Socialized individuals were able to form healthy social attachments to others and tended to perform their antisocial acts within a deviant social group (e.g. youth gangs).

In fairly short order, the American Psychiatric Association decided that these categories failed to accurately categorize psychopathic-like youths and removed the terms from DSM-IV. However, from a conceptual standpoint, this idea of four subtypes of psychopathy is interesting to consider and can help us describe with greater specificity how ASPD might present in someone like Leandra, who would fall under the "socialized-nonaggressive" type. In fact, among certain ADD clients I've seen who live on the border of psychopathy, this is the most common presentation.

ASPD Treatment. Psychopathy in general, and ASPD specifically, create a lot of cognitive dissonance[100] in a provider community dedicated to the remediation of mental illness. That's because the one thing that ASPD is not, is easily treated. The very idea of an ego-syntonic disorder defies intervention because the person who has the diagnosis feels pretty okay about him or herself. There has been some concern (dramatically illustrated in the final season of HBOs *The Sopranos*) that therapy may only serve to hone the effectiveness of the individual's psychopathic tendencies[101], particularly interpersonal, nondirective, or client-focused approaches.

Most therapists have very negative feelings toward clients with extensive histories of aggressive, exploitative, and abusive behaviors. As much as I liked Leandra and found her case interesting and challenging, it was not very fulfilling because all our good work came to naught. While we kept her ADD in check and eventually got her through college (it took eight years), she never accepted the nature, quality, and wrongfulness of her conduct toward others, including friends, family, dating partners, and coworkers. In fact, her situation deteriorated. At

---

[100] Having inconsistence in thought, belief, behavior or attitude about a given circumstance or idea.

[101] journalcswb.ca/index.php/cswb/article/download/25/46. This paper is a seventy-eight page treatise on everything you could ever want to know about treating ASPD, which supports several of the points we make herein.

last check, she was pleading out an assault charge[102]. So much for the "non-aggressive type."

The problem is that Tony Soprano, Leandra and everyone else with properly diagnosed ASPD aren't interested in therapy as a way to develop a conscientious response to the world. At best, they may learn the tangible value of prosocial conduct versus the danger of antisocial behavior. However, given the impulsive and aggressive nature of ASPD, most of these clients are always one bad decision away from the same antisocial path they've trod many times before.

This makes the value of medication for ASPD suspect. What symptoms on the above-cited list would one address with medical intervention? Does anyone make a pill to enhance personal responsibility? Are there any dosing guidelines for increasing contrition or empathy? Instead, any benefit is more likely to come from a successful treatment of co-occurring disorders, in this case ADD. Unfortunately, there are three reasons ADD-ASPD clients are especially difficult to treat with stimulants:

- They tend to abuse and misuse medication either personally or through sale and distribution, as highly sought-after drugs like Vyvanse and Adderall XR can sell for $20 a pill on the raging black market near any college campus.

- Stimulants may raise irritability, making the ASPD person more difficult to live with and, worse, more aggressive.

- Stimulants may improve the ASPD person's ability to focus on getting into antisocial situations. For a well-socialized ASPD client (like Leandra), having good focus doesn't necessarily improve judgment. It may simply raise attention to detail, enhancing the ability to think up and execute criminal hijinks.

Knowing this, many prescribers are unwilling to see such clients, at least outside of a highly organized treatment system, typically in the purview of the department of corrections or court services.

If remediating co-occurring ASPD and ADD is so fraught, you might wonder why we included it in this book. While Kelsey and I have taken

---

[102] Yes, one could surmise that this moved Leandra from the "nonaggressive" to "aggressive" type, but the story that goes beyond what we have space to discuss, suggests otherwise. Such are the annoyingly fine distinctions in such cases.

on some pretty complicated cases of people prone to misbehave, we, too, draw the line at documented ASPD. I never referred Leandra to Kelsey for medication (she saw her PCP instead). I have routinely turned away cases that had the look and feel of psychopathy. Just as Dr. Melphi finally concludes in *The Sopranos*, we're not interested in honing the skills of psychopaths. So, to be honest, we have no good suggestions on how to get the correctly diagnosed ASPD-ADD crowd on the road to a better tomorrow.

Instead, we'll lift up the work of a few dedicated professionals, both clinicians and researchers, who are trying to rehab a vast array of clients with psychopathic tendencies and note that some limited research supports their efforts[103] [104] [105]. A subset of this research suggests that treating criminals specifically for ADD can greatly reduce the likelihood that they will reoffend[106] [107] [108]. It's worth noting however, that these improvements may occur among a broader array of criminals, some of whom do not actually meet the criteria for ASPD. As yet, nobody has done a precise enough study to know.

Here's what we do know for sure about ASPD: an ounce of prevention in childhood and adolescence is worth several pounds of cure in young adulthood. Based on our experience, a key aspect of that prevention could mean treating ADD aggressively. We can't guarantee that will generate a happy, well-socialized, mentally healthy young adult nor will refusing treatment insure your child is headed to the nearest penal institution. But when considering whether or not to try medication for a child's ADD, never presume that declining treatment is cost-free.

Borderline Personality Disorder (BPD)

Second only to ASPD, there's nothing more impactful written into your case record than a well-documented diagnosis of BPD. In fact, if you're an adult who is battling ADD, there's a chance you might get

[103] www.bbc.com/news/health-20414822

[104] journals.sagepub.com/doi/abs/10.1177/1078345808326617?journalCode=jcxa

[105] www.yournacm.com/file_download/b1394ffe-1f58-4e38-97a4-7b17c11eab23

[106] bmcpsychiatry.biomedcentral.com/articles/10.1186/s12888-018-1858-9

[107] Barkley RA, Murphy KR, Fischer M. ADHD in Adults: What the Science Says. New York, NY: Guilford Press; 2008:291-329

[108] www.jwatch.org/jp201211210000001/2012/11/21/medication-adhd-reduces-criminality

tagged with BPD whether you have it or not and that could make a big difference in your treatment. By the end of this section, you'll understand why.

BPD has lived a long and storied life in psychiatry. But even as it has gone in and out of controversy over the years, it remains among the most influential labels in the DSM. Though the symptoms were discussed as far back as Greek philosophy, it was psychoanalyst Adolf Stern who coined the term in a 1938 treatise[109], noting certain patients exhibit both "neurotic" and "psychotic" features such that they lived somewhere along the "border" between the two. Stern actually hypothesized such folks to be experiencing a mild form of schizophrenia, a diagnosis which was, at the time, imagined to be far more common than it is now.

Though the term "borderline" remained, its conceptualization changed throughout the 1960s and 70s to be seen as less a problem of thought and more one of mood, similar in many ways to bipolar disorder, but ego-syntonic. In fact, DSM-II (1968) called the condition "cyclothymic personality disorder[110]" and emphasized intensity and variability of emotion. It was not until DSM-III (1980) however, that the label Borderline Personality Disorder came into diagnostic usage. Thereafter, any connection to schizophrenia or psychosis was shifted to schizotypal personality disorder, a rare condition found only in severe and persistently mentally ill clients. In contrast, BPD has grown in prevalence and breadth and is now given quite often in outpatient populations.

Given this meandering history, one might yet again question the brand DSM has built around BPD. Many authors have[111] and some have gone further, questioning its very existence. A common claim is that BPD symptoms are better explained by post-traumatic stress disorder (PTSD). The problem with that argument is that PTSD does not adequately describe the broader presentation of BPD and most people

---

[109] Stern, A. (1938). Borderline group of neuroses. *The Psychoanalytic Quarterly* 7: 467-489.

[110] Not to be confused with the rarely-given modern diagnosis of cyclothymia, which is also a holdover from this era and describes a lower grade bipolar condition.

[111] Stone MH (2005). "Borderline Personality Disorder: History of the Concept". In Zanarini MC (ed.). *Borderline personality disorder*. Boca Raton, FL: Taylor & Francis. pp. 1–18.

with PTSD show few key symptoms of BPD. While the two may co-occur, they are not the same thing.

Others have critiqued BPD from a political perspective, seeing it as inherently misogynistic because women constitute 80% of the diagnosed population. BPD's proponents counter that it is the symptoms that are gender-specific and reflective of traditional gender socialization patterns and not a flaw in the diagnosis or diagnostician. They add that men with BPD do exist but are less likely to seek help, as is true with other diagnoses.

DSM-5 (2013) took a big step forward with its revised definition of BPD adding several layers of complexity to the diagnosis. Hold on to your hats junior diagnosticians, there's a lot to think about here. We'll begin with a significant impairment in personality functioning in either or both of the following:

a. **Identity:** Markedly impoverished, poorly developed, or unstable self-image, often associated with excessive self-criticism; chronic feelings of emptiness; dissociative states under stress, OR

b. **Self-direction:** Instability in goals, aspirations, values, or career plans.

BPD also requires impairments in either or both of the following:

a. **Empathy:** Compromised ability to recognize the feelings and needs of others associated with interpersonal hypersensitivity (i.e., prone to feel slighted or insulted); perceptions of others selectively biased toward negative attributes or vulnerabilities.

b. **Intimacy:** Intense, unstable, and conflicted close relationships, marked by mistrust, neediness, and anxious preoccupation with real or imagined abandonment; close relationships often viewed in extremes of idealization and devaluation and alternating between overinvolvement and withdrawal.

The client must also show pathological personality traits in any of the following domains.

1. Negative Affectivity, characterized by:

a. **Emotional liability.** Unstable emotional experiences and frequent mood changes; emotions that are easily aroused, intense, and/or out of proportion to events and circumstances.

b. **Anxiousness.** Intense feelings of nervousness, tenseness, or panic, often in reaction to interpersonal stresses; worry about the negative effects of past unpleasant experiences and future negative possibilities; feeling fearful, apprehensive, or threatened by uncertainty; fears of falling apart or losing control.

c. **Separation insecurity.** Fears of rejection by, and/or separation from, significant others, associated with fears of excessive dependency and complete loss of autonomy.

d. **Depressivity.** Frequent feelings of being down, miserable, and/or hopeless; difficulty recovering from such moods; pessimism about the future; pervasive shame; feeling of inferior self-worth; thoughts of suicide and suicidal behavior.

2. Disinhibition, characterized by:

   a. **Impulsivity.** Acting on the spur of the moment in response to immediate stimuli; acting on a momentary basis without a plan or consideration of outcomes; difficulty establishing or following plans; a sense of urgency and self-harming behavior under emotional distress.

   b. **Risk taking.** Engagement in dangerous, risky, and potentially self-damaging activities, unnecessarily and without regard to consequences; lack of concern for one's limitations and denial of the reality of personal danger.

3. Antagonism, characterized by:

   a. **Hostility.** Persistent or frequent angry feelings; anger or irritability in response to minor slights and insults.

Impairment in the client must be relatively stable across time and situation, meaning the symptoms can't just show up, mess with the client's life, go away, and then reappear later on. Nor can they be the result of normal development (read: being a teenager is not a personality disorder) or socio-cultural environment.

Whenever I read over this set of criteria, I am thankful that I do not work for the American Psychiatric Association in the department of typesetting and outlining, because that's a lot of information to format, let alone swallow—and I've tried to make it easier to absorb than how it appears in DSM itself[112].

The World Health Organization (WHO), which marches to its own drum when compared to the American Psychiatric Association[113], has published a similar symptom set for what it calls "emotionally unstable personality disorder," of which there are two subtypes, impulsive and borderline. The impulsive subtype must have at least three of the following:

- a marked tendency to act unexpectedly and without consideration of consequences;

- a marked tendency to engage in quarrelsome behavior and conflict with others, especially when impulsive acts are thwarted or criticized;

- liability to outbursts of anger or violence, with inability to control the resulting behavioral explosions;

- difficulty maintaining any course of action that offers no immediate reward;

- unstable and capricious (impulsive, whimsical) mood.

The borderline subtype must also meet at least two of the following:

- disturbances in and uncertainty about self-image, aims, and internal preferences;

- liability to become involved in intense and unstable relationships, often leading to emotional crisis;

- excessive efforts to avoid abandonment;

- recurrent threats or acts of self-harm;

---

112 As much as we both like simple things, the newest definition of BPD is, in fact, better reasoned and explained. It has been, in the past, a bit too easy to give a diagnosis of BPD and harder to explain why it was given. Revisions in DSM-5 have moved that process forward.

113 This is a great example of how diagnosis doesn't really exist outside of human language and experience as we pointed out in Chapter 2.

- chronic feelings of emptiness;

- impulsive behavior like speeding in a car or substance abuse.

These lists sound familiar, don't they? Reading both APA's description and WHO's, you find many overlapping primary symptoms of ADD, including impulsivity, chronic boredom, failure to persist, mood disturbance, and risk taking. Several others overlap with the secondary symptoms, including feelings of emptiness, poor expression of empathy, low self-worth, poor planning and an inconsistent self-image surrounding goals, values, or career plans[114].

There are two reasons this matters to you if you have ADD or love someone who does, or if you have BPD or love someone so diagnosed. First, BPD clients may want to consider talking to an experienced provider about the possibility of co-occurring ADD. The broad symptom overlap means a fair number of people who have BPD will also qualify for and might best be treated with medication for ADD. However, we doubt most are getting that treatment because therapists who treat BPD typically focus on a traditional theory of personality development related to attachment and trauma rather than on genetics or neurology. In fact, based on the research, the best predictor of BPD is *not* attachment or trauma but genetic predisposition, adding another way in which ADD and BPD are alike and perhaps connected.

Of course, the reverse is not true. The vast majority of people with ADD do not qualify for BPD even if they have a few of its symptoms. While they might benefit from similar approaches to therapy, the diagnosis of BPD would be unnecessary and unhelpful. To make matters worse, clients who have co-occurring ADD-ASD or ADD-BiD tend to look even more like they also have borderline personalities. So much so, that whenever I refer such teens out as they leave for college, I worry that they may be picked up by new therapists who will see them as BPD. It's happened quite a few times. In other situations, only my intervention has stood in the way of a young adult being up-diagnosed this way.

With so much symptom overlap, how can we tell which ADD clients also have a legitimate diagnosis of BPD versus ASD? In one sense, it's pretty easy. As with other co-occurring diagnoses, we look for what

---

[114] In *I Always Want to Be Where I'm Not*, I described this as a lack of psychological integrity.

does not overlap; the unique characteristics of BPD that don't connect to ADD or ASD. The most important of these are:

- **Severity of interpersonal impairment.** While many folks with ADD struggle with personal relationships, those with BPD are so impaired that interpersonal conflict is the axis around which their lives play out. People with ASD are similarly compromised, but there is a decidedly naïve flavor to their interpersonal travails. Where people with BPD deliberately undermine their friendships just to test them, ASD and ADD people stumble into social miscues through a shear lack of understanding and attention.

- **Over-idealization (and over-involvement) versus devaluation of people (and withdrawal).** Like those with BPD, ADD people also pull into and then away from close relationships. However, this is usually in response to boredom and convenience, not interpersonal turmoil or hostility. There's rarely a component of over-idealization or contempt among ADD people unless BPD is also present. People with ASD may also under- or over-value others, but they rarely vacillate so broadly in their loyalties or lack thereof.

- **Separation insecurity and fear of abandonment.** BPD is an externalizing condition where the individual is in constant turmoil with others and then fears they will be rejected. They cultivate dependency and avoid autonomy, often without accepting the flaws in that arrangement and, all the while, testing the limits of their peoples' tolerance. People with ADD may feel dependent on family or friends and fearful of rejection, but that's usually based in fact and not specific to conflict or mood. If they are underfunctioning in school or work, falling back on developmentally inappropriate dependency becomes a survival tactic. Clients with ASD may also be dependent on family support, but rarely do their people feel manipulated or taken advantage of. Many ASD people worry little about abandonment or separation, instead remaining caught up in their own internal processes.

- **Antagonism and hostility.** People with ADD may antagonize others and can be temperamental. However, that's usually based on clearly defined problems and personality conflicts or an ongoing struggle with personal responsibility that frustrates their people. Folks with BPD initiate and maintain seemingly endless quarrels and engage in unproductive attention seeking. Only the rarest of ASD clients would seek attention and many prefer a more solitary lifestyle. Once they deliberately learn the rules of engagement, ASD clients tend to be as conscientious as their co-occurring ADD will allow.

- **Recurrent threats or acts of self-harm.** Most people with ADD have little inclination to self-harm, unless they are also bipolar, very depressed, or face to face with a failure of their own making. Most people with high functioning ASD are at little risk of self-harm unless they are unusually mood-dysreg-ulated. In stark contrast, a defining characteristic of people with BPD are repeated suicidal and self-harm ideations and be-haviors which they use as a lever for influencing a reluctant social support group to respond to their demands.

Listing various characteristics and symptoms is easy. Picking them out of a jungle of conflicting findings, is harder. Some of my ADD-ASD clients self-harm but have no other BPD symptoms. Some of my ADD-bipolar teens and young adults are incredibly antagonistic to their parents or dating partners, but get along pretty well with less intimate relationships.

Of all the myriad diagnoses in DSM-5, we are most reluctant to hand out BPD concurrent to ADD, or at all for that matter. Once you're diagnosed this way, your treatment will never be the same, unless someone else comes along and un-diagnoses you. That happens (I've done it) but it's never great to have the wrong diagnosis stuck in your permanent medical record, even for a little while. The most common example of this is when one is referred for psychiatric hospitalization and the intake worker is trying to justify medical necessity. Remember what I said in Chapter 3 about DSM-5 being an economic document? Not infrequently, hospital staff pull out all the stops to be sure they can access insurance, even though you're only admitted for about three or four days and they barely know you. And not infrequently, one diagnosis that pops up is BPD.

Medical Treatment for ADD-BPD. If it is determined that a client legitimately has both ADD and BPD, the treatment path is neither direct nor easy. It is, however, important to undertake, as treating only one of these conditions risks an unsuccessful outcome, perhaps disastrously so. The power of impairment present in each discrete disorder is severe. When they combine, everyone on the treatment team has a big job and some very specialized treatments, both medical and psychological, will quickly come into play.

Once again, medication may become not only a treatment, but also a tool of assessment[115]. For example, clients who are simply mood unstable will usually get better with medication, sometimes dramatically, supporting the bipolar hypothesis. In contrast, those who better fit the BPD category may, despite numerous attempts at medication management, continue to struggle with mood instability.

The biggest challenge in the medication management of ADD-BPD is the strong possibility that stimulants will spike emotional reactivity and irritability before improving attention. Like ADD-bipolar clients, the client's moods must be kept balanced as attention is enhanced, a perpetual juggling act. This is greatly complicated by the fact that BPD clients may not savor emotional stability the way others do, experiencing a lasting state of calm and organization as abnormal or "not me." Not infrequently we hear the Zombie Effect come up with these folks; that they feel too subdued or pacified no matter what med they're on and despite the fact that their people are excited at perceived improvement. Without stimulants, clients with correctly diagnosed ADD-BPD will struggle mightily to address the neurological difficulties that, depending on how you look at it, either underlie or make worse their personality disorder.

Psychotherapy and Case Management. All the stimulants in the world won't help if a BPD client isn't also in active psychotherapy. When it comes to treating borderline personality disorder, there are generally two groups of mental health providers: those who won't do it and those who love nothing more than to sink their clinical teeth into the complexities and risks inherent to treating these clients.

The latter group has, in the last twenty years, gravitated *en masse* toward Dr. Marcia Linehan's model of Dialectical Behavior Therapy (DBT),

---

[115] If we haven't made it clear enough before, this isn't how we like to think of medication, as a way of figuring out how to treat you, but in practice that's what happens in complicated cases. This is part art and part science and the greatest argument for getting the best treatment team you can find.

honed on the most difficult, brittle, and self-harmful cases and then extended to a wider clinical population. These therapists thrive on delivering a highly structured, skill-based model, enhancing their office sessions with text and phone coaching right at the moment of greatest impact, when a crisis is in progress or a critical decision must be made[116]. They incorporate mindfulness meditation into treatment to help clients recognize both their "rational mind" and their "emotional mind" and to make decisions from a dialectic that expresses the "wise mind" position that is neither and both. Having taken several trainings from both Linehan and her disciples, and employing two therapists at my office who are experienced in DBT, I find many of its principals invaluable in working with ADD clients, and I cite the *DBT Workbook*[117] in *I Always Want to Be Where I'm Not*[118].

Many therapists, however, see BPD clients as presenting an unacceptably high risk and are neither interested in treating them nor sufficiently trained to do so. Many insurance companies refuse to pay for any PD diagnoses because these conditions are, by definition, unremitting, have poor outcomes, and are expensive to treat. Even with two DBT-trained staff, our office always refers clients with this diagnosis to our friends at the local DBT Center[119] which offers a full program of care. This same split also appears in the prescribing community, with some providers willing to work within an integrative model of DBT, others not, and nearly all of them leery about handing out stimulants to these clients.

For people with ADD and Borderline Personality Disorder, this professional split creates a treatment dilemma, carried out well under the client's radar. Providers who are expert in treating ADD usually refer clients with BPD. Providers who become experts in treating the BPD crowd, rarely have training and experience in the nuances of ADD. Many DBT providers, including our local clinic, have no formal

---

[116] Though I don't practice DBT overtly, I've adopted this technique with many of my ADD clients.

[117] amazon.com/dp/1684034582/

[118] A future revision of this book will likely emphasize Acceptance Commitment Therapy (ACT) while still giving a nod to DBT. ACT tends to be much easier to administer in a non-programmatic setting and actually fits better with the more common experience of ADD.

[119] We do offer some DBT groups as ancillary service, but we do not specifically treat borderline personality disorder as we lack the full program needed to be successful.

relationship with a prescriber. Worse, most DBT shops are, by design of their model, closed systems, so all services must be done within their clinic. For exactly the same reasons, our office won't do medication management for anyone not also seen here in therapy, leaving ADD-BPD clients with a difficult choice. This scenario might or might not exist in any given community, but from what we've seen, it's easier to get ADD-BPD clients through the eye of a needle than into a comprehensive, outpatient treatment for ADD and BPD.

Since Kelsey and I don't get to organize the world as we'd like, we don't have a great answer for this problem, but here are our best suggestions should you face it:

- If you're pretty sure you have ADD and you, your people, or your therapist are concerned that you may also have BPD, seek DBT services, even if that interrupts your current treatment for ADD or prevents you from getting one. You're going to need that level of support to manage your foray into stimulants or to improve their outcomes. We suggest doing DBT for say, six months, and then circling back to address the ADD. This isn't a perfect solution, but it may be your only shot to gain some traction on mood management before adding the difficulties of stimulant use.

- If you know you have BPD and suspect you might also have ADD, you may well be right. If you're currently in DBT, ask during a private session if your provider has any experience with co-occurring ADD, and if so, how it's been previously addressed. Once in a while you'll get a DBT therapist who just "doesn't believe" in ADD or maybe doesn't believe that you have it. As discussed throughout this book, that's not evidence-based practice. Normally, we'd suggest you take leave from that therapist and search out a good evaluation for ADD, but in this case, that's not wise or practical. Complete your DBT treatment over six months and then start looking for someone to work with you on ADD, preferably someone who also understands or has training in DBT.

- If the DBT program you select does not have a relationship with a psychiatrist or PMHNP willing to address your ADD symptoms, you'll have to talk with a separate psychiatric practice or, failing that, your primary care physician about integrating medication management into your DBT treatment. Generally a DBT clinic won't object to you having an external prescriber. However, having never tried this ourselves, we don't know how well it would work as any semblance of treatment coordination could be thin to non-existent.

- If you don't already have a DBT therapist, go in search of one who also has a working knowledge of ADD. While we're shooting for the moon, see if you can find one with a good prescriber on speed-dial.

An Alternative Hypothesis for the ADD-PD Connection

Having concluded our oversimplified tour through the complicated subject of personality disorders, we'll wind up with an alternative way to think about the whole ADD-PD connection. It won't fix the many problems of treatment, but we hope it will stir some needed cross talk amongst providers and consumers.

If you research BPD, you'll find its etiology explained as something like this:

> As with other mental health disorders, the causes of borderline personality disorder aren't fully understood. In addition to environmental factors—such as a history of child abuse or neglect—borderline personality disorder may be linked to genetics...and brain abnormalities involved in emotion regulation, impulsivity and aggression. In addition, certain brain chemicals that help regulate mood, such as serotonin, may not function properly[120].

In line with the diathesis-stress model (Chapter 2), this paragraph from the Mayo Clinic points to both environmental and genetic factors in the development BPD. DBT founder Dr. Marsha Linehan agrees, noting BPD emerges "from transactions between individuals with biological vulnerabilities and specific environmental influences."[121] So, a genetic predisposition theory shouldn't surprise anyone. And yet it does. Among most practitioners, little if any emphasis is placed on diathesis when treating BPD. Tremendous—sometimes exclusive—

---

[120] www.mayoclinic.org/diseases-conditions/borderline-personality-disorder/symptoms-causes/syc-20370237

[121] www.ncbi.nlm.nih.gov/pmc/articles/PMC2696274/#S1title

focus is given to environmental factors, most often childhood traumas like sexual or physical abuse or neglect, loss of a parent, parental substance abuse or mental health problems, or unstable family relationships.

There are more logical fallacies in this common view of BPD than we have time to print. Most glaring is the fact that the vast majority of people who endure childhood traumas and hurts do not go on to develop BPD. Likewise, many people who clearly qualify for this disorder do not have histories of serious trauma. Tressa is a good example.

Over the years, my hypothesis about BPD has increasingly diverged from the traditional one. Since the research has yet to prove otherwise, it may be worth considering. I suspect that some portion of BPD cases emerge from co-occurring ADD and bipolar disorder that was insufficiently or un-

I suspect that many BPD cases emerge from co-occurring ADD and bipolar disorder that was insufficiently treated during the teen years.

successfully treated during the teen years; that these highly heritable conditions form the mediating genetic component for many presentations of BPD. I freely admit that this is a Dr. Wesism, but over nearly three decades of practice, I've worked with more kids with combined ADD-bipolar disorder than most psychologists, and I find the similarities striking. For many, we were able to treat the symptoms and help move them to adulthood free of severe personality dysfunction.

Charlotte, a twenty-year-old with ADD-bipolar and mild ASD, whom I've seen since she was fifteen, has never read a draft of this chapter. Yet, while on a recent summer break from college, she noted, "the only reason I don't have borderline personality is because you didn't let me have it," meaning she saw our treatment as a protective factor against an emerging personality disorder. I would concur. Other clients entered adulthood crystalizing fully expressed BPD despite our best efforts. Neither Charlotte, nor the majority of those kids, had the kind of traumatic childhoods seen as underlying BPD. All of them had ADD and some flavor of agitated mood disorder. I'm not proposing that this is the sole etiology of BPD. I'm just saying that it may account for a larger percentage of cases than is currently understood. I'm hoping researchers will eventually examine this possibility. It could explain a lot of diagnostic phenomenon that is presently not well understood.

Given the prevalence of ADD among incarcerated populations, the same might be true for ASPD. Perhaps these folks began as teens with ADD and under adverse environmental circumstances emerged as antisocial personalities. This might not explain everyone who has ASPD, but given the level of co-occurrence it could explain a portion. It can be argued that many antisocial adults come from difficult homes and neighborhoods and, in their teen years began running with other antisocial young adults, and that this better explains the etiology of ASPD than my ADD theory. But many other young folks grew up in those same conditions and did not end up with ASPD. What makes the difference between their life path and that of their antisocial peers? Probably several factors, of which ADD could easily be one.

There are many reasons to care about this hypothesis, but the most important one for readers of this book has to do with prevention, which means treatment of diathesis and reduction of stress. If young people with ADD and mood dysregulation are at higher risk for developing personality disorders later in life, then seeking integrative treatment for these children is critical. Treatment may be more than a means to get a child through school and on to adulthood. It could be a way to interdict, or at least mitigate, some of the most debilitating mental health conditions DSM-5 describes, along with the personal and societal costs they imply.

The Wisdom of Uncertainty

As we wind up this chapter, you may find yourself confused. Great. Let's just go with that. When it comes to psychodiagnosis, certainty isn't all it's cracked up to be, particularly where co-occurring disorders are concerned. The real problem isn't that such diagnoses are so complex that nobody can understand how they go together. It's the fact that as humans, we don't like complexity. We prefer our problems to just lie down before us and offer up clear solutions. "That guy has ADHD. Give him Ritalin." "That woman has bipolar disorder." "That child has ADD and anxiety." Boom, we're done. Or, we hide from reality and claim none of these problems exist.

In statistics, we call such thinking "univariate," meaning that one thing is associated with or leads to another in a predictable and measurable way. That kind of math is only useful for the simplest of life's questions, which means not very often. A higher level of statistics are referred to as "multivariate," and they're used to examine how a series of variables impact another one or, in the most complex equations, another series. Co-occurring and differential diagnosis is a lot like that. You and your team don't need to learn matrix algebra to figure out what's going on with you, but it's best to surrender the idea that a single "obvious" answer is the right one.

This is a bigger problem than you might expect in a field of highly trained professionals. Univariate thinking combines with another human foible, confirmation bias—our tendency to latch onto information that fits with what we think we know and to ignore challenging data. This can lead diagnosticians down the path of simplification error. It's what urges clinicians to have pet diagnoses and prescribers to believe a certain medication is the end-all and be-all, because "it's worked for my other patients." It's both the greatest influence on mental health providers and our worst sin. It's why, at our clinic, we don't give up thinking and rethinking a diagnosis until the client completes treatment.

Figuring out if your ADD co-occurs with another disorder and how to treat it if it does, isn't always as difficult as we describe in this chapter. With a good team, things can be pretty straight forward, requiring only a couple iterations to figure out what works best. Other times, it takes a great deal more time and attention. In a complex case, like Tressa's, we traverse each of the symptom lists above and argue her presentation five different ways. We go back and forth, wondering if any medication can sooth her irritable soul, working with an ASD diagnosis at one point, rethinking it as bipolar at another, and then later as BPD. I recently referred her to a DBT group one week and in the next, I assigned her to read the book *The Journal of Best Practices*[122], written by an autistic man desperately trying to save his marriage. Neither Kelsey nor I are really this flakey. We just try to stay curious long enough for things to add up so we can do what we need to do to make lasting improvement. And when it comes to co-occurring disorders, that's always a work in progress.

---

[122] amazon.com/dp/1439189749/

Finding the Right Prescriber

Mental health problems do not affect three or four out of every five persons, but one out of one.

— William Menninger

- Dr. Kelsey -

Gretchen gave a frustrated sigh as she dropped onto my couch for her psychiatric intake. "I've had a rough time trying to find someone I can work with on the whole ADD thing."

"Where have you tried?" I asked tentatively. It's a delicate question. I want to respect the work of fellow prescribers, but this is one of the most common concerns clients present at our office. Understanding where they've been and what's been tried is crucial to a good start.

"I began at the campus clinic." Gretchen was a college sophomore coming to the end of her fall semester, so it was no surprise she'd started out at the University health center. "They were really happy to hand out the stimulants. I'm sure some people think that's great. You just pop in and they give you drugs."

"Doesn't sound great," I said. "Not if you really have ADD."

"I know that now. I mean that's where my roommate told me to go, and her boyfriend got Adderall there too, along with just about everyone on that end of the dorm. Not one of them really has ADD, but they filled out that checklist and bam, they got speed."

"So, how'd that go wrong for you?"

Gretchen shook her head. "I realized pretty quickly that people who need to be on this stuff actually need more than to be on it. And, it was like they didn't really know much about ADD there. I did my research, so I knew there are different ways to take it and different strengths and types, but that clinic was like, 'Here, take these three times a day,' and I was like 'How about you give me something I can take once?' and for some reason that wasn't what the doc wanted to do."

"That seems to happen a lot," I said. It's odd that a college clinic would prescribe instant release stimulants to a population of teens and very young adults prone to abuse them[123], yet Gretchen wasn't the first client to report this. "So, they gave you three-a-day, fast-acting stimulants?"

"Yep. Generic Adderall. Of course, I'd take the first one and then forget the second one until I was in the middle of a test and then take it too late, which pushed the last one to about 7:00 p.m. and then I got real cute and started taking them later in the evening so I could stay up and study."

"How'd that go?"

"How do you think?" Gretchen let out a wry chuckle. "Before long, I was all messed up. I looked it up online and found I was getting 'sleep dysregulated.'"

"I'm impressed with how much you know about this." Some providers don't like it when a client comes in armed with knowledge. We find that, even if they've found some erroneous info online, their desire to learn makes such clients great students and, eventually, ADD experts. "Where'd you go next?" I asked.

"My mom kept telling me, 'You need a real doctor for this stuff. Go see a psychiatrist.'"

I tried to conceal a knowing smile, but I couldn't.

---

[123] We suspect a key reason for this is that most insurance companies require a prior authorization (PA) for the more expensive extended release products, and as we've learned in our clinic, that gets time consuming in a hurry. In a busy college health clinic, it's much easier (for the prescriber) to hand off a short-acting script and be on to the next patient.

Gretchen noticed. "I know what you're thinking." Her eyes rolled. "I couldn't find anyone who took my insurance, and they were wanting like $400 for an evaluation session. My mom finally said, 'Just go and I'll pay for it.' But everybody I called had like a six week waiting list. Finally, I got in. I gave them my $400, and what I got wasn't exactly a rigorous assessment. That lady seemed interested in just one thing."

"Whether or not you were drug seeking."

"Exactly. So, I go from a place that's throwing pills at me to an office where they act like I'm buying drugs off the street. The only thing that sold her on me not being a cliché study drug addict was that I pulled out this bottle of fast acting Adderall and handed it to her. I said, 'Here, take this. It's not the right medicine for me. I need something that works all day that won't get me all bent out of shape and off schedule."

"So, what did she give you?" I asked.

"Strattera."

"Oh." I didn't have much else to say. While Strattera may work in a very small number of cases, it's among the least used medications for ADD. Despite Gretchen's good faith effort to convince the psychiatrist otherwise, this prescription clearly reflected her concern about stimulant seeking. "How did that work out?" I asked.

"I was pretty skeptical," Gretchen said. "I'd read about Strattera. It's like an antidepressant that didn't make it through its trials and somehow ended up being used for ADD, and it's not very great. But I'm like, 'Okay, whatever. I guess if this doesn't work, I can come back in a couple weeks and let you know.' And she's like, 'Actually, no. I'm booked out about six weeks, and you won't really know how the Strattera is doing until then anyhow.' Then she had her secretary set me up. I asked how long that next meeting would take, because I had a class at four and had to drive across town and she tells me, 'Well, only about ten minutes, but you need to be here about thirty minutes ahead of time to insure your place in line.' I'm like, 'In line?' She tells me that they usually book about six people an hour and sometimes you have to wait thirty to sixty minutes until your turn comes up. I was like, 'Do I take a number or something?' She wasn't amused."

"Yeah," I said. "That's kind of the situation for psychiatry these days. They have to run things a little tight. What did you do?"

"I never went back," Gretchen said. "And Strattera did nothing. I tried another place and that guy like, didn't even believe in ADD. He told me it was overdiagnosed and that most people who think they have it really just need diet and exercise and to sleep more. He offered to prescribe me something to sleep and an antidepressant. I told him Strattera pretty much is an antidepressant and that's not helping. He seemed uncomfortable."

"Are you depressed?" I asked.

"Who wouldn't be?" Gretchen said. "I'm having a hard time in school because I can't keep up, and my mom is mad at me, and I'm spending all her money doing bad. It's like every one of these people has his or her own little theory about what's wrong with me, when I think it's pretty obvious, and I just need help. I'm not depressed because I'm depressed, I'm depressed because I have ADD."

I made a note or two in my chart. "I'm afraid I know the answer, but did anyone actually test you for ADD? I mean before you came here and saw Dr. Wes?"

"Nope. And I wondered about that."

"I'm looking at the printout from the test you did for Wes. You filled out your form and this looks like one from your mom."

"And my dad. They did it together."

"And who is Rudy?" I turned the laptop screen so Gretchen could see the coversheet of Rudy's form.

"My boyfriend. We've been together all year. And I also had my roommate do one. That's Sydney. She's the next one down."

"Wow," I said. "That's a lot of tests and they really converge. Your people see you like you do and your T-scores are really high."

"That's what Dr. Wes said." Gretchen paused a moment. "That was the first time anyone listened to me and made me feel like there was hope. He said that you guys see people like me all the time, and as long as I agreed to do both the therapy and medication, he thought I could survive the semester and maybe make it through college after all."

"I agree. I'm glad you feel comfortable here. There's a lot we have to do, and when you feel comfortable, it makes it easier to do uncomfortable things, like change."

"I'm trying," Gretchen said. "It's just hard when you get ping-ponged around like that. I started thinking, I better just give up and go back to the health clinic, then somebody told me about this office, and it seemed like a way better idea."

"I have one other test I want to do with you. It's a cheek swab so we can tell how your body metabolizes the medication."

"Nobody ever mentioned that either," she said. "Is it new?"

"Not really. But we're using it more often now to hedge our guess as to how you'll respond to medication."

"How come other clinics don't operate this way?"

I chuckled. "That would take a while to explain, and I'd have to get into medicine, psychology, business, economics, and a few other grad school courses. Instead, let's spend our time figuring out how we're going to help you, and maybe someday I'll write a book chapter that answers your question."

Wither We Go for Meds?
- Dr. Kelsey -

Welcome to that chapter I imagined in Gretchen's vignette. To prescribe in the environment we do requires a certain vision for treatment, which we refer to as an integrative approach. As the vignette illustrates, not everyone shares that vision. Thus, it's important to learn a few things about modern psychiatry before you go searching for an optimal treatment environment, and if you can't find one of those, how you can cobble together a workable alternative.

Before you decide this chapter is a big ad for our practice in the heart of America, please know that we're operating at capacity. We actually refer out about half the applicants who want to see the nine providers in our office because they're either out of our scope of practice or they need services we can't provide. Not all of them have ADD or are seeking that diagnosis, but because we're known for that, a good percentage are. Wes and I do a limited number of consultations every year over video conferencing, but we don't open those as clinical cases, continue seeing them on an ongoing basis, or offer medication management. We just send them back to their local communities with our findings and some good ideas, hopefully improving their long-term experience by making them better ADD experts.

Beyond that limited service, please take this chapter in the spirit it's intended, as a guide in your search for a similar practice or at least to help you better organize your own treatment. Because, if you're not being seen in a practice like ours, all case coordination will fall to you.

The Doctor Is Not In
- Dr. Wes -

We borrowed the title for this section from a Fall 2017 article in *ADDitude* magazine[124] which explains why finding a prescriber for ADD is tricky. As Gretchen learned, when it comes to stimulants, prescribers come in several flavors. Some seem very free—perhaps too free—in their willingness to hand out meds. Others are reluctant to the point of suspiciousness. Some pride themselves on their expertise, others feel inadequate, and yes, still others belong to the ADD skeptics club. The *ADDitude* article points out how few specialists really exist who are experts in prescribing ADD medication, which in turn, feeds the problem of misdiagnosis discussed in Chapter 2. So, just who *should* you see for your ADD medication? You have three choices: psychiatrists, psychiatric nurse practitioners, and primary care docs. Let's look at the pros, cons, and oddities of each.

Psychiatrists

If you're like Gretchen's mom and new to this whole psychopharmacology thing, you may reason that psychiatric meds fall within the purview of psychiatrists. Throughout the last half of the twentieth century, the American public became increasingly familiar with psychiatrists,

---

[124] www.additudemag.com/can-a-pediatrician-diagnose-adhd-doctor-report/

even if it still confuses them with psychologists. From the early 1950s through 1980, the psychiatrist was that guy who sat behind you on a couch while you free associated and responded once in a while with an interpretation.

Though he (and for many years, most were "he") might occasionally prescribe medication, it was given in conjunction with an early form of therapy known as psychoanalysis, handed down directly from Sigmund Freud. Believe it or not, our neighbor city to the west, Topeka, Kansas, was once internationally famous for psychoanalysis, because the Menninger Foundation was located there. Begun in the 1920s by Charles Menninger, MD and his sons, Karl and William Menninger, in a large house on the outskirts of town, the clinic expanded first into a sizable campus just north of that old house, and then to an even more sizable campus on a hill in far northwest Topeka. In 2002 however, the foundation moved lock, stock, and barrel to Baylor College of Medicine[125] in Houston. While the older Menninger campus is occupied by various Topeka businesses and clinics, the newer one remains mostly vacant, a vestige of a time when psychiatry was synonymous with couches.

Beginning slowly in the 1960s and then rapidly through the 1970s and 80s, psychoanalysis gave way to several counter-movements based on an improved understanding of psychobiology, more rigorous scientific study, and the deployment of medications to address mental illness at its neurotransmitter level. Early successes with lithium carbonate[126] for bipolar disorder and chlorpromazine (better known as Thorazine)[127] for schizophrenia began a gradual transition in which the primary role of the psychiatrist went from therapist to therapist/prescriber and eventually to just prescriber.

This accelerated considerably with the approval of Prozac in late 1987[128]. While antidepressants had existed well prior to this, they came with complications and intolerable side effects including severe daytime sleepiness, constipation, tremors, and urinary hesitancy. Prozac was, by 1987 standards, a miracle and far better tolerated than earlier meds. Consumers who had not responded well to earlier treatments,

---

[125] en.wikipedia.org/wiki/Menninger_Foundation

[126] en.wikipedia.org/wiki/Lithium_carbonate

[127] en.wikipedia.org/wiki/Chlorpromazine

[128] en.wikipedia.org/wiki/Fluoxetine

or who had never tried an antidepressant, took it in droves, pushing annual sales to a peak of 2.6 billion dollars in the late 1990s. Over that same period, Prozac's many cousins—Zoloft, Paxil, Celexa, and Lexapro—entered the market along with new mood stabilizers and antipsychotics. Just before Prozac came out, a different class of antidepressant, Wellbutrin, hit the market. Though it did not have quite the cultural impact of Prozac, it remains in more common use today.

By the first decade of the twenty-first century, psychiatrists had largely given up couches in favor of prescription pads. Today, you'd be hard pressed to find a psychiatrist who would agree to do psychotherapy and if you could, the price would be exorbitant. For this reason, Gretchen's mom could reasonably assume that her daughter would find lots of psychiatrists out there just waiting for new patients to show up and ask for prescriptions. She would, however, be wrong.

> *There is a severe shortage of psychiatrists, with about 50,000 in practice in the U.S., which the American Psychiatric Association found "wholly inadequate to meet the need."*

Scarcity. When I published *I Always Want to Be Where I'm Not* in 2014, I discussed the severe shortage of psychiatrists, with about 50,000 in practice in the U.S. at the time. The American Psychiatric Association deemed this "wholly inadequate to meet the need," particularly in rural areas where the situation was considered a crisis even then. In 2012, about 96% of medical students entered specialties other than psychiatry[129]. While more students have gravitated toward the profession in the years since[130], that still totals less than three hundred a year. So, with retirements greatly outstripping new-entries, the number of new psychiatrists has actually dropped. In 2018, Forbes found the number of active psychiatrists in the U.S. to be just 28,000, of which three out of five (16,800) were over the age of fifty-seven[131]. The Association of American Medical Colleges (AAMC) referred to this as "an escalating shortage," and warned that the pool could dwindle to the point that the need for psychiatrists would

---

[129] psychnews.psychiatryonline.org/newsarticle.aspx?articleid=1104005

[130] psychnews.psychiatryonline.org/doi/full/10.1176/appi.pn.2017.4b8

[131] www.forbes.com/sites/brucejapsen/2018/02/25/psychiatrist-shortage-escalates-as-u-s-mental-health-needs-grow/#849527a12554

eventually outstrip demand by as much as 16,000. I suspect those numbers are optimistic.

Economics. To understand this, you need to know what happened to the famous Menninger Clinic in Topeka, Kansas. It's not just that psychiatrists woke up one day and decided medication was the one true light of modern mental health. Some think that, but the rest have gotten on that bandwagon largely because they have no other way to make a living. Insurance companies long ago became suspicious of psychoanalysis as an effective form of treatment because it relied on vastly more sessions than newer approaches like Cognitive Behavioral Therapy (CBT), Acceptance Commitment Therapy (ACT), Solution Focused Therapy, and nearly every other model developed since 1960. In the parlance of Chapter 2, psychoanalysis is no longer seen as meeting medical necessity for insurance reimbursement and few clients are willing to dedicate time and money to pay for it out of pocket. This leaves psychiatrists with only one option to generate income: meet the vast market demand for medication.

Writing in 2012 on behalf of The American Psychiatric Association, author Mark Moran couldn't seem to explain the decrease of new psychiatry students in an era "considered exciting for the field." Yet in a different article, he laid them out quite clearly, noting, "When asked why they don't [pursue psychiatry, medical students] cite the opinion of peers and of other non-psychiatric doctors as inhibiting factors.... Students themselves glean from the carveout psychiatric payment system that there must be something off or less valid about psychiatry.[132]" What Moran is saying, in plain language, is that psychiatry isn't considered a cool medical career anymore, nor profitable. Among physicians, psychiatrists are tied for last place in salary, with some specialties paying hundreds of thousands of dollars more per year.[133]

"Hey," you might argue. "I have great health insurance, so I can afford to see a top specialist, just like I do when I have a urological problem or need an orthopedic surgeon." Sorry to burst your bubble, but when it comes to any mental health treatment, especially psychiatry, insurance may be of little to no help. It may even be a hinderance. Over the

---

[132] psychnews.psychiatryonline.org/newsArticle.aspx?articleid=1104028

[133] www.forbes.com/sites/jacquelynsmith/2012/07/20/the-best-and-worst-paying-jobs-for-doctors-2/2/

last fifteen years we've been engaged in a long, painful, and super weird debate about healthcare and how to pay for it. At the time of this writing, a few things have gotten better and others seem to be getting worse. Most (but not all) young adults now have mental health coverage. Pre-existing conditions have somewhat better portability across insurance plans. We're supposed to have mental health parity, in which treatment for conditions like ADD are paid for, though we've seen a plan or two that defy that rule without explanation. For example, one self-insured company[134] lists ADD as the only mental health condition exempted from its coverage. Others offer no mental health benefit at all because, even under the Affordable Care Act (ACA, also known as Obamacare), they just don't have to. Worst of all, at the time of this writing, none of us have any idea what's next for health insurance in general and even less clarity about mental health coverage.

Every time a mass shooting occurs and a politician calls out for better mental health services in the U.S., please know that they are in no way serious. There's no meaningful movement in the U.S. to improve access to affordable mental health care. Quite the opposite, in fact. The community mental health systems developed in the 1970s, 1980s, and 1990s were greatly reduced over the last twenty years, and health insurance companies have been allowed to either cut their allowable charges or at least leave them exactly where they were in the year 2000.

Lack of Private Practices. For your purposes in treating ADD, the only psychiatrist that matters is one who can see you in an outpatient clinic—unless you're headed into a psychiatric hospital, the VA, the military, or prison. Most of the small handful of psychiatrists now work in one of these facilities, because the salary is better than in outpatient practice and less dependent on market economics. Many community mental health centers (CMHCs) take Medicaid and Medicare because their charter requires it, but they may eschew private insurance because it cuts their allowable charge to beneath operating expenses. They supplement their psychiatrist's incomes from the local and state tax base and focus their work on those populations.

---

[134] Some large companies (Walmart is an example) create their own insurance pool and hire a name-brand company like Blue Cross to administer it. The cards look very similar, but when you dig deeper, you find out that the coverage isn't what you'd expect because self-insured companies don't have to follow the same rules and regulations.

Even if you have top-shelf insurance coverage, you'll probably hit a brick wall in seeking a private practice psychiatrist. A handful still accept the best paying plans, but most don't because they don't have to and the economics never add up. To make the spreadsheet balance, private practice psychiatrists either charge a huge hourly rate or carry so many cases that they find it difficult to maintain rigorous clinical standards. As one psychiatrist told *The New York Times,* "We run our office like a bus station," seeing so many patients for five- to ten-minute medication checks that it's difficult to connect to any of them. He adds, "The sad thing is that I'm very important to [my patients], but I barely know them."[135]

Thus, when looking for a prescriber to fit our model of treatment, the biggest obstacle you'll face is weighing your out-of-pocket cost against the quality and expertise of the provider, and figuring that out isn't straight forward. In general, if a psychiatrist takes cheaper insurance, you can expect to be less satisfied, because he or she has to see far more patients per hour than someone who only takes a high cash rate. But the inverse is not necessarily true. If you go out and pay the most you can pay for a prescriber—and that can be in excess of $500 an hour in some zip codes—you may still not get a provider who has pruned his or her caseload to provide the best service possible to a smaller number patients. You may get someone who has successfully advertised his or her practice in a market that has more demand than supply, but who runs it exactly the same way as the person who charges less—like a bus station.

And none of this is getting better. Due to these deteriorating market factors, the psychiatry pool will continue to diminish even as the demand for services increases[136]. And if you're a child, or you have one who needs psychiatric medication, the situation is far more grim. Child psychiatrists are like the proverbial hen's teeth, increasingly scarce, with just 8,300[137] practicing in the U.S. against an estimated fifteen million children in need of mental health care[138]. And many of these

---

[135] www.nytimes.com/2011/03/06/health/policy/06doctors.html?_r=0

[136] news.aamc.org/patient-care/article/addressing-escalating-psychiatrist-shortage/

[137] This is actually a slight increase over the 7,400 Wes reported in 2014, but well short of the need.

[138] www.aacap.org/aacap/resources_for_primary_care/workforce_issues.aspx

doctors are serving in hospitals or other facilities that leave them essentially inaccessible to you and your child.

If this trendline continues, it's possible that outpatient psychiatry as a medical specialty will vanish in the not-too-distant future. Even as it exists now, you'll be hard pressed to see an affordable psychiatrist with any consistency, particularly if you aren't living in a major metropolitan area. Even in New York City, the "bus station" psychiatrist reported a long wait list for intakes.

Psychiatric Nurse Practitioners

The best workaround for the shortage of affordable psychiatrists are psychiatric mental health nurse practitioners (PMHNPs). In most states the APRNs or DNPs[139] are licensed and specialized in prescribing medication for all mental health disorders, including ADD. Whether one might be available to prescribe for you, depends on the state you live in and how these nurses are licensed there. Figure 2[140] illustrates which states grant which prescription privileges to their PMHNPs.

Full practice states allow independent practice for PMHNPs, meaning that if you find one in private practice, he or she can prescribe all the same ADD medications that a psychiatrist would. In these states, PMHNPs have flourished in private practice, and you may have better luck finding one that practices the way we do. However, with that broad privilege have come new business opportunities for nurses. In states like Iowa and Oregon, PMHNPs have made themselves available through telepsychiatry to offer services across state lines to mental health centers and other practices with a shortage of prescriber time. This is still a new and limited area of practice, but it may serve to *reduce* the number of psychiatric hours available to you in your local community, particularly if you need to use your insurance, because those advanced practice nurses can chase better rates elsewhere.

Reduced-practice states grant a conditional, limited, independent practice privilege in which the PMHNP is legally required to practice "on protocol" with a collaborating physician. Many folks—including

---

[139] The difference here is that most APRNs have master's degrees and DNPs have doctoral degrees. Both are advanced nurse practitioners.

[140] www.medscape.com/viewarticle/440315

physicians—mistake this idea of collaborating protocol for supervision. In fact, the sole responsibility of the protocol physician is to approve a list of medications the PMHNP can prescribe once a year. And yet, in these states, PMHNPs struggle to find collaborating physicians and the cost of that signature can range from a few thousand dollars per year to figures so high it becomes impossible to afford to practice. If you're in one of those states, your access to a PMHNP could be limited not by the number of nurses licensed but by the number of physicians willing to provide protocol[141], and it might be worth writing your state legislators to complain. Most state nursing associations are trying to get these laws changed and they could use your help as a consumer.

Figure 2. Restriction of Practice for PMHNPs by State*

Alabama	Reduced Practice	Montana	Full Practice
Alaska	Full Practice	Nebraska	Full Practice
Arizona	Full Practice	Nevada	Full Practice
Arkansas	Reduced Practice	New Hampshire	Full Practice
California	Restricted Practice	New Jersey	Reduced Practice
Colorado	Full Practice	New Mexico	Full Practice
Connecticut	Full Practice	New York	Reduced Practice
Delaware	Reduced Practice	North Carolina	Restricted Practice
Florida	Restricted Practice	North Dakota	Full Practice
Georgia	Restricted Practice	Ohio	Reduced Practice
Hawaii	Full Practice	Oklahoma	Restricted Practice
Idaho	Full Practice	Oregon	Full Practice
Illinois	Reduced Practice	Pennsylvania	Reduced Practice
Indiana	Reduced Practice	Rhode Island	Full Practice
Iowa	Full Practice	South Carolina	Restricted Practice
Kansas	Reduced Practice	South Dakota	Full Practice
Kentucky	Reduced Practice	Tennessee	Restricted Practice
Louisiana	Reduced Practice	Texas	Restricted Practice
Maine	Full Practice	Utah	Reduced Practice
Maryland	Full Practice	Vermont	Full Practice
Massachusetts	Restricted Practice	Virginia	Restricted Practice
Michigan	Restricted Practice	Washington	Full Practice
Minnesota	Full Practice	West Virginia	Reduced Practice
Mississippi	Reduced Practice	Wisconsin	Reduced Practice
Missouri	Restricted Practice	Wyoming	Full Practice

*www.aanp.org/advocacy/state/state-practice-environment

Restricted-practice states grant PMHNP prescription privileges only under the direct supervision of a physician, similar to a physician's

---

[141] Some states allow any physician to provide protocol. Others require it to be a psychiatrist, which, given the aforementioned shortage, causes even fewer PNPs to be available for private, outpatient practice.

assistant (PA). Worse, the statute may require the supervisor to be a psychiatrist, meaning that the psychiatrist shortage will impact the availability of a PMHNP to serve you. If you're in one of these states, make that call to your state house member or senator.

The bottom line is that while finding a PMHNP practicing in an integrative setting is probably easier than finding a psychiatrist, you'll still do a lot of searching and once you've found a good match, you may be put on a waiting list. As we point out in every chapter of this book, there are good reasons to choose your provider carefully, but if you need to get in to see someone while you're out conducting that exhaustive search, there is a third option.

Primary Care Physicians (PCPs)

Given the shortage of psychiatric prescribers, most stimulants and other psychopharmaceuticals are prescribed by primary care docs and in the case of children, pediatricians. You've probably gone down this road yourself. I have. The child psychiatrist who saw my daughter when she first went on medication back in 2005 left private practice in 2007 to direct a local hospital's psychiatric clinic, leaving us with few good options even in a metropolitan area of over 2.3 million people. Because it's unethical for Kelsey to see my kids (because they're my kids), both Alyssa and Alex have relied on their PCP for many years now. And yes, that physician takes most of his cues from me, which we greatly appreciate.

Contrary to what the ADD skeptic press proposes, this trend isn't a product of PCPs and pediatricians seeing a lucrative new market and seizing the day to make big bucks. Not even close. Many PCPs would be quite happy to refer patients to psychiatric prescribers when the topic of stimulants arises, except they haven't anyone to refer to. That article from *ADDitude*, mentioned at the beginning of this chapter, puts a fine point on why. Stephanie Berger, a mom cited in the article, describes trying to get her daughter, Nadia, on stimulants through her pediatrician. Author, Devon Frye, writes:

> "When [Nadia] was four, I went to our pediatrician and told him she was having trouble," Berger said. "He's the first one who said it 'could be' ADHD." Berger, who lives in Brandon, Florida, didn't know much about ADHD, but she could see that Nadia was struggling..."I asked him,

'Can you handle this?' but he demurred. 'I could, but I shouldn't.' He said that they covered [ADHD] a little bit in his medical school training, but it was minute." He would refer Nadia to a specialist.

The specialist was unaffordable, however, so Berger took Nadia to another pediatrician — and, after that, several more. Most said that Nadia likely had ADHD, but each was reluctant to diagnose her. "I couldn't get any of them to say, 'She has ADHD,'" [Berger] said. "They kept sending me someplace else."

Years passed; Berger grew frustrated. "I saw so many people, and no one would help her," she said. Most of the pediatricians she tried said they lacked the expertise to handle Nadia's challenges. Getting the diagnosis would require her to look elsewhere.

Nadia's situation is even worse than what we're used to seeing, but we don't doubt her story. More common are PCPs who are willing to go about halfway in the process, just as Gretchen found, prescribing within their narrow comfort zone and not in response to what might actually work for the person sitting in front of them.

In response, author Frye proposes training modules on ADD for pediatricians in the form of a "three-day mental health intensive, followed by six months of bi-monthly conference calls" along with changes in medical school curriculum to give the physicians most likely to encounter ADHD in their patients, "the confidence they need to handle the cases themselves." We're all for that. We feel great empathy for Nadia and her mom, and we applaud the PCPs and pediatricians who've stepped up to address the shortage of psychiatric care. But even an awesome PCP simply can't afford to spend the time necessary to follow your case closely enough to learn its many ins, outs, ups, and downs. Insurance certainly won't pay for it. I might see a client two to four times a month for an hour each time, then pass my findings off to Kelsey, who sees the client a couple times a month at first and then every sixty to ninety days thereafter. A PCP will see you or your child for a few minutes, three to five times, if that. After things seem to be working, med checks will stretch to every three to six months and, not infrequently, once a year.

Winston Churchill famously said of democracy that it was "the worst form of government on earth except for all the others that had been tried from time to time[142]." This is how we see the PCP model of medication management—if there are no better

If everyone does his or her part, PCP-based medication management can come out okay. And by "everyone," we mostly mean you.

options for psychiatric care, take this one. It's usually better than struggling along without medication. Just know that making a PCP-based approach into the kind of integrative treatment model we describe in the next section requires better-than-average communication between your therapist and your PCP with you in the middle coordinating it all. This is because, as professionals, we're all so busy keeping our spinning plates in the air, that critical treatment dialog will usually come via letter, fax, secure email, or for the less tech-savvy, a flurry of phone messages that run through the physician's nursing staff and could take a week or two to resolve. That's far from ideal, but if everyone does his or her part, PCP-based medication management can come out okay. And by "everyone," we mostly mean you.

A Team Effort (or Not)
- Dr. Kelsey -

The answer to just about any ADD treatment problem is found in this, our most cherished clinical value: the person writing the scripts must talk regularly to your therapist who must talk regularly to you. Unfortunately, the lack of trained prescribers in integrative outpatient settings is the problem to that solution, because few psychiatrists, PMHNPs, and PCPs practice with therapists or even have a working relationship with one.

Below, we've listed the five most common business models in order of most to least integrative. The list can help you know what to look for, what to ask about, and how to sort out your findings to make an informed decision on how to proceed.

Model I: A psychiatrist or advanced nurse practitioner is employed by a larger mental health practice or serves as a private contractor in the same office as the therapists, and part of their job designation is to

---

[142] It's worth noting that Churchill was quoting an earlier source.

interface with the therapists. This is our model. I work for a corporation owned by Dr. Wes, alongside my therapist colleagues. We consult weekly or sometimes daily, share information, and consider each other's recommendations. This is the truest team-based model, because everyone is coequal and bringing something valuable to the table.

Some offices have a "medical director," usually a psychiatrist. While that's also a team model and worth your consideration, it is more hierarchical, like a hospital or large mental health center. In theory, the prescriber runs the team, sets the treatment plan and, at least on paper, oversees everyone else's practice. It is important however, to ask how many clock hours the medical director actually spends on site. We know of practices that pay a fee for a psychiatrist to act as medical director in name only, when in fact he or she provides few, if any, direct contact hours. Such individuals may even hold titles across several different operations. On the other hand, direct services may be provided by PMHNPs under the protocol or supervision of the medical director. That could work out great. Just be sure you ask enough questions to know what you're getting.

Model II: A group of pediatricians or primary care doctors keep on staff at least one licensed therapist, usually a clinical social worker. In this model, the physicians either employ the therapist(s) as ancillary providers or have some form of office sharing or contractual relationship. In researching this style of practice, be sure the therapist is doing more than "care coordination." He or she should be engaging with you and/or your loved one around a clear treatment plan. The extent to which this model constitutes a team depends on the climate set by the prescribers in the practice. If they value the input of the therapists and make time for professional interplay, this can work just as well as our model. If not, this approach may be more about provider convenience than clinical efficacy.

Model III: The prescriber has a handshake relationship with a single group of therapists or, perhaps, several practices. All parties may consult on cases either face-to-face or more often by phone or fax. Or they may not. In reality, most of these arrangements hold themselves out as allied professionals, but don't actually engage in the kind of clinical interplay found in our office. Such arrangements end up more as cross-referral platforms than clinical consultations, allowing the therapist a place to send clients for medication and the prescriber a limited network of therapists he or she can call on when the need arises.

Model IV: None of the above. It blows our minds, but some therapists have no meaningful relationship whatsoever with a medication provider and many prescribers haven't even a rudimentary referral system to therapists. Not your best bet for treating ADD.

This list of models makes it super easy to size up a practice and get going, right? Probably not, because the model a given office uses may or may not be obvious from their webpage or pamphlet. As a rule of thumb, the more they describe working as a team, the more likely it is that they actually do so. Likewise, therapists should mention that while they don't themselves prescribe meds, they have certain providers to whom they refer for that service. They might even list the prescriber and their affiliations on their site. Otherwise, the only way to know is to ask.

When you contact a psychotherapy practice, query them about how they make referrals for medication. When you contact a prescriber, ask for their referral network of therapists. Feel free to be cagy about this, acting as if everyone just expects prescribing and therapy to go together like peanut butter and jelly. If this baffles them, you have your answer. If they offer something vague like "we refer as the need arises," that means they have little investment in integrating treatment and you're on your own to coordinate everyone's efforts. The more they have a clear and confident response and the closer (literally and figuratively) they seem to be to their affiliated providers, the more likely you'll be to find the golden team you're looking for.

You might expect all this questioning to earn a big pat on the back from the practices you reach out to. You're showing great interest in their work, taking the time to read their page. You've done your research and formulated great queries about how they practice. Won't they be impressed? Probably not. We love clients who come with an understanding of what they're looking for—especially if they've read our books! But mostly we're used to something like, "Hey, my kid needs meds and maybe I do, too. Can we come in tomorrow?" Don't be surprised if you run into puzzlement when you call up with a book full of information. Worse, you may get some lightly veiled hostility, implying that you should just trust their judgment about these things and submit your request for services. Don't give up. You're on an important search and you deserve the right program of treatment for ADD.

That's most of what we know about finding a good prescriber. The rest we reserve for private consultation, not because we don't want you to get your money's worth out of this book, but because some of our views are specific to certain underlying dynamics of prescriber-patient relationships and those are best saved for a less public format.

Inside the Medicine Cabinet

The good physician treats the disease; the great physician treats the patient who has the disease.

— William Osler

- Dr. Kelsey -

"I just don't know if my meds are working." Kim's frustration was obvious. "I get tired in the middle of the day even when I've taken them, and I just want to nap. Maybe we need to up the dosage."

"Which medication are you referring to?" I asked.

"I think it's the blue one." Kim dug around in her purse. "I thought I had the bottle in here, but I guess I left it at home."

"You mean the dextroamphetamine?" I was trying to help Kim zero in by saying the generic name for short-acting Adderall printed on the side of the bottle. It wasn't working.

"Isn't that the one I take at night?"

"That would be trazadone, Kim. That one is white and kind of shaped like a trapezoid." I made the shape in the air with my index finger. "The blue one is a stimulant."

"Oh, right." She nodded enthusiastically and made the same trapezoid with her hands. "I haven't been taking that one because it puts me right to sleep."

"That's kind of the point, remember? ADD-related insomnia?" Kim was a sweet young woman in her late twenties. I enjoyed working with her, but at moments like this I wanted to pack her pill boxes myself. "When did you take the blue capsule this week?"

"The square blue one?"

"No, the blue *capsule*."

"Oh you mean the Vyvanse." Kim rested her chin on her fist, her mouth contorting as she thought. "Let me think. So, today is Thursday, right? On Monday I didn't have to go into work until noon so I got up about 11:30 and took it while I was on the bus and I remember it didn't seem to help much until like 2:00, at which point I was really up and going. But then, the next day I almost didn't wake up in time to go in to work."

"Did you do as I suggested? Leave the Vyvanse beside your bed at night, with a glass of water, set two alarms, the first about an hour before you need to get up. Then take it when the first alarm goes off and go back to sleep. An hour later, when the second one goes off, the medication will be in your system in time for work."

"But I don't always know when I'm going to get up," Kim said. "Some days I sleep in."

"I'm talking about work days."

"Right," Kim hesitated. "To be honest, I kind of decide after I wake up how I'm feeling and whether I want to go in or not. I don't want to take the Vyvanse if I'm not going to go to work because I don't like how it makes me feel."

"And that's exactly the problem I'm trying resolve here, Kim. There's a lot more to being on a stimulant than taking a blue capsule so your work is better. You need it most when you have to make the next right decision, like getting out of bed and not calling in. If you take meds as directed, they'll help you ask yourself 'is this what I really mean to do?' and then choose to do what you value. You say you value this job, right? So, with meds, you'll be able to tell yourself 'get out of bed!' and actually do it, not because you feel like it, but because that's how you pay the rent."

"It's just so hard." Kim sighed as she swiped her phone. "I'm checking my calendar for Tuesday. So, okay. I was up late Monday night watching Netflix with my girlfriend and some other friends from the apartment complex, so I took the blue square one at about 9:30."

"Wait." I let my jaw drop for emphasis. "You mean 9:30 at night?"

"Well, yeah, of course." Kim seemed puzzled that I was puzzled. "I told you I didn't get up until 11:30 in the morning, so I got my Vyvanse late and I didn't need the blue square until later in the day after I got off work."

"That 'blue square' is a generic form of fast-acting Adderall, Kim. It's a booster for when you have to work late into the evening. It's not for staying up late to watch movies."

"Right. So, after I took it, I didn't get to sleep for a long time and I had a shift at 8:00 a.m. the next day, so I just kind of napped a little. Then I got up and took the Vyvanse about 7:30 in the morning, and again it wasn't super helpful until maybe 9:30. Then I slept for a while in the afternoon after I got off, and I took the booster pill about 7:00 that evening so I could work on a report for my boss that I didn't get done during the day 'cuz I needed that nap—"

"Kim, this isn't the way I told you to take stimulant medications. Your sleep-wake cycle is really screwed up. I understand that you're working a lot of weird shifts and, as a nurse, I had to do that, too, sometimes, but I also know that the fastest way for someone to get fired is to abuse sleep and call in sick or take home a lot of work assignments. We gave you the trazadone, because even before you started stimulants, you didn't sleep well."

"That's the white weird shaped one—"

"Yes, that's it." I set my computer back on the desk. "I've seen the testing that Dr. Wes did with you. I read your history. I know you have a brother with ADD who takes stimulants and is in med school. I don't doubt you have it, and I don't have any reluctance prescribing for you, but I'm not going to help you stay up all night on speed so that you're even more tired and inattentive, only to have you try to counteract that by taking Vyvanse."

"Other people do it," she said. "I'm doing so much better on meds, and my boss is happier with me, except for the calling in."

"That's great, but you have to think of yourself as being up on a high wire. You have to really pay attention very closely or else—"

"I think I'd be bad at that." Kim laughed. "Even on meds."

"Probably. But you are up there, metaphorically, and what you seem to want to do is waver back and forth and lean to the left so you can see what's going on over there and then back to the right to see that side of things, and you want me to provide you with something that can keep you up there no matter how careless and unbalanced you are. Sure, I could do that, and it will work for a while, but eventually your body says 'no,' and you'll come crashing down. If that's how you want to operate, we won't continue seeing you."

"So, you're saying I can't be wired if I want to get across that wire."

"That's why your boss likes your reports." I smiled. "You have a way with words."

Kim slumped down in the loveseat exaggerating for effect the weight of my instructions. "This is harder than I thought it would be."

"What's harder?" I asked.

She paused, thinking it through. "I guess what I meant is that it's harder than I thought taking meds for ADD and trying to get sleep and go to work and still have some kind of a social life. But as I'm sitting here listening to myself, I think it's even more than that. It's hard being an adult and having to actually set a schedule and get everything done. I've been out on my own for years, and I still don't have it down. And maybe it's hard even accepting that I have ADD. Like, I wanted to just think, 'These meds help, but I don't really have ADD.' I know that doesn't make any sense, but I guess I was kinda in denial, so I wasn't really following the instructions because I didn't think they applied to me." She shook her head, as an exasperated look crossed her face. "I feel really dumb right now."

"Don't. You're still learning all this, and frankly, a lot of people in their first couple of years with this disorder look at it like, 'ADD isn't really me. I'm just visiting here' or something. But yeah, you've got it and it's going to be a lifelong process of coping. Will you commit yourself to doing that from here on out?"

"You and Dr. Wes talk, don't you?" She asked.

"Sure. And he's just as concerned about this as I am."

"I figured he got to you even before I came in. We're working on those alarms and like, a whole bunch of reminders to get me where I need to be. He said that the most important decision I make every day is to get out of bed, and that just sounded so stupid, and then I sat there and thought to myself, yeah, and it's also true."

"Right," I said. "You should only make changes in consultation with us. There are a few ways you can take stimulants strategically. Like on your days off, you could skip Vyvanse, eat three good meals, have fun with friends, and everything will be fine. Just be careful driving off meds. That can be a challenge."

"I've noticed," Kim said. "It gets a little sketchy, and I have to like, double my focus."

"Yes. It's like that with every choice you make about ADD meds. It has to be intentional. The choice has to serve the greater purpose of your treatment, not just solve a short term problem like 'I'm tired' or 'I have to write this boring report for work.'"

She nodded. "So, you're not going to fire me?"

"Not this week. Let's just be sure we're playing on the same team from here on out."

"Okay, coach," she said. "And I'll try and up my game."

Not-So-Scary Science Stuff

Take a deep breath. This chapter details as much information about the various medications for ADD and co-occurring disorders as we can cram into a reasonable space without your eyes glazing over. We hope. It will get a little technical at times, as we get right down to the molecular level of medication management, but bear with me. Why, you may ask, would I even subject you to a ramped up version of undergraduate biology, chemistry, and a little anatomy? Because it's an important part of becoming an expert on your medication management, and I've found that when I break it down for my clients like I will in this chapter, the whole thing gets less scary, more manageable, and less prone to The Zombie Effect.

There are a lot of drugs out there and more seem to appear every year. You can't get through an hour of cable television now without a barrage of ads for new psychopharmaceuticals. How can there possibly be this many ways to treat depression, bipolar disorder, or ADD? This vast medicine cabinet comes from small differences that exist between pharmaceuticals, minute distinctions in their molecular structures that make a big difference in observable outcomes and side effect profiles. Moreover, the impact of those differences isn't consistent across the population of users. These agents interact somewhat unpredictably with all the little differences that exist between you and your neighbor, parents, siblings, or best friend. That's why you won't do great on Adderall just because your coworker Suzi did. You may not even do well on it because your son or mother did. Somehow this critical factoid has remained secret from a lot of prescribers, as clients keep telling us that Dr. So-and-So said, "I've found that most of my patients do better on Vyvanse (or Concerta) than Adderall (or Mydayis)." This is nonsense. No one can predict stimulant efficacy based on a tiny cadre of their ADD patients. We can't do it with our huge cadre.

Becoming an expert on your medication also means not thinking or talking about it as "the pink capsule" or "the blue tablet," especially when meeting with your prescriber. In the opening vignette, I wasn't upset with Kim because she didn't know how to speak my language. I can figure out what she's talking about because I know what most of the meds I prescribe look like. What concerned me was her lack of understanding and respect for these powerful medications. My goal isn't to have clients take their meds like mindless automatons. I want them to really understand why, how, and when those meds should be taken and what to expect, positive and negative, in response.

In this chapter, I'll do the same for you, lay out a broad array of medications we use with our clients to treat ADD, ADHD, and several intertwining disorders including anxiety, depression, insomnia, and bipolar disorder. I can't replace your prescriber with a book chapter, and as Wes noted earlier, please don't go in with my advice highlighted and demand your prescriber "do it just like Dr. Kelsey." My goal is to hone your medication literacy so you can have informed, meaningful discussions with your prescriber, improve the efficacy of your medication regimen, reduce side effects, and raise your overall satisfaction with treatment, thereby improving your compliance.

Neurotransmitters R Us

All our physiological systems are designed to try and replicate a master evolutionary blueprint passed down and slowly modified across scores of generations to produce the optimal healthy human body. This innate regulatory process, known as homeostasis, is a key survival mechanism that's helped us adapt and survive as our environment changed over time. The homeostatic process isn't something that we can influence or improve upon with practice. It's mostly involuntary and initiated by biological triggers. For example, as your shoulders shiver and your teeth chatter, these small expenditures of energy generate warmth in an effort to survive cold environments.

The brain also maintains stability for survival partially through a complex and ongoing balancing act between neurotransmitters[143], receptors, and neurons that impacts every aspect of our mental state—perception, memory, motivation, focus, and so on. ADD results from dysfunction in the transmission of two naturally occurring neurotransmitters: dopamine[144] and norepinephrine[145] which makes it difficult for the body to achieve homeostasis. This ultimately results in limited focus, inattention, impatience, low persistence, and poor planning. If you read a lot of these books, you've seen the old saw about how people with ADD are really the evolutionary descendants of hunters, which puts them at odds with today's society of information managers.

---

[143] Think of these as chemical messengers that facilitate communication between two nerve cells causing either an excitatory response, like increased focus, or an inhibitory response like sedation.

[144] Dopamine originates in the hypothalamus, a region of the brain that regulates emotional activity. The release of dopamine triggers the simultaneous release of an enzyme that is designed to transform and convert dopamine into norepinephrine necessary to maintain homeostasis.

[145] Norepinephrine originates in the adrenal glands, which sit atop each kidney. It is within these glands that norepinephrine combines with a specialized enzyme converting it into epinephrine or adrenaline when necessary.

There's no evidence for this clever idea. In fact, anyone who's done it knows that hunting, while adventurous and energetic, is the art and science of patience, observation, more patience, precision, persistence, and then more patience. ADD inhibits adaptation now, and it's likely to have done so in past generations.

Let's take a look at how each neurotransmitter works in both neurotypical and ADD brains and how we intervene to level the playing field between them in ways that our evolutionary ancestors could not.

Dopamine. This neurotransmitter is released when we indulge in activities we enjoy, feel love or sexual desire for someone, receive praise, etc., leading us to feel bliss and accomplishment. In the face of pleasing stimuli, our internal dopamine surge is such a pleasure-packed sensation for our nervous system that we cognitively associate the stimulus with the sensational reward of the dopamine boost. It's not hard to see how this reward process can go awry, particularly in the context of substance abuse, falling in love with a problematic person, overeating, or any other potentially harmful but pleasing behavior that causes a dopamine release.

As far as dopamine goes, the goal of treatment is very simple. We want to replace exactly what's missing exactly where it's missing. When that works, our clients tell of drastic improvements in behavior, efficiency, and persistence within a few days of initiating treatment, as their dopamine supply goes from dysregulated and insufficient to more or less where it should be.

Although a stimulant itself may lift mood by increasing the dopamine supply, the mood elevation that comes from improved performance is the real boost to one's sense of self-efficacy and self-esteem. Feeling good about yourself and your ability to function in turn creates a dopamine boost that doesn't come from a tablet or capsule, but from success, and with time that can become self-perpetuating by leading the ADD client to seek out more opportunities for the inciting action. Getting kudos on performance from someone you trust or admire boosts dopamine again so you connect working diligently and interacting positively with others as a source for future dopamine spikes. Or, in the language used earlier in this book, it helps you care more.

Norepinephrine. As a big fan of coffee, I refer to norepinephrine as our body's natural espresso shot to illustrate its arousal and activating effects. Norepinephrine is essential for survival. Upon release in response to a sudden stressor, it increases blood pressure, heightens alertness, and boosts energy to our muscles to assist in fighting or fleeing a dangerous situation. These examples of a norepinephrine flood come in response to an exciting or traumatizing event, and are eventually broken down by the enzymes monoamine oxidase (MOA) and catechol-O-methyl transferase (COMT), which then returns the body to homeostasis.

Our treatment goal here is to increase the availability of norepinephrine in the affected neurons which will in turn, improve ADD symptoms by activating anxiety, exciting the body, and creating a sense of urgency, followed by committed action, rather than collapsing in a heap[146]. This increased norepinephrine also creates a heightened awareness of impending deadlines, lowers procrastination, and improves efficiency in your work product by lighting the proverbial fire beneath you.

Purposefully triggering your stress response (either behaviorally or chemically) works pretty well for clients who are singularly diagnosed with ADD, but it gets those who also have anxiety, overstimulated in a hurry. That's why we try to manage anxiety symptoms with medication before moving on to stimulants.

What Stimulants Do and How They Do It

Let's start by clarifying this word "stimulant," which is also bad branding because people associate it with words like "uppers" and "energized." Despite what you've heard and maybe wanted to believe, that's not the kind of stimulation we're looking for when treating ADD. We're trying to stimulate the release of dopamine and norepinephrine in your frontal lobe to compensate for a lack thereof which, in turn, reduces inattentive symptoms, improves impulse control, and decreases hyperactivity. That leads to a calming effect for ADD people of all ages, not the white-knuckled, overcaffeinated image a lot of clients imagine when they first hear the word "stimulant."

At the time of this writing, there were over twenty different stimulant medications the FDA had approved to treat ADD/ADHD. Some are

---

[146] See chapters "A Right Path!", "Going Down the Drain", and "Radical Honesty" in *I Always Want to Be Where I'm Not: Successful Living with ADD and ADHD*

now generic because their time-limited patents ran out. Others are brand name only because a pharmaceutical company has mixed up the core chemicals or revised the release mechanism enough to receive a new patent. However, at their most basic level, each is comprised of one of two molecules: amphetamine or methylphenidate. If you know something about medication already, you'll recognize these as the key components of Adderall and Ritalin, respectively.

Adderall is really a brand name for what is variously called "amphetamine and dextroamphetamine mixed salts," "amphetamine salt combo," or most commonly just "mixed amphetamine salts." Hereafter, we'll refer to this class collectively as "amphetamines." They've been in use for many decades. Ritalin is a brand name for methylphenidate. First approved in 1955, it's the same ingredient we find in several other modern products, including Focalin, Concerta, JornayPM, and the Daytrana patch. As a group, we'll hereafter refer to them as "methylphenidate" types.

Generally speaking, all stimulant medication for ADD will fit pretty well into one or the other of these categories, though some newer brands offer unique spins on the old ingredients. The main differences between stimulants within a given class are their modes of entry into the body (pill, patch, liquid, gummy, oral dissolvable tablet, etc.) and, once it's there, the way the body delivers the stimulant to your brain and nervous system. Each mode and method varies in how long it takes to enter the body and how quickly the effect becomes and remains active on the nervous system.

Despite being based on different chemicals, amphetamine- and methylphenidate-type medicines share several characteristics. Both work primarily by enhancing the amount of dopamine in the synaptic gaps of your brain, though the mechanism of each is a little different. Ritalin medications are norepinephrine–dopamine reuptake inhibitors. Adderall medications are reuptake inhibitors and they push dopamine, norepinephrine, and serotonin out of the neuron's intracellular fluid and into the synaptic gap, similar to the action of caffeine, but with greater potency.

Once they're in your system, both kinds of stimulants essentially block the reuptake of norepinephrine and dopamine into the presynaptic neuron, increasing their release in the neuron. Amphetamines do this by binding to the chemical messengers norepinephrine and dopamine, getting their foot in the door and riding the coattails of the these messengers all the way into the neuron.

Once inside the neuron, the amphetamine or methylphenidate molecules cause a cascade of events. You may have read that we "don't understand" how these medications work[147], which the ADD skeptic press always points out quite ominously. That's not the whole story. We do understand *what* happens when the stimulant molecule sneaks in. The process we don't completely understand, even after years of research, is *how* the stimulant causes the release of dopamine and norepinephrine back into the synapse making more chemical messengers available to transmit faster messages to our reward center. Think of it like this: Norepinephrine and dopamine get special backstage VIP passes to a concert that is you. Amphetamine or methylphenidate get to go in with the band just because they tagged along. Everyone is glad to see them, but nobody knows quite why they got those passes. But once they arrive, the party begins.

How Much Stimulant Do You Need?

One of the well-worn and persistent myths among prescribers is that you can estimate a person's dosage of stimulant by looking at their age, height, or weight[148]. Charts still exist which recommend dosing based on the these factors, but in practice, none of that has anything to do with how a given person will process any given type or level of stimulant. We have small teenage girls on big doses of stimulant and hefty football players on comparatively small doses. When we take an interest in weight, it's not because it tells us how to prescribe, but because we want to monitor weight loss as a side effect of the prescribed dosage (Chapter 8).

> *One of the well-worn and persistent myths among prescribers is that you can set a person's dosage of stimulant by looking at their age, height, or weight.*

---

[147] Every FDA-approved stimulant (and most other psychopharmaceuticals) has to mention in a large newspaper-like pamphlet given out at the pharmacy that "The mode of therapeutic action of this product on ADHD is not known." In reality, many aspects of the pharmacology of stimulants are well understood and their impact on humans quite predictable.

[148] www.additudemag.com/adhd-medication-mistakes-adderall-dosage/

The potency of a stimulant on your particular ADD is instead determined by the speed of a few enzymes in your body called cytochromes P450, which are produced in your liver for the sole purpose of processing and eliminating foreign substances of which medicine is one. Think of these enzymes as being like the Pac-Man video game with a couple of twists: your Pac-Men run at a different speed than your neighbors' do, and there's no Inky, Blinky, Pinky and Clyde to show up and shut them down. The little dots in your brain game represent the medicine flowing through your body. These Pac-Men go through your body at the molecular level and dispose of your medicine by turning it into waste that can be eliminated through the kidneys and, eventually, though urine. We call this metabolism. Having a fast Pac-Man in this analogy means having a fast metabolism.

Some enzymes are drawn to stimulants, making them especially interesting for readers of this book. If you have fast stimulant Pac-Men, your Adderall or Ritalin will get "eaten up" and disposed of much more quickly than your neighbor who has slow Pac-Men, even if you're on the exact same stimulant. It would be awesome if we could know ahead of time how fast your Pac-Men run. Then we could pull out a chart and calculate how potent you and your neighbor's stimulants need to be to work around them. We might find that you want to take twice the dose that your neighbor takes because the disposal of your medication is so much faster.

The cool genetic test I used with Gretchen in the Chapter 5 vignette, and which I'll discuss later in this chapter, helps us guess how your particular Pac-Man metabolism breaks down medication, even before you start taking it. The experiment we'll discuss in Chapter 7 gives us a way of sneaking up on the right dose over the first six weeks you're on medication. That reduces the chances that you'll be sucked into the Zombie Effect with excess medication.

Adderall vs. Ritalin

Which Is Best?

How can we know before prescribing whether you'll do better on an Adderall- or Ritalin-type medicine? We can't. There is some research based on fairly small samples from many years back that suggests three groups of stimulant responders. One responds better to Adderall types, one responds better to Ritalin types, and a plurality respond to both types.[149] That's not super helpful, is it? This lack of clarity has given rise to all sorts of stimulant myths from some pretty odd sources.

We love Consumer Reports (CR) for buying cars and dishwashers, but please (please!) ignore any advice they offer on stimulant medication. In a 2012 article, CR looked at various treatments for ADD and puzzlingly concluded:

> Stimulant medications, such as methylphenidate (Ritalin), might be slightly more effective than non-stimulant medications also used to treat ADHD, which include Intuniv, Kapvay, and Strattera. Our findings indicate that none of the stimulants are clearly more effective than any other.[150]

From this, CR concludes somehow that the clear choice for treating ADD is generic methylphenidate (Ritalin) and generic methylphenidate sustained-release tablets or capsules, of which there are several. As with all things CR, cost seems to have influenced them. They note "Methylphenidate has a long track record that shows it is generally safe and effective. The monthly cost ranges from $15 to $196, depending on strength."

This article is so dumb that it made Wes go back and question his dishwasher purchases because if the "analysis" they did here matches their appliance tests, we're all in for some dirty dishes. It's a good example of how wrong-headed non-experts can be in trying to ref the game of stimulant management. The idea that one could pick a stimulant for readers of Consumer Reports through statistical analysis and assign it a "Best Buy" as one might a Honda lawnmower is nonsense, which is probably why the article hasn't been updated in seven years.

We have only one clue in choosing your stimulant. The enzyme processes mentioned above are impacted by genetic factors, which can hint at whether you'll do better on one or the other classes of stimulants or equally well on both. For this reason, it's valuable to know how any first-order relatives responded to stimulants if they ever took them for ADD. That won't offer a perfect correlation, but it gives us

---

[149] adhd-institute.com/disease-management/pharmacological-therapy/differential-response-to-treatment/

[150] www.consumerreports.org/cro/2012/03/best-treatments-for-children-with-adhd/index.htm

somewhere to start. If you know both dosage and class, share that with your prescriber. If your first-order relative has tried both classes and many doses of stimulant, their pharmacy list is a great document to bring to a first session, often saving time and aggravation. Other times, this just doesn't help because, in the end, your brain chemistry is uniquely yours.

Going, Going, Gone

Unlike say, antidepressants, stimulants are what we term "Here Today, Gone Tomorrow Meds." They wash out of your system within eight to thirteen hours and, unless you take them the next day, the main-effect of the medication goes right along with them. Both are sold in short-acting (IR)[151] and long-acting (XR, ER, or LA)[152] formulations. Short-acting means the medicine's effect is gone in roughly four hours. Long-acting means that you'll feel the effect about twice that long[153]. At least in theory. In practice, your mileage could vary considerably.

All things being equal, you'll want to be on a long-acting medication. Yes, Adderall IR can be used to mimic its extended release (XR) version but that requires taking one tablet two to three times a day exactly four hours apart. As a matter of diagnosis, people with ADD have enough trouble remembering one pill in the morning. Two is pushing the limits and three is just not going to happen. Often, while still in my office, clients assure me that taking multiple stimulant doses per day will be no problem. However, the research and all our experience says otherwise. Increasing daily administration by just a one dose results in a twofold reduction in treatment compliance[154]. No matter how well matched they may be to your system, medications don't work if you don't take them. Be transparent with yourself and your prescriber

---

[151] IR stands for instant release.

[152] Talk about bad branding. Both XR and ER stand for extended release, but the XR people must have an extra cute creative department. LA stands for long-acting. Some medications, like Concerta, are long acting but don't actually state that in their title. And yes, you need to know this.

[153] You may also hear these referred to as "fast acting" and "short acting," both of which are misnomers. Neither one acts any quicker than the other, the short-acting medication just goes away faster than the long-acting one.

[154] Srivastava, K. A. (2013). Impact of reducing dosing frequency on adherence to oral thera-pies: a literature review and meta-analysis. Patient preference and adherence, 7, 419-34.

when thinking through which regimen will work for you. In the long run, most clients find long-acting stimulants an organizational gift.

Conversely, clients can get a bit too attached to taking those short-acting pills and, like Gretchen in Chapter 5, keep on taking them to do things like pull all-nighters. Repeated use of short-acting stimulants, even when used as prescribed, can lead to a saw-tooth pattern in stimulant blood levels, creating a quick rise and deep fall with each additional dose administered.

Amphetamines: The Adderall Types

There are really two types of amphetamines within this category: dextroamphetamine (d) and levoamphetamine (l). These are called isomers, two types of amphetamines with identical molecular formulas but different molecular structures, meaning the arrangement of the atoms within each molecule gives it different properties that yield different results depending on the type of amphetamine being ingested. Think of molecules and their isomers as you would the genus and species in the animal kingdom. The genus we know as *Panthera* includes both tigers and leopards, both of which are big-cat mammals with long tails, powerful jaws, and striking fur. But you wouldn't mistake one for the other because they reside on different continents, differ in size by about 300lbs, and their coats look nothing alike.

L-amphetamine reduces symptoms of inattention and d-amphetamine reduces impulsivity and hyperactivity, meaning the proportion of each in a given medicine will differentially impact your personal symptom set. The several medications within this class are made up of various combinations of these two amphetamine isomers. Knowing how each medication is proportioned can help you and your prescriber tailor your stimulant regimen to your body and your daily lifestyle. Unfortunately, as we'll see in the next chapter's vignette, not all providers understand these formulations, approaching stimulant trials as a bit of a crapshoot. Or maybe they read Consumer Reports. If your prescriber is one of those, you may need to offer some respectful but better informed input.

Adderall. Perhaps the most famous of all stimulants, Adderall comes in both IR and XR formulations. Both contain 3:1 ratios of d-amphetamine to l-amphetamine. As noted, the instant release form is inactive within four hours, sometimes less.

Adderall XR capsules have a 50/50 mix of immediate release and delayed release beads which results in a two phase dosing within a once daily capsule. The immediate release beads are activated thirty minutes after swallowing. The delayed release beads go into action four hours later, for a total duration of 10-12 hours.

Vyvanse. Vyvanse is produced by Shire, the same company that produced Adderall. It's been a big hit among clients with ADD and a financial bonanza for Shire. Many clients find Vyvanse lasts longer than Adderall XR with fewer side effects, though some clients find the opposite to be true. It's available in both capsule and chewable formulations.

Prodrugs require the body to metabolize or change the substance in order for it to become an active stimulant.

Vyvanse is unique among stimulants in that it's comprised not of a d-amphetamine to l-amphetamine ratio but of a different amphetamine molecule called (take a deep breath) lisdexamphetamine dimesylate, a prodrug of dextroamphetamine. Prodrugs sound like something an athlete would get kicked out of a competition for taking, but they're really just compounds that require the body to metabolize or change the substance in order for it to become active.

Understanding this unique molecular makeup can help you assess the duration of a given dose, plan when to take it, and manage your expectations of the result. For example, most amphetamines start reducing symptoms within thirty minutes after swallowing, allowing many who take them to start feeling the effects on their way out the door in the morning and coming to full flourish by the time they arrive at school or work. However, given its mechanism of release, Vyvanse may not impact your symptoms for sixty to ninety minutes after swallowing. Where I might suggest a client take one of the other amphetamines right after breakfast in order to get a good meal in before appetite suppression begins, I typically advise those taking Vyvanse to get it into their system as soon as they get out of bed. Sometimes I even suggest they take it before they wake up, as I did with Kim in the opening vignette. An advantage of this prodrug mechanism is that you can still get a good breakfast after taking it, which, as we'll discuss in Chapter 8, can be a challenge with other stimulants.

Another nice, but little known, feature of Vyvanse is that prescribers can tune in exactly the right dosage by having you dump the capsule contents in an empty pill bottle of water, shake it well, and then drink some smaller portion of the solution, say two-thirds. This lets your prescriber titrate[155] or temporarily reduce your dose. You may want to try this system to reduce your normal dosage on weekends or to lower the side effects of irritability and appetite suppression. This also works well when starting back on meds after a stimulant break (Chapter 9).

Figure 3 shows how to make a two-thirds solution by mixing one pill bottle of liquid containing two capsules into three pill bottles of the same size with equal amounts of the liquid from the first. You would then drink one of the three bottles to get the two-thirds ratio you mixed. You can vary this formula to say three-fourths, by adding three capsules to the first bottle and then distributing that solution into four bottles. The numerator (top number) is always the number of capsules you put in

Figure 3. Mixing Vyvanse into a Two-Thirds Solution.

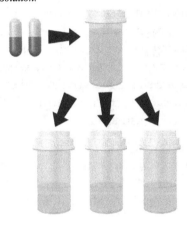

the shaker and the denominator (bottom number) the final number of bottles you distribute it over. Before doing this, however, go over the formula with your prescriber so you're both on the same page about how and why to do this. Be careful. It's very easy to short yourself or exceed your dosage if you're not doing it exactly as described.

Be aware that while the whole "dissolving it in water" thing is FDA approved, dose titration is not. That's between you and your prescriber. It's usually recommended that you not store diluted Vyvanse, but based on our experience and client report, that doesn't seem to be a problem. Wes did it for many years with his kids and found no reduction in efficacy.

---

155 The process of raising or lowering the dose of a medication for the maximum benefit without adverse effects. The purpose of titration is to find as perfect a balance as possible of a particular medicine for your body.

Few prescribers will know about this option. Of those that do, some will love this idea. Others won't get it. So, be ready to make a respectful suggestion if the approach makes sense to you.

Adzenys XR-ODT. This stimulant entered the market in 2016 for use with both child and adult populations. It has a ratio of 3:1 d-amphetamine to l-amphetamine. Adzenys uses a completely different method of delivery via a once daily oral dissolvable tablet. It has a fruity flavor which has proven a great option for clients of all ages who have difficulty swallowing tablets or capsules. The tablets are individually wrapped in foil packs to maintain their integrity before use, which makes them easier to transport in a pocket or backpack. Though it lasts ten to twelve hours, Adzenys releases in an arc similar to Adderall XR, allowing half of its medication to become active immediately and the other half to begin a steady release four hours later until it runs out. Despite sharing its core ingredients with Adderall XR, I've had several adult clients prefer Adzenys XR-ODT because of its ease of transport and administration.

Clients also like the price. As we'll discuss in more detail at the end of Chapter 7, the manufacturers of Adzenys and its methylphenidate counterpart (Cotempla) were, at the time of this writing, offering some pretty good incentives. Older extended release generics, like Adderall XR can run $60, even on some of the better prescription formularies. Cost certainly isn't the only reason—or even the best—to go with a given product, but if the medication fits the client, incentives can help decrease a big, long-term, monthly expenditure.

Other than a name nobody can seem to pronounce or remember, there's only one downside to Adzenys relative to our treatment model. The manufacturer offers several dose options that should, in theory, allow us to sneak up on your therapeutic dosage as we'll describe in Chapter 7. However, in real life that doesn't work very well. Unlike traditional capsules or tablets, the foil-wrapped packets come in a box of thirty, so your prescriber can't order you say, five days at 9.4mg, five days at 12.5mg, and then five days of 15.7mg. To try and compensate, I usually start clients off at the lower dose and then schedule us to meet again in ten days before considering whether to double up. Or we may try a more conventional medication to find our range and later make the switch. Either way, it's more complicated than anyone would like.

Mydayis. Shire claims that Mydayis is the longest acting stimulant on the market, with a single dose remaining active for up to sixteen hours—the full extent of most people's waking day. It does this by releasing in a single capsule not two but three amphetamine doses, each with a different release arc. Each dose is activated throughout the day by the acidity in your gastrointestinal tract providing a steady release pattern intended to create fewer ups and downs than other Adderall XR types. Like Adderall and Adzenys, Mydayis capsules contain a 3:1 ratio of d-amphetamine to l-amphetamine. For some clients, it's proven a great way to avoid late day stimulant boosters (more on that later). For others, it's just too much for too long and they ask to fall back to a different long-acting stimulant that's not quite so long-acting.

Dyanavel Oral Solution. Get ready for some (brief) advanced chemistry, readers. Dyanavel is a once daily extended release liquid that contains a 3.2:1 (three point two to one) ratio of d-amphetamine to l-amphetamine with both immediate release and extended release components controlled by a pH-independent polymer, meaning that it will have a delayed release once one of the molecules is at a certain point in your GI tract. This product has only been on the market since 2016, and we have limited experience with it in our clinic; but it sounds marvelous, particularly for those who don't like capsules or dissolvables.

Evekeo. This product was released by Arbor Pharmaceuticals in 2015 and combines equal parts (1:1) d- and l-amphetamine. With this ratio, the manufacturer claims fewer central nervous system side effects (like increased heart rate) and less appetite suppression[156]. In practice, we've found Evekeo works best as a way to boost other longer-acting stimulants. In 2019 the company developed an oral dissolvable tablet, perhaps in response to that market.

D-Amphetamine-Only Products. Both ProCentra and Zenzedi are comprised of 100% d-amphetamine. If you're following the molecular logic here, it stands to reason that they would target the ADHD spectrum, emphasis on the "H." That's how the FDA saw it, too, during the approval process. The theory is that those with hyperactivity won't need levoamphetamine's wakefulness properties. That said, these medications shouldn't be ruled out for primarily inattentive clients. They may not be the best choice to start a medication trial, but if other

---

[156] www.evekeo.com/hcp/evekeo-pharmacology

formulations aren't getting the job done, a high d-amp might be worth trying.

Methylphenidate Types

Methylphenidates are a class of medication most commonly associated with medications like Concerta and Ritalin. They include two isomers: d-methylphenidate and l-methylphenidate, which are varied in ratio to produce several products. Once again, it's important to discuss the similarities and differences of the methylphenidate molecules in order to consider which medications may be worth trying first in your case, or which you might go to if you and your prescriber are considering a medication change. For example, once it gets into your body, d-methylphenidate is about ten times more potent than l-methylpheni-date. While d-methylphenidate is correlated with improved focus, it also tends to show greater adverse effects like nausea and tics, meaning different formulations may have more or less efficacy versus side effects. Let's take a look at some of the products available to deliver methylphenidate.

Daytrana. In theory, it's a simple idea—methylphenidate on a trans-dermal patch ranging in size from two to six square inches—the larger the patch, the higher the dose. Once a month you get a box of thirty patches. Each morning you peel the plastic backing from the patch and push it firmly onto your skin somewhere around your hip. Depending upon your reach and size, it's probably easier if your loved one sticks it there for you. It's even better if that person applies it thirty to forty-five minutes before your alarm rings, for the same reasons I suggested Kim take her Vyvanse before getting up. Because Daytrana steadily transfers medicine through your skin over many hours, it takes a while to kick in.

Despite nearly fourteen years on the market, Daytrana has struggled to gain acceptance and sales. Still, despite several shortcomings we'll discuss in a moment, we've found Daytrana to have some pretty great attributes in the daily treatment of ADD. Here's why we like it:

- **There's no pill or liquid to swallow.** Some clients with sensitive stomachs report fewer gastrointestinal side effects with Daytrana, and people who hate taking pills or drinking solutions think the patch is pretty neat.

- **You can leave it on longer.** Though the instructions say to remove the patch after nine hours, Daytrana will keep working for about fifteen hours. Its manufacturer, Noven, originally asked for a thirteen-hour period of use, but the FDA rejected that and came up with the number nine. We have no idea why. How long you wear your particular patch on your particular body is up to you and your prescriber to decide through trial and error.

- **You can take it off earlier.** Whenever your focus day is done, you can remove the patch and its effect will ebb in two to three hours. This makes Daytrana the only stimulant medication you can shut down after it's taken. Until you've experienced this for yourself, you may not understand how awesome it really is. People who can't sleep well on stimulants or have severe appetite suppression, can talk with their prescriber about removing the patch earlier so they're hungrier in the evening and/or more able to fall sleep. Those who occasionally need to take their medication later in the day, as Kim did in the vignette, can apply the patch and then pull it off in a few hours, essentially turning it into a short-acting stimulant as needed. However, once it's off, you can't stick it back on.

- **Better release.** Daytrana's release arc goes up slowly, hangs there more evenly over the day than most medications, and doesn't drop off until you remove it or it runs out of stimulant.

There are some good reasons to not like Daytrana—or, more correctly, reasons why it may not be the right medication for you. Let's explore each, along with some workarounds if you decide to try it:

- **The patch hates water.** No matter what they've done to the adhesive over the years—and they've done a lot—Daytrana doesn't respond well to moisture, including sweat, swimming pools, showers, etc. If you want to put it on early, we suggest showering at night. If you prefer to shower in the morning, do so immediately after you get up, then put the patch on right after you dry off and your skin is clear of oil.

- **You forget to take it off.** If you get busy and forget about your patch, you risk greater than necessary appetite suppression late in the day and trouble sleeping. We used to worry a lot about this, but it hasn't turned out to be a problem. Most people can feel the patch and are ready to get it off, which leads directly to its next shortcoming.

- **It can be annoying to wear.** Many folks with ADD struggle with things like scratchy tags or fabric textures. For some, Daytrana feels a lot like that. I've seen clients cringe and shiver when I'm simply explaining it to them. The FDA-approved instructions are astoundingly specific about where they want you to stick it, because that's where they stuck it in the research trials and nobody is going to spend any money to research sticking it anywhere else. As you can see in the FDA-approved handout[157] linked via this footnote, that spot is beneath your underwear just south of the elastic line. In real life, no one can stand a Daytrana patch rubbing against their underwear all day and any but the loosest undies will snag the patch and start pulling it off. Since where you put your patch is up to you and your prescriber, you should consider that some spots are less annoying than others. Most clients prefer to wear it above the elastic line around their lower abdomen. However, you must select a different site every day, preferably using each site only once per week.

- **It creates a skin reaction.** You'll probably see a red spot the size of the patch on your skin after removal. That's a normal response to the patch dropping medication into your skin and the reason you want to move the stick-spot each day. After removal, an ointment like A&D works well to cover the patch site and ease irritation. Once in a while, we see a more severe reaction that doesn't remit for days. If you get something like that and it isn't gone by the next time you want to stick a patch, your skin may be too sensitive for Daytrana, just as some people's skin doesn't take well to adhesive bandages.

- **Yucky residue.** The patch may leave a little gray gunk on your skin. The Daytrana instructions suggest putting lotion on the patch site to fix this. Apparently they've never actually tried this because it doesn't work. A couple of wipes a week with

---

[157] www.accessdata.fda.gov/drugsatfda_docs/label/2010/021514s009s010MedGuide.pdf

athletic bandage adhesive remover does. There are many such products available locally and on Amazon.

- **It can occasionally be hard to find.** For many reasons, Daytrana has, at times, been out of stock at pharmacies and, worse, the subject of recall as Noven has struggled to get the adhesive to stick all day without causing skin irritation. This has turned out to be more difficult than anyone imagined and probably why nobody has used this technology to create an amphetamine patch. Given that planning can be a critical problem for the ADD crowd, out-of-stock meds are burdensome and inconvenient, which may lead to giving up. It's best to take your prescription in a few days before you need a new box or, in the case of e-prescribing, get an appointment with your prescriber and request a new prescription a week in advance. That way the pharmacy can send away for it and it will be ready when you need it.

You may find your prescriber has little experience with or faith in Daytrana. Many remember its early dark days of bad adhesive and scarcity and haven't come back to it since. We think it's worth considering and we use it often in a variety of situations where nothing can match it.

Concerta. Concerta is an extended-release medication that has a slow build throughout the day and reaches its peak blood concentration after about five hours, before gradually decreasing. It's one of the oldest and most reliable methods for getting methylphenidate into your system. If you don't like Daytrana, Concerta is a great alternative and for most insurance carriers the generic version is on the lowest cost tier of your drug formulary (Chapter 7). Concerta is a mixture of d-methylphenidate and l-methylphenidate, although the exact ratio is not made available to the public.

Concerta's mechanism of release works differently than any other stimulant. It uses an "osmotic-controlled release oral delivery system (OROS)". A little less than a quarter of the medication is sort of painted across a cylindrical outer covering that is tinted a different color based on the dosage. The rest is split between two layers of different concentrations. As the cylinder passes through your body, water enters it via an osmotic membrane, creating a pressure that expels methylphenidate through the laser-drilled hole on the side.

This ingenious system gives Concerta (and its generic knock-off) both an immediate release starter dose and a long, fairly even distribution arc across the day. After the stimulant is expelled, it enters your body conventionally, through the gastrointestinal system, so if you have digestive issues with other forms of methylphenidate, Concerta may not solve that problem.

Other than it's cool, the most important thing to know about the OROS delivery system is that unlike a normal capsule or tablet, the cylinder is not dissolved and digested. More than one client has called me or the pharmacy wanting to report a defective batch of Concerta after finding the cylinder floating in the toilet.

And with that factoid told, let's move on to more appealing imagery.

Quillivant XR. Because it comes in liquid form, Quillivant allows the most gradual rate of titration possible, thus your prescriber can direct you through micro-dose increases, much as we discussed in the Vyvanse dilution section, above. Similar to Concerta, at the molecular level Quillivant is a mix of d-methylphenidate and l-methylphenidate. But the peak of the medication's effectiveness (its peak blood level) is reached slightly faster, in about two hours for adolescents and four hours for adults and children.

Like several of the medications we're about to discuss, the way Quillivant XR works can be greatly impacted by what and when you eat. The time it takes to reach its peak blood level can be sped up by as much as one hour if Quillivant XR is taken with food, while its overall potency can rise by twenty-eight percent if that meal includes a lot of fat. When was the last time you heard a recommendation from your nurse practitioner for more cheesy ham and eggs in your breakfast diet? If you don't go overboard, it's a great way to get this medication into your system and keep weight on in the process.

QuilliChew ER. Quillivant XR also comes in a chewable form. I primarily use it with those kids who are "too grown up" for liquid medication, which they consider to be appropriate "only for babies," but who cannot reliably handle tablets or capsules yet. I've had debates with people who think gummy medications are a method of tricking kids into taking medication outside their awareness or consent. Most of those folks have never had to fight with an eight-year-old in the morning about whether or not they are going to take their gross-tasting, bitter medication. Rough mornings make for rough days at school, which make for rough evenings. For parents needing a break from pointless power struggles, ask your prescriber for this product. No medicine works if a child won't take it.

Aptensio XR. Another d- and l-methylphenidate mixture, this extended-release medication reaches peak concentration within two hours of administration, followed by a gradual decrease over four hours. A second peak is reached approximately eight hours after administration, followed by another four hours of gradually decreasing effect. The capsule can be swallowed whole or the contents can be sprinkled on something like applesauce.

Metadate ER. This is an older medication dating back to the late 1980s. Metadate is a combination of seventy percent extended-release and forty percent immediate-release d- and l-methylphenidates with a rapid onset of two hours or, if given with food, one hour. If that's a high fat meal, the overall blood concentration is increased, so grab another sausage and egg biscuit.

Cotempla XR-ODT. Speaking of palatable stimulants, this is an oral, dissolvable mixture of d-methylphenidate and l-methylphenidate with a fruity flavor. Like its cousin, Quillivant XR, it comes in individually wrapped foil packets that make for easy administration on the go. However, eating a high-fat meal actually *decreases* the overall maximum blood concertation of Cotempla XR-ODT, so it's best given on an empty stomach and then followed by a breakfast high in complex carbs but low in fat. Oatmeal for this one, dear readers.

Methylin. Continuing our theme of easy to swallow meds, Methylin is an immediate release product that comes in either a chewable tablet or liquid. It combines d-methylphenidate and l-methylphenidate and is essentially equivalent to a short-acting Ritalin tablet for anyone who cannot swallow tablets.

Focalin. Think of this product as a molecular mirror image of Concerta but with a higher concentration of d-methylphenidate. Focalin acts much faster than Concerta, reaching full absorption in your blood in one fifth the time, and it comes in extended- and immediate-release formulations. It is also considered a bit more potent than Concerta, and as such, it should be deployed carefully in children or those who are stimulant naïve. We've had more than one client who found it too harsh. However, it can be a great option for those who underrespond to other methylphenidate products as it has a very wide dosing range that comes in increments of just 5mg. This allows for easy creation of a starter pack of 10mg for five days, 15mg for five days, and then 20mg for five days before follow up.

Give Me a Boost

If you're taking copious notes, reading and re-reading every word of this chapter, preparing a list of questions for your physician, and re-naming your pets Adzenys and Cotempla, you're: a) maybe getting a little too obsessed with this fascinating subject, and b) realizing there's no one perfect medication for ADD. For any given person, some medications, even extended release products, don't last long enough while others hang around too long. Some don't kick in quickly enough.

Nobody wants to function for just eight hours a day, nor even ten, but getting the right release arc dialed in can be tricky. That's why we're always interested in medications like Mydayis or Adhansia that attempt to solve this problem in one easy dose. But even with long-acting agents, achieving wakeup-to-bedtime coverage without side effects (Chapter 8) may require adding a short-acting (IR) dose as a "booster." If you're trying to extend the day, we suggest taking it in the late afternoon. If you need to accelerate the slow morning release of say, Vyvanse, we'll have you take it right when you wake up. Occasionally, with clients who have high metabolisms for stimulants, we'll do both, but only after several trials and careful analysis.

Yes, this violates our "once-a-day is best" recipe, and it adds to your cost even with health insurance. With the exception of Daytrana, most super-long agents create inflexibility, because once they're in you, you can't untake them. Some clients, like Kim, find this problematic. They need to vary their schedules from one day to the next. If a student has a late class on Tuesday and Thursday, she may not want to take a stimulant that's active for sixteen-hours seven days a week if it interdicts eating or sleep, and she sure doesn't want to wait until she's going to her first class a 11:30 a.m., lest she be up 'til 3:00 the next morning. Stimulant tolerance (Chapter 9) can also necessitate use of a booster as we try to extend your working day without exceeding reasonable dosing guidelines. This is most often true when a student has reached tolerance at the end of a semester, inconveniently right before finals.

Looking only at my caseload, I would estimate that some sixty-five percent of our clients are prescribed both a long acting stimulant and a short booster. None of those decisions were made lightly. Those clients are great team members who we monitor closely. It takes that kind of effort to safely prescribe anyone multiple stimulants. If you work as well with your prescriber as our clients do with us, tailoring your medication this way won't be a problem.

If All Else Fails: Non-Stimulants

Strattera. Back in 2002, when Strattera was first approved to treat ADD, everyone was excited. Finally, prescribers had a non-stimulant, non-controlled substance in their toolbox. And, unlike Adderall or Ritalin, Strattera built up in your system so you'd get 24/7 symptom control. What was there not to like about it? Efficacy, it turns out.

When it was first developed, Strattera wasn't even meant to treat ADD. Ely Lilly intended it to compete in a class of antidepressants called selective norepinephrine reuptake inhibitors (SNRIs). Unfortunately for the stockholders, Strattera failed its U.S. test trials as an antidepressant. Not to be undone on an expensive product development, the company researched and received approval for Strattera as a treatment for ADD.

That might have worked well in research trials, but among clinical populations of children, teens, and adults things have turned out differently. Early on, prescribers gave Strattera every possible chance, raising the dosage beyond recommended levels, giving it six to eight weeks to work, and offering magic incantations to frustrated clients imploring them to "hang in there" until it started working. Such patience is rare in anyone who seeks assistance from medication. It's even rarer for folks with ADD. Most discontinued Strattera, and those who did hang on were rarely rewarded.

When it does work, we find its fans usually have underlying anxiety or depression that the norepinephrine components of Strattera may help to treat, much as Lilly had hoped in its original, failed trials. However, with those clients we greatly prefer Effexor or Wellbutrin, which we'll discuss in the last section of this chapter, and which are usually better tolerated and more effective. We only go to Strattera when those medications aren't working or when a parent is vehemently against their child being on a stimulant.

Strattera's lack of efficacy is reflected in sales data. In 2012 the drug grossed just $620 million in sales, making it second to last for the Lilly line of products.[158] By 2016 sales had dropped to $535 million, a trend that should continue as Lilly ceased promoting the drug after its patent ended in 2017. By comparison, gross sales of Vyvanse in 2012 were $1.6 billion and had risen to $2.4 billion by 2018[159] making it Shire's number two seller.

Intuniv. Shire announced FDA approval of this non-stimulant in late 2009. Once again, prescribers felt hopeful, until they dug a little deeper and realized nothing was new about this product. Intuniv is just a time-released version of guanfacine, not to be confused with guaifenesin, the mucus reducing agent in Mucinex[160]. Guanfacine (brand named Tenex for the short acting version) is an old blood pressure medicine that was once used to treat symptoms of ADD, but hasn't been considered a front-line solution for many years.

As a first line of treatment for ADHD, Intuniv (and Tenex) haven't proven effective because, while we find it can reduce irritability in ADD children, it does little to improve focus and attention. It may also quell the behavior of that small group of hyperactive, impulsive children who become dysregulated in no time flat and then calm back down just as quickly. In other words, similar to Strattera, when these medications work, something else is amiss, most likely an anxiety disorder or underlying mood disorder. We're not the only ones who've moved away from guanfacine-based meds. Shire sells only about $287 million worth of Intuniv each year, putting it near the bottom of their product line[161].

We used to see, and occasionally still do, clients who did a trial of Strattera or Intuniv, saw no improvement, and gave up on treatment completely.

---

158 investor.lilly.com/releasedetail.cfm?ReleaseID=736234

159 www.takeda.com/siteassets/system/newsroom/2019/shires-full-year-2018-results/shires_full_year_2018_results_clean_en.pdf

160 This little branding problem caused a spate of dispensing errors in pharmacies around the country.

161 en.wikipedia.org/wiki/Shire_plc#cite_note-prelims-1 citing data compiled from www.shire.com/shireplc/uploads/report/Shire_FY2012EarningsRelease_14Feb2013.pdf.

Unfortunately, the presence in the market of Strattera and Intuniv has created at least one unintended and unfortunate outcome. We used to see, and occasionally still do, clients who did a trial of these meds with a primary care doctor or pediatrician, saw no improvement, and gave up completely on treatment for ADD. This may have occurred because no one explained that failing a Strattera or Intuniv trial says literally nothing about how one might do on a stimulant.

This may also reflect, in part, discomfort among prescribers about prescribing stimulants to children, thinking that the child should at least try a non-stimulant first in the hope that this might tide him or her over. This is completely illogical. For most clients, stimulants are the best treatment available. Deviating from that protocol should be done only with very good reason—like the client failing several Adderall and Ritalin type stimulants—but never as a first line treatment. Moreover, the many months it takes to get a client up to a therapeutic dosage of Strattera while waiting for an effect that probably will never come is, in the life of a child, precious time wasted.

Generics Anyone?

- Dr. Wes -

Throughout this chapter, we've mentioned both brand name and generic medications. It's important to understand generics because ninety percent of all medications dispensed today come this way, and there are several generic stimulants you'll need to know about. This is a relatively recent development. A decade ago, if you compared a list of generic stimulants with a list of brand names, you'd find the generic list pretty scant, with only a couple short-acting products and no long-acting agents. This was super annoying because insurance companies didn't want to pay for brand names, so many consumers were stuck taking an instant-release generic two or three times a day, leading to all the problems discussed earlier and a lower level of compliance.

What a difference a few years make. There are now several long-acting generics in both the amphetamine and methylphenidate categories alongside the newer products mentioned above which are still only available as brand names. Does this mean ADD medication is now in its golden age with something affordable for everyone; a land of stimulant milk and honey sold at a reasonable price?

> *The emergence of generics has actually complicated the prescribing and dispensing of stimulants, and our experience is still evolving.*

Not exactly. While things are better today for consumers, the emergence of generics has actually complicated the prescribing and dispensing of stimulants, and our experience with them is still evolving. As with every topic in this book, we want you to understand not just the "what" and "how" but also the "why," because (repeat after me) if *you* don't master this material, nobody else will do it for you. So, let's take a look at generic stimulants with an eye toward the two issues of greatest import: cost and quality.

Generics Are Cheap and Cheap Is Good, Right? If you've ever filled a prescription, you know that "brand name" rhymes with "expensive," so the only benefit of a generic drug is that its cost is lower. This isn't always the case, however, particularly for stimulants. Most drugs go generic in two phases. In the final year or two, as the manufacturer's patent nears the end of its ten to twenty-year term[162], the medication is often licensed to another manufacturer. That tends not to lower costs much because demand remains high and the manufacturer is still getting a cut of the profits due to the licensing deal.

In the second phase, the patent expires and other companies become free to create their own versions of the original product. If you're a fan of *How I Built This*[163] or *Shark Tank*[164], you've heard the term "knock-off," meaning an imitation product that's supposedly identical to and intended to compete with the original. In most cases these are unwelcome intruders that violate patent law. In the pharmaceutical industry however, knock-offs are seen as a way to lower prices and create a broad health benefit for the public, so the government limits the patent's duration to stimulate competition.

For most pharmaceuticals, this second phase does lead to a price drop. The extent of that discount can be hard to gauge however, because, believe it or not, you can't just go into your pharmacy and ask for the cash price of any given medication without presenting a prescription. And if you do have a prescription, you'll get the retail price and the

---

[162] www.upcounsel.com/how-long-does-a-drug-patent-last

[163] www.npr.org/podcasts/510313/how-i-built-this.

[164] abc.go.com/shows/shark-tank

price you'll pay after several kinds of discounts are applied (more on that later). So, who really knows the cost of your prescription until you run your credit card?

Apparently, Walmart does. They're the third largest pharmacy network in America with 6,300 pharmacists nationwide. You can probably guess that the top two are CVS (24,000 pharmacists) and Walgreens (10,600)[165]. A few years ago, Walmart started posting many of its generic drug prices online[166]. Most of the medications we use in our office for treating depression, bipolar disorder, and anxiety are listed on their website as costing around $9.00 per month, including several we'll discuss at the end of this chapter. Because Walmart competes with the other big chains, that list gives you a good guess as to the market price for a long list of generic drugs.

However, Walmart lists no cash price for stimulants, probably because stimulants never cost $9.00 a month. GoodRx lists a Walmart price of $60.75 per month (using their coupon) for generic Adderall XR, which the site claims to be "seventy-nine percent off the retail price of $207.88." GoodRx lists $94.46 for generic Concerta with a retail price of $276.48. However, you can't take these numbers to the bank because, as GoodRx also notes, "many pharmacies won't honor coupons for controlled substances." A client recently told me he used GoodRx to get Adderall XR for about $54.00. So, we're back to "who knows?"

While those retail prices sound pretty close based on our experience, I offer them here only to challenge the notion that generic stimulants are as cheap as other generics. For any medication, price is driven not by what name you call it or who manufactures it, but by the price the market will bear. Generic or not, there's a burgeoning demand for stimulants, so prices stay high for your insurance company or, if you have a high deductible plan, for you. In fact, stimulants are even more costly than popular generics of Cialis or Viagra.

They All Come out of the Same Bin, Don't They? When I was a teenager, Martin Ward, my venerable auto mechanics mentor, always told me to order my engine overhaul parts from the Sears Catalog. They were a lot cheaper than the brand name parts at the local

---

[165] en.m.wikipedia.org/wiki/Pharmacies_in_the_United_States

[166] www.walmart.com/cp/$4-prescriptions/1078664

automotive store, but still… "Sears?" I asked. "Is that stuff any good? I don't want my truck to like, blow up on the highway."

Experience has proven that generics may be exactly the same as brand name products. Or not.

"Humph," Martin scoffed. "They're auto parts. They all come out of the same bin."

Martin was right about this and most other things. Back in 1978, car parts did all come from the same U.S. factories and my old truck ran for many years thereafter until I sold it to another eager young man. He texted me later to say that it had fired right up after installing a new battery and oil. Go 1970's Sears!

Experience has proven that when it comes to medication, generics may be exactly the same as brand name products. Or not. They might even come out of the "same bin." Or not. You probably thought the FDA regulated all this very carefully, didn't you? They sure claim that they do[167], but an article by Katherine Eban *The New York Times* (2019) suggests otherwise[168] as does her bestselling book on the topic[169]. Anna Edney raised the same questions writing for *Bloomberg*[170] [171]. Well before that, a 2013 article in *Fortune*[172] cited Dr. Janet Woodcock, then director of the FDA's Center for Drug Evaluation and Research, admitting in a speech to the Generic Pharmaceutical Association, "I've heard it enough times from enough people to believe that there are a few products that aren't meeting quality standards."

Compared to other psychopharmaceuticals, generic stimulants came late to the game. In 2009, Shire's patent came due and it began marketing its own Adderall XR generic through two companies, Teva and Imax. Shire still manufactured the drug, but it distributed through

[167] www.fda.gov/drugs/generic-drugs/generic-drug-facts

[168] www.nytimes.com/2019/05/11/opinion/sunday/generic-drugs-safety.html?auth=login-email&login=email

[169] amazon.com/dp/0062338781/

[170] www.bloomberg.com/news/features/2019-01-29/america-s-love-affair-with-cheap-drugs-has-a-hidden-cost

[171] www.bloomberg.com/news/articles/2019-03-27/tainted-generic-drugs-force-fda-to-tighten-safety-regulations

[172] fortune.com/2013/01/10/are-generics-really-the-same-as-branded-drugs/

these companies[173]. This may seem odd—a pharmaceutical company creating its own knock-off drug—but it happens all the time and it can be profitable. However, not long after that, Shire ended up in patent litigation with Teva and Imax after these companies attempted to produce their own versions of Adderall XR. Finally in 2012, Shire lost its battle to retain its patent[174], and unlicensed generic versions of Adderall XR began to hit the market.

From our perspective, this did not go very well. Insurance companies were excited to cut costs, so they immediately required all Adderall XR clients to begin taking the generic versions. Shire countered by pushing its then-new product, Vyvanse[175], even while it was still manufacturing both brand name and generic versions of Adderall. And then things got really weird.

Clients who had for years taken Adderall XR with great success were happy to cut their copays by half to two-thirds—until they started taking the new generic XR and finding dramatically reduced efficacy. Or as one of my client's put it, "What the hell was that stuff, a sleeping pill?[176]" She wasn't alone. A stimulant is different from most medications in that you can really can feel it working, so there wasn't any lag time in finding out that these new generic prescriptions were junk. The people who'd transitioned were instantly frustrated and ready to pay the higher price for the real deal. So, for about a year, we asked that all prescriptions for Adderall XR be "dispensed as written (DAW)" or, even more often, we just went right along with Shire's advice to prescribe Vyvanse instead. What else were we to do, prescribe generic XR as a sleeping aid for people with ADD? Eventually, the quality issues with generic Adderall diminished, and it is now the substantial equivalent of the brand name version. At least we think so. Literally nobody we see is on brand name Adderall anymore, so how could anyone tell if a difference existed?

Shortly after we got past those initial hurdles, we began seeing national shortages of Adderall, both short and long acting, which Shire blamed

173 www.pharmexec.com/sandoz-and-shire-settle-adderall-xr-dispute

174 www.gabionline.net/Generics/News/Generic-Adderall-XR-approved-in-the-US

175 ocweekly.com/adderall-maker-to-patients-dont-take-adderall-6465225/

176 Obviously not. What she was reporting was actually the withdrawal effect of suddenly being off her stimulant—except of course, she wasn't supposed to be off of it.

on the DEA limiting the supply of its ingredients. The DEA denied the shortage existed and many who knew it existed argued that Shire was intentionally withholding stimulants in order to drive up the market for Vyvanse[177] [178]. I don't recall how long this fiasco lasted, but in reading articles from that period, it seems to have resolved by the end of 2012 and by the time I published *I Always Want to Be Where I'm Not* in 2014, it was a thing of the past.

A similar problem occurred when Janssen licensed Concerta to Watson Labs (now Activas), except it was even worse, better documented, and remains unresolved. In 2013, Watson began manufacturing a licensed knock-off product with exactly the same OROS delivery system as Concerta. However, in 2014 when the patent expired, two additional generic versions came out, one by Mallinckrodt Laboratories and the other by Kremer Laboratories which later changed to Kudco or Lannett Lab[179].

And that's when things went whacky for Concerta. Although these two products were completely different in design, the FDA approved them both as "AB-rated generic equivalents" to Concerta and its licensed Watson knock-off. Remember this "AB" designation. It becomes critical as we move through the story; plus, you'll want to use the term when you talk to your prescriber and pharmacist both of whom will be super impressed and a little confused that you kind of know what it means. The product insert approved by the FDA was nearly identical to the one included with Concerta and the Watson/Activas product. But it didn't take long to realize that these Kudco/Lannet/Kremer and Mallinckrodt generics were in no way equivalent to Concerta or the Activas generic.

The OROS product did perform just like Concerta right out of the chute. But the other two did not. Nobody complained about it being a "sleeping pill," but everyone who took it after taking Concerta noticed that it simply didn't work very well. And this time, it wasn't just

---

[177] www.reuters.com/article/us-adhd-adderall-shortage/insight-shortage-of-adhd-drug-adderall-seen-persisting-idUSTRE80009E20120101

[178] www.nytimes.com/2012/01/01/health/policy/fda-is-finding-attention-drugs-in-short-supply.html

[179] All this company name changing doesn't seem sketchy at all, does it?

anecdotal. The FDA acknowledged the problem in late 2016[180], admitting they'd had concerns about the non-OROS knock-offs as early as November 2014 but did not remove them from the market, nor have they since. The FDA only changed the designation of the non-OROS generic from "AB" to "BX", meaning the data were insufficient to determine whether they were equivalent to original Concerta.

For some reason, it took a long time for this to really sink in. It wasn't until 2018 that the popular ADD press[181] [182] [183] spread the news that only Concerta and the Activas generic worked effectively, and for quite some time, we found that pharmacies continued to distribute the less effective knock-offs as if they were no different. To this day, we have to instruct clients to be sure they are getting the AB drug.

The Bottom Line. As I wrote in *I Always Want to Be Where I'm Not*, and confirmed many times thereafter, you can't count on the FDA to assure the quality of generic stimulants. At this point we feel pretty good about the Adderall XR generics and the AB-rated Activas product, and Kelsey prescribes them with confidence. But as brand name drugs continue to come off patent over the next decade, we advise caution for prescribers, pharmacies, insurance companies, and consumers. You may need to think of generics as experimental at first, instead of assuming they work as they're supposed to. And you'll want to keep your eye on the ADD press to keep updated.

As we move into the next section discussing common medications for co-occurring disorders and how they interact with stimulants, be aware that many of the drugs we site are generic. In general, they've worked quite well for us, but unlike stimulants, it's harder to tell in head-to-head comparisons. For example, in about 2006, one of the manufacturers of trazadone began distributing a product that was far inferior to others. None of us would have known this had we not all been comparing notes through the clinic and all been switched by our pharmacies at the same time to this brand. Our calls to the FDA went

---

[180] www.fda.gov/drugs/drug-safety-and-availability/questions-and-answers-regarding-methylphenidate-hydrochloride-extended-release-tablets-generic

[181] www.additudemag.com/generic-concerta-is-not-created-equal/

[182] adhdrollercoaster.org/medication/authorized-generic-concerta-update-6-1-19/

[183] beingwellcenter.wordpress.com/2018/03/23/concern-over-concerta/

unanswered, despite several concerns found online about the quality control at this now-defunct manufacturer's facilities.

Medication for Co-Occurring Disorders
- Dr. Kelsey -

In Chapter 4, we discussed in general how we treat co-occurring disorders like anxiety, depression, insomnia, and bipolar using SSRIs, SSNIs, and mood stabilizers and alluded to how these medications may play with and against stimulants. In this section, I'll provide an overview of the most common medications I use in tandem with stimulants so you're familiar with them if and when you need to discuss them with your prescriber.

You'll want to know both the brand name and generic because a) the brand names may sound weird but they're often easier to remember, and b) many of us still refer to sertraline as "generic Zoloft" or fluoxetine as "generic Prozac." Sometimes we even forget the word "generic." So, before we go on, please review Figure 4, just enough that you remember that the brand name equivalents are listed there.

The use of multiple medications for a given client is called "polypharmacology," and it requires the prescriber to consider several factors that have nothing to do with symptoms and a lot to do with "pharmacodynamics" and "pharmacokinetics," meaning the way in which medications affects the body and vice versa. Here's an example. Remember our Pac-Man analogy from Chapter 6? Depending on your genetic predisposition, even small doses of Vyvanse and several other medications can inhibit the Pac-Man-like enzyme known to eliminate Lexapro. We'll call him Pac-Man2D6. Slowing the elimination of Lexapro allows it to linger longer which may increase the risk of Lexapro side effects, like shaking, sweating, and nausea.

Imagine that you were genetically predisposed to have little to no activity in Pac-Man2D6. This would mean that the rate of Lexapro's elimination from your system is severely impaired. The combination of your slow 2D6 and a medication (Vyvanse) that relies on 2D6 to get rid of it could turn out badly if you're also taking a med (Lexapro) known to interact with your genes (referred to as a gene-drug interaction), and/or you're taking a medication known to inhibit the elimination of another drug that you're also taking (drug-drug interaction). So, does this mean that anyone with ADD who is taking Lexapro shouldn't also be taking Vyvanse? No. We have many clients on this combination, even some of whom are known to be slow metabolizers of CYP4502D6. It just means that you need to have an awesome prescriber who pays attention to things like this and helps you piece together the puzzle of how to keep your meds working for and not against you.

Figure 4: Brand Name and Generic Equivalents

Depression and Anxiety			Mood Stabilizers		
Brand	**Generic**	**Class**	**Brand**	**Generic**	**Class**
Celexa	citalopram	SSRI	Risperdal	risperidone	Atypical
Cymbalta	duloxetine	SNRI	Depakote	valproate	Anticonvulsant
Effexor	venlafaxine	SNRI	Invega	paliperidone	Atypical
Fetzima	levomilnacipran	SNRI	Seroquel	quetiapine	Atypical
Lexapro	escitalopram	SSRI	Tegretol	carbamazepine	Anticonvulsant
Luvox	fluvoxamine	SSRI	Geodon	ziprasidone	Atypical
Paxil	paroxetine	SSRI	Latuda	lurasidone	Atypical
Pristiq	desvenlafaxine	SNRI	Trileptal	oxcarbazepine	Anticonvulsant
Prozac	fluoxetine	SSRI	Abilify	aripiprazole	Atypical
Celexa	citalopram	SSRI	Zyprexa	olanzapine	Atypical
Viibryd	vilazodone	SSRI	Lamictal	lamotrigine	Anticonvulsant
Zoloft	sertraline	SSRI	Rexulti	brexpiprazole	Atypical
			Vraylar	cariprazine	Atypical

Anti-anxiety Sedatives			Blood Pressure		
Xanax	alprazolam		Catapres	clonidine	
Klonopin	clonazepam		Intuniv	guanfacine	
Valium	diazepam		Tenex	guanfacine hydrochloride	
Ativan	lorazepam				
Restoril	temazepam				

Remember that genetic test I used with Gretchen in Chapter 5? This is one way the results help your prescriber make a better choice on which medications will work for you and how they'll work together. The test also suggests which medications are gene-neutral, meaning that the meds pose no special dosing considerations or have potentially greater side effects.

As we look at each co-occurring diagnosis and the meds we use to treat it, I won't go into the same detail about release, ratios, and boosters as I did earlier. That's in part because this book is about treating ADD, but also because none of these medications can be tuned-in or strategically deployed the way stimulants can. Once we get to a therapeutic dosage, they either work the way they were designed to work, or we need to try something different, or we need to add something. The recipe for success in any given case is so complicated that it goes way beyond the scope of this book. But it pays to know the ingredients.

Anxiety and Depression

Generally speaking, there are three types of medications used to address anxiety, both as a standalone disorder and as it co-occurs with ADD: benzodiazepines, selective serotonin reuptake inhibitors (SSRIs), and selective serotonin-norepinephrine reuptake inhibitors (SNRIs).

Benzodiazepines. The best known medications in this group are Valium and Xanax, but the most commonly used are Klonopin and Ativan. Benzos, as they are known in the biz, are among the oldest psychopharmaceuticals. All are considered Schedule IV controlled substances, and they are highly susceptible to misuse and abuse.

Valium's patent dates way back to the late 1950s, though it did not enter the market until 1963. By 1968 it was the top selling medication in the United States and continued to be so until 1982. At one point the company sold two billion tablets a year[184]. That's *billion*. With a "b." Though its popularity has waned over the last thirty years, even today about six million prescriptions are written for Valium every year.

Valium did mad business for one simple reason. It works. A bit too well, really. Or as one of Wes's client's described it, "Wow. That could knock the spots off a leopard." The problem to the solution of Valium is that it builds tolerance and physical dependence, which leads to a physical withdrawal so severe that it becomes very difficult to discontinue. In fact, doing so too abruptly can have serious health implications such as hallucinations and seizures. In Chapter 9, we'll explain how stimulant medication builds tolerance; but the tolerance that comes with Valium is on a whole other plane of serious.

The widespread use of Valium came and went well before I became a PMHNP (actually, before I entered middle school), but Wes describes working with other prescribers, trying to help clients wean off of it in the smallest increments possible and literally never succeeding. For this reason, I don't prescribe it. It can be useful as a rescue medication[185]

---

[184] en.wikipedia.org/wiki/Diazepam

[185] A medication used once, or very infrequently, to bring the client out of a state of acute psychiatric distress such as panic, mania, or a psychotic break.

when anxiety or panic are at devastating peaks and as a treatment for muscle spasms. However, even this brings a risk of behavioral dependency as the client becomes quickly reliant on the sedative effect of the medication to regulate anxiety (or muscle spasms), and upon gaining that benefit, uses it more often and at a lower and lower threshold.

Klonipin was brought to market in 1975 by Roche Biomedical with the intent of providing a less-addicting answer to Valium. This was not altogether successful as most users found Klonopin very sedating and thus less useful for daytime panic attacks with little decrease in the potential for dependency. I will continue clients on Klonopin if they're already taking it without experiencing sedation, but in my experience, that's rare. In fact, this med is far more useful as a short-term (less than two weeks) treatment of severe anxiety-related insomnia precisely because it makes clients so sleepy.

Upjohn developed Xanax in the 1970s, and it entered the market in 1981 as a competitor to Valium and Klonopin. Having begun his career in the early 1990s, Wes recalls the initial pitch for Xanax was that it carried the same benefits of Valium with a lower risk of dependency. However, over the long haul, that's proven optimistic as Xanax has many of the same problem attributes[186] as its older rival. In our experience, it is possible to prescribe Xanax in a way that is therapeutic, but it is unwise to consider it far safer than Valium. It remains best used as a rescue med with a careful eye toward behavioral dependency and only in tandem with one of the longer-acting agents described in the next (SSRI and SNRI) sections.

When we must use benzos, we lean toward Ativan which was introduced in 1977 by Wyeth Pharmaceuticals, and even then, only within a larger treatment protocol. Unlike its cousins, Ativan poses a lower risk for physical dependency due to its longer-acting and more gradual start-up effects. We've been able to move clients on and off of this medication with greater ease, as long as it is withdrawn slowly.

---

[186] en.wikipedia.org/wiki/Alprazolam

Both Valium and Xanax have a long history of misuse and abuse, making them unsuitable for people with ADD who often struggle with issues of addiction and dependency.

Both Valium and Xanax have long histories of misuse and abuse, both in tandem with other drugs and as standalone party drugs. This makes them quite unsuitable for people with ADD who often struggle with issues of addiction and dependency. The other obvious shortcoming of benzos for the ADD crowd is illuminated by our "caring" model of anxiety and in-attention (Chapter 2). If we greatly reduce your anxiety with one of these medications, we are very likely increasing the effects of ADD because we're getting you to "care less," when you need to care more.

Selective Serotonin Reuptake Inhibitors (SSRIs). As discussed in Chapter 5, antidepressants existed for many years but did not reach their modern formulation until the late 1980s with the first successful SSRI, Prozac. Thereafter, a whole slew of these meds came into being, most notably Zoloft, Lexapro, and Celexa. They are among the best known medications, owing in large part to the early Prozac boom, but also to the ease with which primary care providers have been willing to prescribe them. If a client comes in and says, "I went to my PCP for depression medication, I can say, I bet he or she gave you Zoloft or Lexapro, and I'll be right about eighty to ninety percent of the time. This has nothing remotely to do with the efficacy of SSRIs for depression and everything to do with the prescriber's level of comfort with these long-established drugs, which are seen as easy to get on, easy to get off of and comparatively innocuous.

A common misconception about these medications is that they provide a new ingredient needed to reduce anxiety or depression symptoms. In fact, they merely stop the overly rapid recycling of existing serotonin—which can occur due to genetics, trauma, or life circumstances—so that your anxiety-modulating neurotransmitter can do its job helping you keep your cool. As you might gather from the name, the medication blocks the absorption of serotonin out of the synaptic gap and into the neuron, allowing your brain more accessibility and use of the serotonin that your body naturally makes.

Unfortunately, based on a great deal more dialog and personal interaction with clients than the average PCP or psychiatrist can provide, we've learned that SSRIs aren't very effective for depressive symptoms. They tend to leave the depressed client with a sense of "blah," or what we call "malaise," feeling little range of affect, perhaps okay but not much better. Prozac tends to be among the worst offenders in this regard, but the others can also create the blahs.

Not infrequently, we've seen new clients previously misdiagnosed with depression, when they clearly have ADD, and put on an SSRI. If you follow our caring-model, you can imagine how poorly this turns out. You take someone with ADD and give them a drug that makes them feel comfortably numb. Clients with co-occurring ADD and well-diagnosed depression will get much the same result.

For this same reason, however, SSRIs have proven terrific at treating anxiety, and as a result, most of these meds are now on label for treating it. If you care too much, have intrusive thoughts, excessive and/or unrealistic worry, and a variety of accompanying physical symptoms, a medication that can calm you down won't feel numbing, it will feel lifechanging. Unlike benzodiazepines, the SSRIs don't sedate you, and because you're on the medication daily, you don't have the kind of hand-to-mouth symptom chase that leads to behavioral addiction.

For people with ADD and anxiety, SSRIs can work in tandem with stimulants as the two medications will tend to balance each other out, increasing attention and decreasing unhelpful anxiety. It's a little harder to tune-in than I'm making it sound, but the basic thesis has worked in many cases.

That said, SSRIs have their shortcomings. At the top of the list are sexual side effects. When they first hit the market in the 1990s, the drug trials identified low libido, anorgasmia (exactly what it sounds like) and erectile dysfunction to be among the most prevalent side effects. However, the researchers proposed the rates to be comparatively low. Over the last three decades culture has changed. We now talk more about sex and sexuality, and clients are more open to discussing sexual dysfunction with trusted professionals and at least some of those professionals have learned to ask. What we've found in response is that SSRI-related sexual side effects are far more common than the original drug trials proposed—rising to perhaps fifty percent of users. Nobody knows the real number, because all these medications are now generic and nobody is going to pay for research to learn more about their side effect profiles. But the anecdotal evidence is so clear that we go over this topic with every client we see, including teenagers, to be sure we're not creating more problems than we're solving.

For ADD clients, the malaise effect of an SSRI can overwhelm a stimulant's improvement in focus, leading to lowered motivation. So, if we try an SSRI and find an ADD client caring too little, even while taking a stimulant, we typically move to an SNRI. In many cases involving ADD, we're now forgoing the SSRI trial and moving straight into this next class of meds.

Selective Serotonin-Norepinephrine Reuptake Inhibitors (SNRIs). Just as the SSRIs were gaining a foothold, a new class of medications came to market for treating both depression and anxiety. Known as selective serotonin-norepinephrine reuptake inhibitors (SNRI) these medications began with Effexor (1994) and continued with Cymbalta (2004), Pristiq (2008), Fetzima (2013), and most recently, Viibryd (2015).

Serotonin-norepinephrine reuptake inhibitors work just as the SSRIs do, but they also block the absorption of norepinephrine, a neurotransmitter that is both uplifting and suppressing in the best of ways. Norepinephrine's uplifting properties can improve your energy, motivation, focus and concentration, which makes it an ideal paring for someone with ADD. Its suppressing powers are in how it regulates anxiety. Think of norepinephrine as being like the sorting hat in Harry Potter. Its job is to categorize the ten thousand situations we encounter each day into "Worry About This" or "No Big Deal." When your brain is in hyper-drive norepinephrine recycling mode, absorbing the neurotransmitter so quickly, it's as if you have no sorting hat, so everything goes straight to "Worry about This." When the sorting hat is working at its best, your experiences are sent where they're supposed to go, generating a sense of calm clarity in which you feel more in control of your anxieties.

Effexor in its generic form (venlafaxine) has become our most commonly used medication both for stand-alone anxiety and for co-occurring ADD-anxiety and ADD-depression. Across many cases, it has proven to generate fewer sexual side effects than SSRIs and, rather than increase the sense of malaise, it often improves motivation and energy.

As with all clinical experience, our love affair with Effexor comes directly from daily conversations with clients who express higher satisfaction[187] with this medication than any other in the SSRI or SNRI class. We've had people come in who've tried multiple meds from several classes without success. Despite their molecular similarity, we've not had the same positive experience with Cymbalta and Pristiq—and believe me, we've tried. While they will work in certain cases, those are the exceptions. We're still working with Fetzima and Viibryd to see how they impact ADD and non-ADD clients; but their additional cost has proven too great to justify except in cases where Effexor just isn't cutting it.

Here's the downside. All SSRIs and SNRIs can have something called discontinuation syndrome (DS)[188] which includes a variety of symptoms both mental and physical that occur when you stop taking the medication. Some people are far more prone to this than others. For some medications, like Prozac, which sticks around in your body for weeks and weeks, there's very little likelihood of DS in anyone. But for some medications, the risk of DS is high. Effexor is among the best known examples. Clients are warned on the day I write their first script that if they forget to take a dose of Effexor they will, within a few hours, have something ranging from severe emotionality to flu-like symptoms. We also walk them through a protocol for how to handle a missed pill: carry one pill at all times, take it when you realize you forgot your normal dose, move your next dose back by a few hours to compensate for that day's late administration; then work your way forward the next day to the normal dose time. Every client makes this mistake once and, after experiencing the consequences, never makes it again—or at least they know how to handle it.

Depending on therapeutic dosage, if we need to take you off Effexor, the correct procedure is to withdraw slowly in the same increments you went up. Occasionally, we'll also prescribe Prozac before you begin discontinuing Effexor, and then taper you off the Prozac in a few weeks. This can help dampen DS symptoms in people particularly

---

[187] We don't actually have a scale for this, but more people state positive experiences with Effexor, remain on it, and express fewer complaints about it.

[188] en.wikipedia.org/wiki/Antidepressant_discontinuation_syndrome

prone to them. And in case you're wondering, every SNRI has some risk of DS, so trying a different brand may not resolve this problem.

While most clients are a bit taken aback by the prospect of DS, very few have refused or quit Effexor because of it. They like the main effects and are thankful for its relatively low side effect profile. Learning to take it consistently and enacting the back-up protocol is worth the risk of DS, which can usually be managed as described above. What has caused pause among clients, particularly young adults, is Effexor's tendency to enhance the impact of alcohol on the body. That's true for other psychopharmaceuticals, too, and we warn every client who's about to take a new medication about this possibility. With Effexor, however, lowered tolerance for alcohol is almost a sure bet. For some clients who really like to drink, that's intolerable. However, these tend to be folks whose substance use makes it difficult to treat any mental health condition without additional recovery work, so taking a specific medication may be the least of our worries.

All in all, SNRIs have proven invaluable for treating ADD folks with co-occurring depression and anxiety without the problems that come with SSRIs. While a few primary care physicians know and use these meds, most don't, perhaps because they can't spend the necessary time to counsel clients on how to use the medications or to monitor them to assure success.

Wellbutrin. In 1985, Wellbutrin entered the U.S. market, actually predating Prozac by a couple of years. We've given this medication its own section in this discussion because it belongs to an odd category of medications known as norepinephrine–dopamine reuptake inhibitors (NDRI). Others in this category include a broad array of medications for very different conditions, including all of the methylphenidate products we discussed earlier and a few lost antidepressant and amphetamines you probably haven't heard of.

Given that connection, you might think Wellbutrin ideally suited to treating folks with ADD. As a standalone, that's not usually the case, though it often works well in tandem with stimulants for people having co-occurring ADD and depression without features of anxiety. Since it works only on norepinephrine and dopamine, it tends not to create a malaise, has a low side effect profile (including those related to sex), and can complement rather than stem the effect of stimulant medication. Though we've seen it happen, Wellbutrin is not known for discontinuation syndrome. Many primary care doctors know about and like to use Wellbutrin, but are less likely to do so in tandem with stimulants.

Bipolar Disorder

The goal in treating bipolar disorder is to bring down the highs and lift up the lows so, not surprisingly, the medications used in such cases are known as term mood-stabilizers. That is, however, a pretty imprecise term for a wide range of different medications. Let's take a look at each.

Lithium. When you think of bipolar disorder, you may think first of lithium, some form of which has been used for mood stabilization for over a hundred years. Lithium is principally used to treat mania.

Though it ebbs and flows in prescribing popularity, Lithium brings with it some significant and long-recognized problems. Because it is a naturally occurring salt, its side effects include increased urination, hypothyroidism, and something called lithium toxicity which occurs when too much of the drug builds up in the body. Toxicity usually comes not from a mistaken dosing, but from other changes in the body that affect how the lithium is absorbed. These can include inadequate hydration, an increase or decrease in sodium intake, and other subtle changes. Worse, the therapeutic blood level for lithium is very narrow, so blood has to be regularly drawn and several pre-lithium screenings performed to ensure your kidneys are in good working order. For this reason, lithium is most commonly started during an inpatient stay where mental and physical health screenings can be managed quickly under one roof. Outside the hospital, this protocol poses a difficult laundry-list of tasks for a person in the throes of a manic episode, and the regimen can be difficult to maintain in daily life.

Lithium is also known to cause weight gain, which can place clients at greater risk for developing heart disease[189] so, in addition to lab monitoring, your weight should be watched closely to ensure you're not solving one problem and causing another. Lithium should be used with special caution in anyone known to have heart rhythm abnormalities as it can induce minor changes in the heart's electrical rhythm.

---

[189] De Hert, M., Detreaux, J. & Vancampfort, D. (2018). The intriguing relationship between coronary heart disease and mental disorders. *Dialogues in Clinical Neuroscience*, 20(1), 31-40.

Given these issues, clients don't tend to like lithium very much, and their compliance is poor. Yet, because of its age, lithium is very inexpensive, making it a treatment of choice for those with limited means and no insurance. For folks with ADD who abhor complex medication regimens and blood tests, lithium will do more to annoy than to please. For this reason, we almost never use it. In its place, there has grown a shelf of mood stabilizers drawn from three very different categories: anticonvulsants, blood pressure medications, and atypical antipsychotics.

Anticonvulsants. Also known as anti-epileptics, this category of medication was originally produced to treat seizure disorders, but several have been repurposed to manage bipolar disorder, with varying levels of success. These include Tegretol, Depakote, Trileptal, and Topamax. Each of these medications has its own share of side effects. Trileptal is particularly worrisome for young heterosexual women because it can inactivate their hormonal contraception and allow them to become pregnant. Topamax can cause significant loss of appetite which, on top of a stimulant, can be quite problematic. It can also lead to memory problems.

By far the most effective and best tolerated medication in this class is Lamictal, known generically as lamotrigine. It has, for some twenty years, been a first line treatment for bipolar disorder, particularly of the depressive variety. It is not, however, ideal for BiD individuals who are experiencing mania or mixed manic-episodes. In fact, it can actually make them worse by triggering mania, as can SSRIs or SNRIs. There's not a lot of research on why this happens, but the case studies are clear—mania-prone clients do not do well with the addition of Lamictal, even with a concurrent mood stabilizer or antipsychotic.

Blood Pressure Medications. This category, known as Central-Alpha2 Antagonists, includes Catapres and Kapvay, the short- and long-acting versions of clonidine, which are used be to treat ADD-related hyperactivity and impulsivity. They may also be used off-label[190] to reduce symptoms of low-grade mania in clients with BiD. The principal concern in using these drugs is that their main effect is to lower blood

---

[190] Meaning they are not approved for this use because research is lacking but have been found in clinical use to have value.

pressure, which can lead to rebound[191] if the drug is suddenly discontinued.

Atypical Antipsychotics. I can visualize jaws dropping all across our readership at the thought of taking an antipsychotic medication or giving it to a loved one. Don't get too freaked out. If you're facing a correctly diagnosed case of bipolar disorder, these medications can be literally lifesaving; and if I don't tell you up front what they really are, you'll balk when your prescriber wants you take one and you get online and find out for yourself.

Although it's not completely understood how these medications work, one biochemical theory of BiD involves the dopamine receptor sites being more sensitive to dopamine. Where folks without BiD may simply experience satisfaction or mild happiness when their dopamine molecules enter their receptor sites, people with BiD overrespond with euphoria and mania. Atypical antipsychotics work by seeking out the D2 receptor sites and filling the spaces where the dopamine might otherwise enter, thereby reducing the overresponse. Once again, the medication isn't providing an ingredient for stability or correcting a "chemical imbalance," it's just regulating the process so you can use your own neurotransmitters for mood stability and not instability.

Over the last twenty-five years, atypical anti-psychotics have become mainstays in the treatment of bipolar disorder.

Over the last twenty-five years, medications of this class have become mainstays in the treatment of BiD, specifically to hold down mania, but also to address symptoms of depression by activating a receptor for a specific subtype of serotonin, 5-HT_2[192]. That hasn't always been a smooth road, however.

The first atypical was Zyprexa, approved in the U.S. in 1996. While that's before my time as a PMHNP, Wes remembers its impact on clients with BiD who found it a miracle drug that worked like nothing they'd ever tried before. Jennifer, Tressa's mom from the Chapter 4 vignette, found her life changed in her first months of taking Zyprexa,

---

[191] A sudden increase in a symptom, in this case a spike in blood pressure.

[192] Serotonin's proper chemical name is 5-hydroxytryptamine or 5-HT. There are seven 5-HT families (5-HT_1–5HT_7) and each has several subtypes (ex. 5-HT_{2A}).

until she and most of the clients who joined her on that journey began gaining substantial weight. Many also saw blood sugar spikes, a few to the point of diabetes. For this reason, we no longer use Zyprexa except as a rescue med[193].

Shortly thereafter, in 1997, Seroquel came to market, and it remains one of the best tools in our mood stabilizer toolbox. I often use it in conjunction with Lamictal as an adjunct mood stabilizer when the primary symptom concerns are agitation, irritability, or persistent lack of interest in life. It is effective for both the acute and depressive phases of BiD, though it can be sedating, particularly in lower doses. Yes, I meant that. Lower doses of Seroquel are so sedating they can be used for severe insomnia—though there is controversy over the efficacy of that approach, and we only try it when all else has failed. Higher doses are less sedating. Seroquel has been found to pose less risk of weight gain than other atypicals. It is nearly impossible to overdose on Seroquel, making it safer for people at risk of self-harm.

Geodon was approved in 2001 and was briefly used to treat BiD, but it ended up causing many of the same side effects as Zyprexa. It is reserved for last-resort use in children and teens with early-onset symptoms of bipolar disorder and is typically only started during an inpatient stay.

With these mixed results, you can imagine how skeptical prescribers were when the second wave of atypicals came into clinical use, beginning with Abilify in 2002. However, with seventeen years of experience, Abilify has proven its benefit with BiD. We use it often to treat these folks and also in cases of very agitated unipolar depression.

Latuda was approved in the U.S. in 2010, though it was not on-label for treating BiD until mid-2013. It has been found more helpful for treating the down periods of BiD than for managing manic episodes. Similarly, Rexulti came to market in 2015 and is produced by the same company as Abilify, which went generic (aripiprazole) that same year. It is unique among atypicals in that it is approved only as an adjunct treatment for resistant unipolar depression and not for BiD. The manufacturer gave it a good shot in the original drug trials, but early in

---

[193] Zyprexa works quickly and over the short term its negative side effects are minimal.

2019, Lundbeck (in partnership with Otsuka) announced that the drug had failed to show efficacy for the treatment of BiD.

All atypical antipsychotics carry the same warning for possible extrapyramidal[194] symptoms. Adding to the growing list of dopamine's duties is its involvement in directing impulses and messages to the extrapyramidal system, the part of our brain and spinal cord responsible for our motor functions and reflexes. Atypical antipsychotics are also called dopamine antagonists, because they block or antagonize dopamine receptors to produce a therapeutic result. These extrapyramidal side effects can range from a mild reversible tremor to permanent abnormal jerking motions in the arms or legs.

That said, when compared to the early antipsychotics of the 1950s like Haldol, which effectively blocks all dopamine receptors for long periods of time at small doses, atypical antipsychotics are much less likely to cause extrapyramidal symptoms. The greatest risk for these side effects comes within the first four weeks of initiating or increasing dosage, so you should be monitored closely during this time. As always, if you're put on one of these medications, it's up to you to become the expert, keep an eye out for both good and bad results, and report them to your prescriber.

Insomnia

Whether a sleep problem is primary, ADD-related, or the result of stimulants, it's serious. If sleep hygiene and strategic medication management fails to correct your insomnia, you may need to turn to additional medications to get you the length and depth of sleep you need. This is an uncomfortable space for both client and prescriber, because there are so many "sleepers," as we call them in the biz, from so many different classes, and so many problems with each of them. Because the main effect of a sleep aid is pretty straight forward to assess (you do or don't sleep), we'll focus on the shortcomings and side effects in this section.

Longevity of Use. At the top of the list of shortcomings is that most sleep medications don't work well over the long haul. They build

---

[194] Physical symptoms, including tremor, slurred speech, akathisia, dystonia, anxiety, distress, paranoia, and bradyphrenia.

tolerance quickly and lose efficacy, sometimes within a few days. For example, the most common over-the-counter medication for sleep is diphenhydramine, which is also the ingredient in Benadryl. The original intent of Benadryl was allergy relief and the chief side effect, drowsiness. It's actually used intravenously to sedate patients before a variety of medical procedures.

For most folks who took Benadryl as an allergy med, that side effect wore off after a few weeks of use. Great for the sneezers, but if you're taking it regularly to fall asleep, the same will apply, making it of limited use after a week or two. This is also true for many prescription sleep medications, which stop working after a comparatively short period of time. If you have more than occasional insomnia, particularly if it's ADD- or stimulant-related, you're not going to get over it quickly, so a medication that works well for a long time is preferable.

While benzodiazepines can be used to aid sleep with less risk of dependency than if they are used for anxiety, they won't do the job for long. Medications like Ambien will conk out after two or three weeks, and anyone who tells you they've been on such meds for years has long since entered the valley of the placebo—believing so strongly that the medication still helps, that it does. Lunesta, which came to market in 2004, is supposedly less prone to tolerance, but there's no real evidence that's true.

Without a doubt, the best long-term medication for treating insomnia of any sort isn't even on-label for that use. Yet it's the second most widely prescribed medication for sleep on the market[195]. Trazodone was approved in 1981 as a serotonin antagonist and reuptake inhibitor (SARI), a unique class of medications with very few meaningful peer drugs and none of them still on the market.

Trazodone was intended to be an antidepressant, and it passed its trials as such, but it was a complete failure because it caused extreme drowsiness. And unlike most medications with that side effect, the drowsiness continued unabated for years on end[196]. While most patients will

---

[195] It was hard to get data on this, but the several formulations of Ambien appear to be the top seller.

[196] This is a clinical anecdote, but a very robust one. There's been no research beyond four weeks of use. As noted, this is typical in the field of psychopharmacology, and nobody is going to spend a dollar to run longer studies on a medication that can be bought for less than three dollars a month at a chain pharmacy.

need to increase their dosage over time to keep the effect going, the increase is very slow and the dosing range wide, from 25mg to 400mg. It does have a significant discontinuation syndrome and must be reduced very slowly over time. Not everyone responds to trazodone, and others will experience negative side effects. But if it works, there's no better long-term option, and there's no risk of abuse or dependency aside from the discontinuation syndrome.

Next Day Hangover. The second problem with nearly all these medications is impairment in mental and physical functioning, particularly in the morning. The precarious balance we want to strike is between getting you to sleep, keeping you asleep, and letting you wake up. You'll become very aware of how your body processes these medications by how this balance plays out, because each body is very different.

Using trazodone as an example, some people find it helps them get to sleep and stay asleep, which is a great joy until the alarm clock rings. One of my clients coined the term "trudging" to describe how the morning went after the alarm clock rang. We gave the medication time, and for this client

> *The worst thing about all the problems related to sleep medications is that we cannot know how they will affect you until we try them.*

that "trudging" effect eventually wore off; but for others, it never does. Likewise, we have occasionally taken advantage of Seroquel's low-dose side effect of drowsiness, only to have clients discontinue after a few days because the sedative effect lasted all day. Ambien comes with a warning not to drive the day after taking it due to its residual effects.

The worst thing about this issue, and really all problems related to sleep medications, is that we cannot know how they will affect you until we try them. Even with genetic testing, we can only get a hint and then try to avoid the meds that appear to have the worst match with your DNA. How you do the next day, or how you'll do after a week of next days, can only be learned by trial and error; and where hangover is concerned, that's a pretty rough trial. And yet, trudging is nothing compared to…

Strange (Even Dangerous) Nighttime Behavior. Ambien is very well known for this one, prompting a new set of warnings on its label long after it was initially released and went generic[197]. Ambien can cause those who take it to sleepwalk, sleep drive (!!!), have sleep sex, and even sleep, get up, make a three course meal, and sleep eat it. While we've read about some of the side effects with sleepers or heard tales told in prescriber gatherings, we've actually seen situations like this, all of which are frightening and give us pause before prescribing Ambien, even for short term use. We typically ask clients to give their car keys to a partner or roommate and to ask them not to surrender them at night, even if the client seems quite coherent.

Ambien is not alone in this regard. Two other sleep medications, Lunesta and Sonata, are also prone to cause night venturing and thus require warning labels. We've yet to have a client do this while taking these two medications, but we would rather be safe than sorry. While trazodone isn't known for this sort of thing, it can cause dizziness and falling, particularly in older patients. We advise everyone who takes it to be sure the path to the bathroom is clear should they need to go at night, even after they are used to the medication.

Abuse. We only see this occasionally, but it's worth mentioning. Some of these medications can get overused or even abused. Some can be taken in such a way as to simulate the sedation effect of benzodiazepines. Most are listed as posing a risk of dependency. This is particularly true of Ambien and unheard of for trazodone.

Nature's Way. If you want to try natural methods of insomnia management, melatonin should be your first choice. It's both a supplement used for sleep initiation and a hormone produced by a tiny gland in our brains. When melatonin is released by this gland into our bloodstream, our sense of alertness fades and sleep starts to entice us. Melatonin is kind of like Dracula. It only comes out and does its bidding in the darkness of night. This is why you'll notice a sharp melatonin spike during a matinee movie or classroom slideshow leaving you in need of a nap. You're not just bored. Melatonin is calling for you.

Taking melatonin as a supplement can make that happen when your body is acting like an angry toddler at night-night, saying "No, I won't go to bed. I won't!" We find over-the-counter melatonin supplements between 1mg and 5mg most effective for helping to initiate sleep. There's also a controlled release (CR) variation you can find online

---

[197] www.nytimes.com/2019/04/30/health/sleep-drugs-ambien-side-effects.html

that's a single tablet with two releases of melatonin, four hours apart. This is ideal for those experiencing both difficulty falling asleep and/or staying asleep. And if you're worried that taking a melatonin supplement will dampen your body's ability to produce its own melatonin, don't be. While I do get patients reporting tolerance to melatonin with sustained use over a period of years, there's no evidence that taking it as a supplement impacts your natural production.

The primary downside of melatonin is shared across every other insomnia remedy. Where some people swear by it, others find it just doesn't work. But of all the possibilities, melatonin is the least likely to be sworn at. It's either going to help or not and you're not likely to have any of the problems or side effects we mentioned.

There. You made it through our unbelievably long and yet, all too brief overview of the medications used to treat ADD and its co-occurring disorders. We don't expect you to commit this chapter to memory. If you tried, you'd be getting dangerously close to psychopharmaceutical geekdom. We do hope you'll remember enough to trigger your curiosity at the point you need to know more, so you can come back to this chapter and find what you need when you need it.

You Are the Guinea Pig

Science, my boy, is made up of mistakes, but they are mistakes which it is useful to make, because they lead little by little to the truth.

— Jules Verne, *Journey to the Center of the Earth*

-Dr. Kelsey-

McKenzie shook her head with a hint of frustration and looked sideways at her husband. "I feel like we wasted a lot of time with our primary care doc. He let Calvin pick out his stimulant medication from an online drug company ad, and then he gave him a ninety-day prescription and didn't even do a follow up."

"We're more into the scientific method," I said. "The media gives a pretty mixed up message about stimulants. On one hand, you hear they're overprescribed. On the other, people want to just roll up on their doctors, grab the pills, and expect the medication to make all the difference in the world."

"Doing that seems to work," McKenzie groaned. "But not for long. The first few days he's on something, he's doing great, cleaning the house, finishing work he brought from the office. Then it just wears off."

"Right," I said. "You have to understand that 'being peppy' is more of a side effect than a main effect. It may seem nice, but it's not how the meds are supposed to work. They aren't going to give you motivation, Calvin. They just help you channel the motivation you do have into action. That's a key reason our clients have to be in therapy along with meds. We want to be involved in how that plays out."

Calvin leaned forward, rested his elbows on his knees, and glanced down at the floor. "I guess my expectations were too high. This friend at work has ADD, and he's taken medication for a long time, and he says it changed his life. I wanted that to happen for me, too. And for McKenzie. I'm not as great at relationships as she wants me to be."

"Let's see what we can do." I glanced at the intake form the therapist had completed the week before. "First of all, you're on a whole lot of stimulant for somebody who's not getting much effect. I'm not saying we don't have anyone on 60mg of Adderall, but you also have a 20mg short-acting booster going on here. Has anyone ever talked with you about taking periodic breaks?"

"What? No." McKenzie's brow furrowed as she turned to Cal. "I mean, *did* your doctor ever say anything about that?"

"I don't think so."

"Are you sure?" McKenzie's voice was skeptical.

Cal hung his head. "I don't know. I can't remember."

I stepped in before McKenzie could scold him. "It's entirely possible that nobody mentioned it." We talked a bit about how to keep ahead of stimulant tolerance using the method we'll explain in Chapter 9. Then, I explained our method of starting clients on medication. "Some prescribers don't see this as very complicated, but it really is. Think about Type-2 diabetes as an example. There are several ways to treat it. You start a medicine, and then they check your blood sugar, and then you try an additional one or maybe a different one, and so on. Maybe you eventually have to take insulin. They know there's going to be some experimentation and a lot of doctors know exactly how to do that. Maybe they want your morning sugar to be below 120 and your A1C to be about 6.5, and so on. We think of stimulants more like that, except we can't look at your blood or tap into your brain to know what's going on. We have to listen to you, try some things, see what happens, and maybe try something else."

"We didn't do any of that at my primary care doc's," Cal said. "I just kept going back, and he kept upping the medicine."

"We also have to balance side effects," I said. "We have to do what works with as few side effects as possible and then work around the ones we can't eliminate. That's true of any medication for anything, but with ADD it's tricky. For example, how's your sleep?"

"Not good. I toss and turn all night."

"Okay. Is that new or something you were dealing with before medication? Think about it hard."

The couple exchanged glances.

"I'm going to say it's always been this way," Cal said. "I can remember that I didn't sleep well in high school or early in college, even before I was on Adderall."

"I agree," McKenzie said. "But I think it got worse when he started taking that booster in the afternoon. He's kind of dependent on that to finish out the day now and then he's wired at bed time." She turned to Cal. "Don't you agree?"

"Yeah. I guess that while I take that stimulant break you were talking about, I could see if anything changes at night. But I'm pretty sure I'm going to still struggle with sleep either way."

"Could be," I said. "Did you and your doctor ever talk about sleep problems?"

"Yeah, but he just said to take the stimulants earlier in the day. I'm not sure I even realized I was sleeping badly before stims. I associated that with taking Adderall. I don't think I asked enough questions."

I smiled. "We're all about the questions here. I agree, a two-week stimulant break would give us some good data and get you ready to start over on finding the right medication."

"Two weeks!" McKenzie said. "That sounds horrible. For us both."

"It can get rough," I said. "But starting over will let us study how different medications work for you. For example, have you ever tried a Ritalin-type medication, like Concerta or Daytrana?"

"No," Calvin said. "My doctor read an article that said extended-release Adderall was just as good as some of the expensive name brands and now that it's generic it's cheaper. He said most of them are made of the same stuff anyhow."

"He's kind of right, but how that stuff is put together and delivered into your body can make a big difference. We'll try different formulations and see how each performs for you in the real world."

"I have another question," McKenzie said. "Calvin's uncle has ADD, and he also takes something for anxiety. I think it's Effexor. Shouldn't you look at that too?"

"Sure, we can," I said. "Did you and your therapist talk about that before she referred you over to me?"

"A little," Calvin said. "But she wanted McKenzie to come in first before she made another diagnosis, she wanted her to come to this appointment too. I never thought of doing that."

"That's another difference in how we operate. We want to see not only how you view yourself, but how your people view you as well. It helps us get the experiment right with fewer trials and errors."

"Experiment?" Calvin chuckled. "Like I'm a lab rat now?"

"Running through our maze." I smiled. "We'll try and keep it as easy as possible with few blind alleys and more happy turns toward the cheese."

"I like this idea," McKenzie said. "When I'm involved, I feel like I understand Cal better and know whether what I'm doing is helping or hurting his progress."

"That's how we like things to work," I said. "I'm going to write you one more script for the current medication to get you by, and then you two work with the therapist to schedule a break so it creates the least hardship at home and at work. Then we'll start from scratch."

Into and Out of the Maze
- Dr. Wes -

What We're Going for Here

In a perfect match between stimulant and stimulant user, we want the experiment to conclude by you jumping up and shouting, "Eureka! Is *that* how the neurotypical people think!?"

That really does happen. On the day I wrote this paragraph, I was in Ann Arbor training at the University of Michigan. At the morning snack break, a colleague approached me and said, "You're that guy who wrote that book on ADD, right?" Sometimes answering this question turns out well, other times not so much, but I did 'fess up."

"Wow," the colleague said. "After I finally started taking stimulants, it was just…wow. I don't know how I ever got anything done before."

"That's so cool!" I said as I took a bite of my oatmeal bagel. "My wife told me about when she was a kid and she got glasses for the first time. Until she put them on that day, she didn't realize trees had leaves."

"Yeah!" The colleague said. "That's exactly what it was like. I never thought of it that way before. Leaves. Those are like all the little details I never noticed before."

With stimulant medication, we want you to concentrate better and longer, to care just enough about what you need to care about to get it done, and to pay attention to little details like time and place and who and where and why. We want you to remember things better, either because your memory works more efficiently or because you've encoded the details more fully. We want you to make decisions based not on how you feel from moment to moment, but on chosen values, and to persist enough to follow through on what you decide. We want you to understand boredom as the rest of us do, annoying but tolerable on the path to a valued end. And we want to see these improvements play out in real life—at your job or school and in your social relationships.

We see many versions of this outcome daily, so we know stimulants work across the population of clients we see. But even if you're correctly evaluated as we described in Chapter 3, the road from diagnosis to "Wow!" isn't always a direct one. This chapter will help you get there as efficiently and effectively as possible by turning you into the single subject of your very own scientific experiment.

You remember science, right? You and your eager friends gathered around a flaming Bunsen burner to conduct an experiment from the recipe in a textbook. It might not have been apparent back then, as you sat clad in lab coat and goggles on metal stools, but you weren't really learning which chemical combinations do and do not explode. You were learning the scientific method. Based on how badly Americans misunderstand research, perhaps high school science class wasn't altogether successful in that mission. That's too bad, because experimentation is at the core of all learning.

When the subject of inquiry is you and your meds, the scientific method becomes critical because, more than any other form of medical practice, getting meds right for a psychiatric condition is a process of trial, error, observation, and communication. We used to hear the term "guinea pig" muttered by frustrated clients as we toiled in earnest in this process, and eventually, we decided to embrace the guinea pig model. With that level of honesty on the front end of the experiment, clients began to have more reasonable expectations and greater enthusiasm for treatment.

If your prescriber is an ADD medication management expert, he or she may already have a protocol to do this experiment. However, based on experience, that's unlikely, so we'll use the rest of this chapter to offer our protocol. As always, share it wisely and gently with your prescriber.

Preliminary Assessment

- Dr. Kelsey -

Before we[198] start the experiment, I'll do my best to tease out of your medical history any co-occurring diagnoses (Chapter 4), health conditions like tic disorders, heart arrhythmias, neurological issues, nutritional malabsorption, and any developmental or physical delays. If I become concerned about how a health condition might change the way

---

[198] In most of this section, I'll speak to you as if you were in our office doing this experiment. I'm not presuming to speak for all prescribers, but this makes for an easier and more comfortable read.

stimulant medication impacts your body or vice versa, I'll request a medical workup and consult with the specialist before proceeding and as often thereafter as necessary.

It's critical that you disclose your medical history to the fullest extent possible.

For this reason, it's critical that you disclose your medical history to the fullest extent possible. I'm especially interested in any family or personal history of glaucoma or an increase in eye pressure, tic disorders, abnormal heart rhythm, fainting at rest or during exercise, or psychosis. I'll want to know if you've have ever had issues with your kidneys or suffer from a chronic kidney condition as this may affect the dose of your medications. I may want you to visit with your parents, if they're still living, asking questions about family history and health, looking for any counterindications for stimulant medication, especially anyone who experienced cardiac events before age fifty, particularly those that ended in death.

I'll ask you about all prescription and over-the-counter medications you take, including antihistamines, vitamins, and nutritional or pre-workout supplements used regularly or as-needed. Many supplements contain caffeine which can greatly enhance the effects of stimulant medication. I'll also do a detailed assessment of what a typical day of eating looks like in your home in order to get a sense of what drives you or your child to consume food: hunger or social cues. This will play a key role in managing the impact of appetite suppression, discussed in Chapter 8.

Step 1: Pharmacogenomic Testing

Several times in this book, I've mentioned genetic (pharmacogenomic) testing. While still optional at our office, I'm increasingly using it to improve our medication hit rate. The company we use at the time of this writing is Genomind[199]. As always, neither Wes nor I own stock in this or any similar product, and we don't even charge for or get a cut from its use in our practice. Our only stake in this game is improving client outcomes. There are several other companies that offer the same service. However, not all of them include stimulant medication, because the research isn't as strong for those agents as it is for say, SSRIs

---

[199] genomind.com

or SNRIs. Not every company wants to risk selling something that turns out not to be useful.

We appreciate that sense of caution, particularly in a chapter dedicated to the scientific method. However, we've decided to offer Genomind to clients with full disclosure that its application to stimulants is still experimental, so everyone can give fully informed consent before spending their money with this company. We're monitoring the results over many trials to see how accurately it predicts the class of stimulant we end up finding to be most effective. When we have a clearer sense of its efficacy, we'll publish that on our blog at www.familypsychological.com. For now, here's a short FAQ on pharmacogenomic testing:

What Is It, Exactly? A panel of tests designed to reveal how your genotype or genetic makeup influences the way a given drug impacts your body and how your body may impact the drug.

How Much Blood Do I Have to Give? Not a drop! With Genomind I'll take two buccal samples (cheek swabs) with a Q-Tip, one from each side of your mouth. With OneOme you do the same thing at home. The samples are mailed to a lab where technicians extract DNA from your cheek cells and observe (literally look at) the DNA sequence and compare that to a norm-reference template. Their goal is to identify genetic deviations known to influence how medications interact with your body. These variations impact two mechanisms— pharmacodynamics and pharmacokinetics, respectively—which influence the level of medication that constitutes your therapeutic dose, the likelihood of side effects or adverse reactions, and whether or not the medication is likely to work as expected.

How Do I Get It? Genomind requires a physician or nurse practitioner to order the test. If your provider isn't already signed up, he or she need only establish an online account and complete a credentials verification to order the test. In the case of OneOme, you order the test online as you would say, 23 and Me. The company sends you the kit and you perform the mouth swab at home. OneOme offers a video consultation with a genetic counselor to answer questions and discuss results. However, that consultant is not a prescriber, so to get any benefit from the package, you'll still need to share your results with a current or future psychiatrist or PMHNP. You may want to ask your provider to set up a free OneOme account to help with that process.

How Long Does It Take? About thirty seconds to do the swab and about a week for your results to become available online to your prescriber, who will then share them at your next appointment. If the provider asks you to drop by just for the swab outside of a regular session, he or she should not charge you.

What Can It Tell Us? Enough to make it worth considering and not as much as we'd like. When these tests were more expensive, we used them only after a client had failed several medications, particularly when we needed to start polypharmacology[200] for co-occurring disorders. Now that pharmacogenomic testing is more affordable, it's proving an efficient way get some hints before I start prescribing. It also offers some limited guidance on how to dose other medications appropriately when we know the potential gene-drug interactions that exist within your profile. It may even let us reconsider failed medications by helping us understand and correct what went wrong.

For example, we sometimes get clients with no evidence of another underlying mental illness who nevertheless overrespond to a low-dose of an antidepressant (let's say Cymbalta) in the first few days of initiating treatment. After pharmacogenomic testing, we might learn that the client is an ultra-slow metabolizer of Cymbalta, meaning the medicine was acting on their body as if double the prescribed dosage. With this genetic data, we might be able to use a different SNRI that did not show a gene-drug interaction or we might try the client on one third of the normal starting dose of Cymbalta and monitor their response.

What Can't It Tell Us? Exactly what to prescribe. The test does include information on the pharmacodynamics and pharmacokinetics of many common medications, including recommendations for dosage based on an individual's enzyme speed specific to the elimination for that particular drug. However, many common medications have been around so long that no information is available on their use with individuals known to be slow metabolizers of certain enzymes. For this reason, your prescriber should walk you through a detailed plan of how to use your test results with the medication's dosing recommendations if a gene-drug interaction appears in the report.

It would be great if this sort of information told, "Susan will respond best to Vyvanse and Effexor," and we gave you those medications, and

---

[200] The use of more than one prescription medication for one or more conditions.

you were forever grateful for our wise and precise clinical intervention. Unfortunately, the tests aren't that sensitive, and they probably won't ever be. Too often, clients miss this limitation and are disappointed when we show up with a "red, yellow, green" chart of medications and then say, "Well green doesn't really mean 'go for it!' And red doesn't mean 'no, don't!'" The test also can't suggest exact dosages or indicate how long-term use will affect you. Pharmacogenomic testing is a tool for clinical decision making and treatment plan development. It can't substitute for clinical judgment and careful experimentation.

What Does It Cost? We'd like to say, "Just $99.95, but if you act now we'll also throw in a second test for free, but wait there's more…" Unfortunately, the cost is a little difficult to calculate up front which makes it the most vexing step of the process. At the time of this writing, a quick Google search will return a price for pharmacogenomic testing of as much as $7,000 (yikes!). However, due to a steep discount program offered by Genomind, the exact cost is based on a sliding scale taking into account family size and income. People with commercial insurance (meaning not Medicaid or Medicare) should pay no more than $330. If you call your insurance company to verify whether they will cover the testing, the short answer will be, "No, we don't."

Confused yet? Just focus on this: Genomind offers this maximum $330 out-of-pocket deal to those with insurance regardless of what your insurance reimburses to Genomind. Our clients usually find that it's worth that price considering the wealth of knowledge gained from the test for both patient and prescriber. OneOme is currently priced at $349. It has the added benefit of providing information on treatments for other medical conditions as well, including allergy, dermatology, and cardiovascular conditions.

Wait. Aren't "Deep Discounts" Usually Scams? Wes and his daughter, a forensic accounting graduate student, love to study and pick apart cons and swindles and there are plenty of scams in our business worth studying. Wes will discuss some of them in Chapter 11. Things that sound too good to be true usually are, like $7,000 worth of testing for three hundred bucks. This deal, however, is legit. Think of it as a "loss leader[201]" for the company, rather than a sketchy act of false beneficence. What they get in return is data. To complete the

---

[201] Taking a loss on some item or service in order to make money later.

Genomind order, the prescriber must provide your age, sex, and your geographical region, and all past and current medication failures. This yields a ton of monetizable data even before they get your DNA! They're also raking in millions of test results they hope will build a case to insurance companies that using their system will result in fewer costly medication errors and provider visits. So, this discount is just good business. Take advantage of it.

How Does It Work? If you're feeling really sciencey today, think back to Chapter 6 when we discussed the CYP450 enzymes, the Pac-Men that eliminate medications and other foreign substances at a genetically pre-determined rate. Several factors like aging, the presence of other medications in your system, and having certain health conditions can also impact what stimulants do in your body.

Remember our Lexapro-Vyvanse interaction example from Chapter 6 in which Lexapro showed more side effects, like nausea, headaches, lethargy, and jaw tension, when paired with Vyvanse? That's an example of a gene-drug interaction that might well show up on a pharmacogenomic test. We've had several cases like this with both SSRIs and SNRIs and knowing it beforehand helps us understand what we're getting into genetically with a given case. That, in turn, pushes us toward greater creativity, teamwork, and discussion, and guides us on when to stay the course with a regimen and when to bail.

Step 2: Selecting a Trial Medication

We'll use a few other strategies to hedge our bet as to which class of medication—amphetamine or methylphenidate—is likely to work best for you. First, we'll look in the low hanging branches of your family tree. I'll ask if you have any first order relatives diagnosed with ADD and if so, what medication they take now and what they've tried in the past. If you don't know the answer and you don't mind letting your family members in on your assessment, I'll ask you to text them and ask. Most clients have no problem doing a little detective work, and the information gathered is invaluable.

There are a few other concerns that impact which stimulant we start you on. Most are economic, however. Because treating ADD is a long-term process, we want to prescribe a product that's cost-sustainable over time. A free month's trial of the latest ADD medication might work wonders, but if the second month costs you $250 out of pocket because it's not covered by your insurance, it's better to start off cheaper. Later in this chapter, we'll teach you more than you even want to know on the topic of insurance and how it impacts our experiment.

Step 3: Testing a Trial Dosage

With our best guess in hand, we're ready to prescribe your first dose. While every trial is important in the larger experiment, the first is especially so because you enter it "stimulant naïve," meaning your body has no experience with ADD meds. There are however, three exceptions to this, all of which should be disclosed and discussed before you begin, as they will impact the results of your first trial.

- You come in, as Calvin did, while taking a stimulant with another provider, or you took them in the past and you're wanting to up your game to a more integrated approach. I may ask that you discontinue that medication, as I did with Calvin, before we start this experiment. Otherwise, the initial trial isn't much of a trial. It's just more of the same. Other prescribers may not approach it this way, but then they really aren't using an experimental model. It's not our place to judge their work, but if you want to do this the way we do it, simply tell your prescriber you'd like to take a break and start fresh. That's also a fine time to have a talk about stimulant tolerance (Chapter 9).

- Like Lisa in Chapter 2, you may have "borrowed" someone else's stimulant or purchased it from one of those people around town who traffics in such things. We absolutely do not endorse this because it's a level one felony and clinically unwise, but it's so common that we've begun asking about it at intake. A prescriber cannot report you to the police for doing this, because you have a confidential relationship[202], so you need to provide as much information as you can recall about the medication brand, its dosage, and how it worked. That helps us determine the impact stimulants have on your system before beginning the experiment. And, if you're thinking,

---

[202] A prescriber can, however, look up your history of stimulant use online. It's in a registry available to DEA-approved prescribers. We'll discuss this more in Chapter 10. So, if you have a history of stimulant abuse, the prescriber may decline to see you. However, he or she still can't turn you into the police.

"Wow. Street drugs! That's a great idea. I never even thought of—" Just stop right there. Did we mention level one felony?

- You've been taking another form of stimulant in large doses. The most common examples are caffeine and nicotine, particularly now that vaping is so popular. We've had enough people come to see us who are drinking two or three pots of coffee a day or using caffeinated workout supplements, that we've also included that question on our intake form (see Dan's vignette in Chapter 3). Far worse, we've had a few people come in who are legitimately ADD and have turned to methamphetamine as their drug of choice. These folks are definitely not stimulant naïve and the effects of meth, even if it's been awhile since last use, must be examined before proceeding. We've successfully treated a handful of these clients after they've entered recovery; but that only works if you're honest with the prescriber, he or she is knowledgeable about substance abuse, and you have unusually good family support. Otherwise, most prescribers won't work with you (Chapter 10). We're no exception.

If you don't fit into any of the these categories, then you're stimulant naïve, and our primary goal on Step 3 will be to figure out whether first exposure makes you better, worse, or does nothing at all and whether it causes more side effects than you can accept after a two-week starter period. The entry dose for this step is usually about 10mg for Adderall XR, 20mg for Vyvanse, 18mg for Concerta, 10mg for Focalin XR, the smallest Daytrana patch, or Adzenys XR-ODT 9.4mg. You and your prescriber will choose which one makes the most sense. Very rarely will an entry dosage be therapeutic, but it's the safest way to gauge main and side effects, so don't expect super-great results in the first day or two. A few clients do get a big surge right off the bat, but that tapers off quickly.

This protocol requires careful prescriber/client monitoring and modification in the first eight to sixteen weeks, so before you leave our office, you'll set up another appointment for exactly two weeks out.

Step 4: First Five Days

At the first appointment, I'll ask you to take only a single dose of the prescribed stimulant for about five days, while carefully noticing how you're feeling throughout the day. To help track progress, you may want to do a daily journal of one or two sentences in the morning, mid-afternoon, and night reflecting how the medication is impacting you. You can also use any of several handy smartphone apps to both note your progress and remind you to take your meds. Medisafe is my favorite and believe me, I have tried them all. It has an interaction checker to highlight potential risks of combining over-the-counter supplements with existing medications. It counts down how many pills you have left in your monthly supply. It even allows you to customize your reminder to feature Morgan Freeman gently prompting you to take your meds at your chosen intervals throughout the day. Its diary option is a quick and easy way for you to take time- and date-stamped notes on any main or side effects noticed. That's essential when we have our next meeting and try to look back at how your functioning has changed over the first weeks of your trial.

Step 5: Second Five Days

At your first appointment, I'll ask you to double your entry dose on the sixth day after starting the medication by taking two of the pre-scribed pills. Please color inside the lines. I'll know if you've gone rogue and taken more than that, because you'll run out of medication early. Breaking protocol is a great way to get off on the wrong foot with any prescriber.

I'll ask you to notice how you feel over the second five day period on the double dose and how that compares with the first five. If you feel fewer symptoms and have no major side effects, other than appetite suppression and modest irritability at washout, I'll ask you to you go up to a triple dose on the eleventh day. That means you'll be taking 54mg of Concerta, 30mg of Adderall, 60mg of Vyvanse, or 37.5mg of Mydayis, etc. If you feel focused and have few side effects at that level, we've probably hit your therapeutic dose. If you feel overmedicated after two or three days, we'll take you back down and wait for Step 6 to consider whether to take you up again or leave you at the second level.

Step 6: Second Appointment

You'll return to our office for the two-week appointment, report your findings, and agree upon a correct dosage, probably either the second or third level of the medication tested in Step 4. I'll prescribe you a month's supply at that dosage. If instead, you've experienced little effect even on the triple dose or the effect was negative, we'll likely try the other class of medication and run a similar trial to test how that works.

Step 7: Find Your High End.

Once you're on the right medication, you'll come in about four to six weeks later and again in another four to six weeks. Our goal at these appointments is to find your personal ceiling between breaks, which as noted earlier, varies from person to person regardless of gender, height, weight, etc. By using the stimulant break protocol discussed in Chapter 9, you can maintain some headroom if you do need to go up one or two dosing levels between breaks.

Cost-Benefit Analysis

If the world was organized as we think it should be, this entire experiment would come pre-packaged in a trial box of stimulant medication with the above instructions attached. Some pharmacies can set up a trial pack like this at the direction of your prescriber, either in a pill box or bubble pack, but the cost will exceed the value added, so I usually just write the prescriptions as I want the experiment to play out.

While writing this chapter, Wes and I realized that neither of us knew why drug companies had never offered this arrangement. In the past, several medications, like Effexor, came boxed in exactly this way with a 37.5mg dose and a 75mg dose and a 150mg dose so the client and prescriber could test various ranges and, in the case of that medication, titrate the client slowly. We wondered if the DEA didn't like starter packs of stimulants, or was it just that nobody else had seen the value of this before? Might there be some hidden royalties we could leverage? Just kidding. Mostly.

We wrote a major pharmaceutical company and got this answer back:

> Thank you for your question. We found your idea intriguing. To our knowledge, there is no regulatory barrier that would prevent pharmaceutical companies from offering starter packs or kits as it is largely just a packaging change that would be a good way to further limit unused pharmaceuticals in medicine cabinets. We're familiar with an approved starter kit for lamotrigine which is used for

epilepsy. We are going to follow up with our customers to see if there would be interest in your idea.

Bingo. Royalties!

We appreciate this unnamed company's interest in our little plan, but their idea of testing it on customers presumes that customers understand why it would be valuable. We're not sure most prescribers would get it, let alone the consumer. So, for now, this cool starter pack thing will remain in the imagination of Drs. Wes and Kelsey.

And why do you care about our rather dry fantasy life? Because without that packaging, the downside of this experimental protocol is its increased cost to you and your insurance company, via copays for prescriptions filled during the trial phase in a less than efficient manner. Our experimental package would instead come as a loss leader to market the company's medication, at reduced cost to the consumer, and greatly ease how the experiment plays out.

The DEA and You: Managing Stimulants

These medications are called "controlled substances," and the first time you fill a script for one, you'll learn why. While all prescription medications are regulated by the Food and Drug Administration (FDA), certain classes are additionally regulated by the Drug Enforcement Agency (DEA). These include hormones, benzodiazepines, pain medications, and yes, stimulants. Of these, stimulants and pain meds are controlled at an even higher level.

Taking medication for ADD requires you to change how you engage with and plan your trips to the pharmacy to avoid future confusion and frustration.

This means that taking medication for ADD requires you to change how you engage with and plan your trips to the pharmacy to avoid future confusion and frustration with the pharmacy and your prescriber.

We have an entire protocol within our office to help guide clients when they encounter the inevitable hang-ups that haunt stimulants. It takes some getting used to, but we'll try to prepare you for what to expect as an engaged medication expert in your treatment. Aside from dealing with insurance, this is the most irritating logistic of stimulant management.

Here's a list of policies required of prescribers and pharmacies by the DEA when dealing with stimulants. They aren't negotiable:

- If you're taking a non-controlled substance, your prescriber can write you a year's worth of medication, say eleven monthly refills after your initial dose[203]. Stimulants cannot be refilled even once. Only one prescription can be written per month and it must be for no more than a thirty-day supply, even in months that have thirty-one days.

- Depending on your treatment plan, you'll eventually need to meet with your prescriber less often. At that point, he or she may issue more than one stimulant prescription on a paper document or electronically[204]. Each script will include a date upon which it can be filled. While a normal prescription may say, "3 refills before September 9," stimulants will always say "0" refills or "Dr. Authorization Required" even if your prescriber has written for a ninety-day supply. This is because that "ninety-day supply" is really three separate and distinct prescriptions, each for thirty-days. The first script can be filled close to the date it was issued. The second, thirty days later and the third, sixty days after issuance.

- Even if your prescriber accidentally circles "1" on the refill line of your paper prescription, the pharmacy will not honor the refill due to restrictions within their system designed to track all medication leaving the pharmacy. Prescribers who submit stimulant prescriptions electronically are also prohibited from putting refills on an e-script.

- The frequency with which a stimulant can be filled is typically mandated by state law, usually no sooner than twenty-eight days from the previously filled prescription. We recommend filling the prescription on that twenty-eighth day so that, over time, you build up a small reserve and thereby reduce the

---

[203] We don't do that because we want to see medication clients at least every ninety-days to keep closer track of the impact any medication is having on emotion, cognition, and behavior. But our policy is above the standard required by law.

[204] While the FDA approved e-prescribing for stimulants in 2010, it took a long time for the industry to catch up, so electronic scripts for stimulants only became "a thing" in the last five or six years.

likelihood that you'll run out of medication. It's also wise to put refill dates on your calendar or as an alarm on your phone, spaced every twenty-eight days along with notations on when you need to come back in to see your prescriber for a renewal.

- The "three separate scripts" rule means your stimulant prescription may not sync properly to your pharmacy's mobile app or online portal, even if your pharmacy has additional pre-dated prescriptions saved to your profile. This means you may not be able to determine how many "refills" you have by looking at the refill count online, even as this is incredibly important in determining when you next need a med check to get another refill. Thus, you'll need to calendar that yourself, planning your med check at least a week *before* your script runs out. Better yet, make your next follow-up appointment before you leave the office, even if that's ninety days in advance.

- An app like Medisafe helps immensely. Its refill reminders send push notifications when your pill count drops to a certain pre-set number, which is fantastic when managing stimulants. If you're not a digital fan, just copy the template below, enter the information at the time of your appointment and hang it somewhere you'll notice before you need it. Since our office requires follow-up appointments at least every three months, this template provides only three lines. You can easily modify this reminder chart to reflect your prescriber's protocol.

-My Stimulant Prescriptions-

My prescriptions can be filled on or after the following dates:

Script 1 Date: _____

Script 2 Date: _____

Script 2 Date: _____

Did I make a future medication appointment at the interval recommended by my prescriber?

☐ YES: Date_____   Time_____

☐ NO: But, to avoid running out of medicine, I will need to make an appointment by this date: _____

Dealing with Insurance

- *Dr. Wes* -

Unless you're independently wealthy, your insurance coverage will heavily influence how you manage your meds. Sometimes, it's more significant than any other single factor in your care. Nothing frustrates us or our clients more than dealing with the interplay between big pharma and big health insurance.

You or your ADD loved one may have little previous experience with health insurance. The only prescriptions you may have filled were for antibiotics, allergy medications, contraception, etc., none of which have the same dynamics at play. Once introduced to this dysfunctional world, many clients, and particularly those with ADD, become over-whelmed. Often, a key job of a treatment team is helping clients navigate the strange twists and turns of health insurance. That's a nice thought isn't it—having to get mental health treatment to counteract the stress of paying for mental health treatment? It is, as they say, what it is. So, here's a primer on managing your plan.

Formularies

As the breadth and number of medications for all conditions grew in the 1980s and 1990s, a complex dance emerged between the pharmaceutical companies and the insurance carriers. Manufacturers needed to create new and supposedly better medications and get them to market at a price that turned a profit for their investors. As any *Shark Tank* fan knows, if you don't have enough margin between the cost to research, manufacture, and market a product and the price you charge at point of sale, it doesn't matter how many units you sell. Drug manufacturers either make their money this way or get sold to the highest bidder.

Insurance companies make their profit on the margin between what their covered lives pay in premiums and their cost of administration, marketing, and payout on medical claims for products and services rendered. Over the last thirty years, prescription costs have risen to constitute about seventeen percent of total healthcare expenditure[205]. Of this, seventy percent goes to "retail drugs" which are sold direct to consumer through a local pharmacy, just as we're describing in this

---

[205] aspe.hhs.gov/system/files/pdf/187586/Drugspending.pdf

chapter. The rest were dispensed as a part of inpatient care at, say, a hospital or other care facility.

To try and keep their margins high (sometimes wildly so), health insurance companies began creating "drug formularies," commonly defined by insurance companies as:

> A list of prescription drugs, both generic and brand name, used by practitioners to identify drugs that offer the greatest overall value. A committee of independent, actively practicing physicians and pharmacists maintain the formulary[206].

As is typical in the insurance world, this makes the formulary sound quite beneficial to the covered life (you). Highly qualified folks are taking the time to sit down and figure out the best medications for your situation, so you and your doctor don't have to. Except if you read the definition that way, you missed three words: "greatest overall value."

A drug formulary is not a list of the best medications for your condition. Not by a long shot. It reflects the cheapest medications the drug company can get its hands on, meaning either generic or discounted. We discussed generics in Chapter 6. Discounted means that the drug company incentivizes the insurance company to feature its medication on the formulary. This is why, back in the day, brand name Concerta was on many formularies right from the start. Janssen had some kind of arrangement with many companies to carry it, whereas Shire did not market Adderall XR in the same way and it was left off many formularies.

There are several ways formularies can be laid out, but the most common includes three "tiers." The lowest tier is all generic. In order to incentivize consumers to select one of these, the insurance company charges the lowest copay, usually at or below $15. The second tier usually contains a few more expensive generics and the brand name drugs that either don't have a generic equivalent or are incentivized by the manufacturer. The copay here is usually $35 to $40. The third tier contains approved brand name products with copays of $60 or more.

There's usually an unlisted "fourth tier" of medications that the insurance company simply will not pay for. These typically have a less

---

[206] secure.wecareforwisconsin.com/customers/formulary/what_is_a_drug_formulary/

expensive "preferred" alternative on a lower tier, which is supposedly equivalent to the brand name drug.

None of this has anything to do with making the correct prescription choice for you. It simply means the "qualified professionals" decided the insurance company could get away with refusing to include a specific product in favor of a cheaper one. It's kind of like Consumer Reports, except in this case the pharmaceutical company has a stake in what you decide to do, and thus they cannot be seen as unbiased.

Prior-authorization (PA)

The bane of a prescriber's existence, nearly every psychopharmaceutical not listed on the first or second tier of a formulary requires your prescriber to fill out paperwork, usually online, to explain why the "qualified professionals" in the insurance company are wrong and that yes, the prescriber wasn't kidding when she wrote the prescription, and this really, really is the right medication for you. And how big a pain in the butt is this? Kelsey spends more time doing PAs than anything else except face-to-face time with clients, and none of that time is paid for.

At the risk of being reductive, prior-authorizations come in two flavors. The first serves no purpose except, in our estimation, to make it aversive enough for prescribers that they give up and prescribe on the lower tier of the formulary. No, really. We believe this is an intentional ordeal to discourage prescriptions outside of tier one, because under this condition, the prescriber only has to say, "I authorize this" and sign off. That's it. Yet, the time it takes to coordinate this, get it done, and get it submitted, is just enough to make it annoying.

The second flavor of PA, is the one that requires you to have a prior history of "failing" two other medication trials. This is the insurance company's attempt to join the experiment by proposing that you first try lower tier medications before moving on to something more expensive. On the surface, this seems pretty sensible. Why pay more money out of your pocket or theirs for an expensive drug when a cheap one will do?

The problem lies in what it means to "fail" a medication. If the med runs out too early in the day, is that a failure? If it interrupts appetite, is that a failure? This whole concept is drawn from other classes of medications where it makes more sense. A drug either does or doesn't lower your blood pressure, or it does or doesn't give you side effects while doing so. Impact, efficacy, and side effects are more abstruse and subtle in the world of psychopharmaceuticals. While we do sometimes get negative results, "failing" isn't how we'd describe the process. More like "tuning" your medications as if they were delicate instruments. But that's not how insurance companies want to spend money. Good enough is good enough, as long as it's cheap.

We resist the temptation to give up and go low. We try to tailor exactly the right stimulant to each client, so Kelsey ends up writing a lot of prior-authorizations and then having to renew them at least every year—which also makes no sense outside of our "ordeal theory." And this doesn't just happen when we finally get the right drug figured out. She has to do a new PA every time we try something new that doesn't appear on the company's lower tier, and considering how limited most of those tiers are, that's eighty to ninety percent of the time.

Deductibles

Over the last decade, insurance companies have also increased their profit margins by offering high deductible plans. If you're coming at this cold, you probably haven't given your deductible much thought, particularly if you're on your parents' or someone else's plan. So, here's a checklist of what you need to know to make sensible treatment decisions. I realize it's super boring, but you must know the answer to each question, or you could end up with a very exciting bill in the mail.

What Exactly Is a Deductible? That seems like an easy question to answer, doesn't it? Nope. In its simplest form, the deductible is what you pay for a service or prescription before the insurance company starts paying whatever they're going to pay at whatever rate they are going to pay it.

Some plans really are simple. You pay the first, say, $5,000 on all your medical treatment over a given year[207], at which point the insurance company starts paying either a set amount per claim or a percentage of the claim. Other plans, including my wife's (on which I am covered)

---

[207] Different plans have different cycles. Most are January 1 to December 31, but many schools and colleges follow the academic year. Some plans use your start date and then reset your deductible on that anniversary. Know when your plan resets.

are set up so that the insurance company pays a copay or coinsurance[208] from day one on all office visits and the deductible is only relevant to certain services like surgery, emergency room visits, MRIs, x-rays, and so on. For this, and most similar plans, medication is also paid on a copay using the aforementioned multi-tiered formulary.

How Much Is It? This seems easy, too, like you'd just look on your policy and see the word "deductible" and know what it is. That's usually true if you're the only person on your policy. However, many people are on a family policy, particularly if they're under age twenty-six or married or have kids of their own. Those policies typically have two deductibles, one for the individual and a higher one for the family.

For example, a common policy we see has a $2,700 deductible for the client and a $5,400 deductible for the family. If Eliza meets her $2,700 deductible, her services will then be paid in part by the insurance company. If she goes to the emergency room for a broken leg and pays out $5,400 (which is entirely possible, ouch), she's not only covered her deductible but also her family's. Now everyone on the policy—even if it's a family of ten—will have their services covered in part by the insurance company for the rest of the policy year. If Eliza meets her $2,700 deductible and her sister, Angelica, meets her $2,700 deductible, both young women and everyone else in the family will have met the deductible because, together, the sisters spent $5,400. So, when Peggy goes in for knee surgery, the family will pay a fraction of the cost out of pocket[209] with no deductible left to worry about.

Beyond this distinction between individual and family, insurance plans come in two general forms. Low deductible plans run somewhere between $1,000 and $2,000 for the individual and $2,000 to $3,000 for the family. We count high deductible plans as anything over $6,000 for the individual and $10,000 for the family.

When Does My Deductible Apply? Yet again, the answer is as clear as mud, particularly when it comes to mental health coverage. As noted, some plans require you to pay everything out of pocket until

---

[208] These represent the cost you pay for a given service. A copay is a set amount, like $25 for an office visit or $100 for a trip to the ER. Coinsurance is a percentage, often 20 to 50% of the cost of the given service.

[209] Speaking of which, most policies also have an "out of pocket max" meaning that at some point the insurance company takes over at 100%. That's usually a pretty hefty figure and rarely relevant unless something really bad happens.

you meet your deductible. Other plans allow you to pay a copay or coinsurance for office visits but then apply certain procedures like surgery and ER visits to the deductible.

There's a third condition that we've only run into with a single insurance company in a single city. Kansas City Blue Cross claims that it can differentially reimburse medical providers and mental health providers, despite federal laws that require parity between the two. This means that they will pay for Dr. Kelsey's medication services because they fall under an "office visit," but they impute all my fees to the client's deductible, requiring the client to pay 100% out of pocket until that deductible is met, usually at least $1,000. When challenged on this, Kansas City Blue Cross essentially said that their billing process is legal because they say it is and no one has challenged them. This leaves middle and lower income people out of luck when it comes to mental health coverage.

The higher the deductible, the lower your premiums, so there's a calculus at play that only a few people spend time figuring out in advance.

Should I Pick a High or Low Deductible Plan? This is complicated, too. The higher the deductible, the lower your premiums, so there's a calculus at play that only a few people spend time figuring out in advance. About ten years ago, my wife's employer offered a high deductible plan for the first time. I sat down and developed a huge spreadsheet that extrapolated our cost savings over ten years, factoring in the substantial savings in premiums against our substantial outlay of cash for services and medication. After two and one half years, the retention/expenditure lines finally crossed and we would begin saving a little bit of money. However, in that two years, we'd have paid out of pocket tens of thousands of dollars for costs that the more expensive plan covered on a copay basis. In the end, I determined it just wasn't worth it.

Given my Type-2 diabetes and high blood pressure, I'm a high-end user and perhaps not typical among the covered lives on my wife's plan. So, I asked around to see how others' calculations had come out. Every person I spoke with stared blankly at me. One asked if I could run his numbers through my spreadsheet. At that moment, two things became apparent to me: not many people are skilled at Microsoft

Excel, and if one is not good at longitudinal analysis of health care cost and payment curves, one probably should not purchase a high deductible plan.

That said, a high deductible policy can be a good deal for some people if *all* of the following conditions are met:

- The premium is so much lower on the high-deductible plan than it is for a low plan that the person saves enough money over the course of a year to pay all of their out-of-pocket expenses and still has money left over.

- The person is in excellent health and is unlikely to need any services other than routine prevention and an occasional trip for minor medical attention.

- The person has access to a Health Savings or Flex Benefits account (see next section) that creates a tax-deferred bank account that will cover most of the deductible.

However, there's a catch. People tend to make three huge mistakes with higher deductible plans:

- They don't keep the money they saved from lower premiums and put it toward their health care, either in a health savings account (best) or in an interest-bearing bank account. The only way high deductible plans work well is if you plan for the worst and hope for the best. If you don't create that savings account—and most people don't—you'll end up with big medical bills and no financial reserve. That's the number one reason for bankruptcy filings in the United States.

- They're so frugal with healthcare spending that they only meet their deductible in the last two or three months of the year. One cannot predict the future, but if you know you'll always meet your deductible by the end of the year, you shouldn't hold back on medically necessary spending. I have one family who just can't get the hang of this. They scrimp on their child's care all through the year, choosing the cheapest medication and down-sizing the number of sessions she comes in. Then, when they meet her deductible in October[210], the last two

---

[210] Their deductible turns over on January 1 every year.

months of the year they enjoy an 80/20 coinsurance, which they can easily afford, and want to start experimenting with different meds and coming to therapy more often. While we don't condone splurging on unnecessary treatment, we do recommend getting what you or your child need when it's needed not when it's cheaper. Better to meet the deductible in May or June and gain the benefit for the year than to wait for it to be paid and then play catch up.

- They don't seek routine preventive care and end up spending more in the long run when serious illness catches up with them. One of the best arguments for a copay-based system is that it keeps people healthier and thus, in the long run, spending less on medical care. While remodeling, I recently jammed my left hand into an exposed stud. When it still hurt the next day, I feared a fracture in my pinky and/or ring finger. Since it was only a $50 copay to see an urgent care doctor and I'd already met my deductible, I didn't hesitate to go in on a Sunday morning for an x-ray. It was close, but no fracture, so I didn't gain much for my cautious approach. But had the hand been broken, and I didn't seek immediate diagnosis and treatment because it cost too much out of pocket, things could have turned out much worse—including a delay on this book because, typing.

Persons who do sign up for high deductible plans may find it helpful to seek out a concierge physician, a doctor who takes a monthly subscription, usually under $100, to provide all needed medical attention. This won't cover medication, testing, surgery, or hospital stays, but it will definitely address the problem of avoiding services.

To answer this question for readers of this book, we must ask ourselves whether the average person with ADD is likely to meet all of the above criteria to benefit from a high deductible plan. In general, the answer is "no." The annual cost of treatment with the best (affordable) medications and therapy we recommend here will likely be around $6,000 depending on the severity of the case. That includes only a single medication (I used Vyvanse in my calculation) and twenty-four total sessions of assessment, therapy, and medication management. One would be better off paying for a plan that covered part of that cost up front than paying all that out in cash.

By definition, a person with ADD is not in "excellent health" because he or she has a long-term, expensive condition requiring ongoing treatment. Moreover, if the annual cost is $6,000, one is better off paying for the more expensive policy and getting more health care for the same price. Folks with ADD are especially prone to avoid routine healthcare to begin with. If they start having to pay out of pocket each time, their motivation won't improve. Finally, it's hard enough for neurotypical folks to set aside money for future health care. For those with ADD, prone to quick gratification, saving money is usually the problem not the solution. We're not in the insurance business (don't own any stock there either) but we've seen many folks make the wrong choice on this and end up paying more than they expected for unexpected healthcare costs, while getting a lot less than what they need.

Health Savings (HSA) and Flex Spending Accounts (FSA)

For employer-based insurance, one or both of these plans is usually available. HSAs can be unlimited in how much is withheld or retained each year, and they are often used to offset the high deductible plans. Some HSAs are directly tied to them. Most start at zero and have an employer contribution and an optional employee contribution that builds monthly. An HSA can be rolled over year after year, indefinitely so you can keep paying into it and, presuming you don't need to access the money, building up a sizable account. The only catch is that the money can only be used for health costs.

FSAs are funded by the individual, not the employer, through payroll withdrawal. They're limited to around $2,650 per family and are usually fully funded at the beginning of the policy year, then paid back over the next twelve months. If you have a sudden expense early on, the FSA can pay it, up to the full-funded amount. The HSA can pay only what has been saved. On the other hand, the FSA does not "rollover" on an annual basis. You must spend it or lose it during the policy year.

FSA accounts don't draw interest. HSA accounts may draw a small interest and others can be invested in stocks and bonds like an IRA. Beyond making sure you have a financial reserve, the main benefit of an HSA or an FSA is that both offer a tax shelter. That's especially true for people who cannot deduct medical expenses, which is just about everyone who isn't very old or who does not have a medical condition that consumes a far greater than average portion of his or her income. This is because the money that goes into these accounts is drawn from your paycheck before taxes. The HSA is paid as an untaxed benefit or withdrawn in the same way from your salary.

How Much Should I Save? With the HSA there's no downside to accumulating as much money each month as you can afford because you'll use it eventually for a major medical event or even in your retirement years for services Medicare doesn't cover. Because it doesn't roll over, the FSA is trickier to calculate. If your total cost for medication, med checks, and therapy combined with all other medical expenses for you or your family are likely to reach the yearly maximum, you should put the full amount into your FSA plan. It's like getting $2,650 off your taxable income and it's available on day one. If, instead, you find that your projected expenses for treating ADD and all other health costs in the family are say, $1,200 a year, set the withdrawal at $100 a month for twelve months. Just don't set the FSA withdrawal higher than you can reasonably use up in the policy year or they get to keep it. If you do that, talk to your HR person. It may be possible to use your FSA plan for over-the-counter drugs if your prescriber will write a script for you. So if you take, say, Claritin or melatonin you can have your physician prescribe it and then pay with the FSA.

Discount Cards

One of my kids has taken stimulants for fifteen years, the other for ten. Neither has ever paid the formulary price for Vyvanse or Daytrana, even when it was on tier three. I've often gotten copay discounts for my diabetes and high blood pressure meds too, you can do likewise, and it's easy. Before you start any brand name medication for ADD (or anything else), go to the manufacturer's website and see if they offer a discount program. If you Google "Vyvanse discount card" or "Mydayis discount card" you should go straight to the button you want to click. Each year, you'll click the same button to get a new discount card. Just be sure you're really on the website for the product and not an aftermarket coupon. As we'll discuss later, there can be value in cards like GoodRx, but only in the generic market. Here, we're talking about getting hundreds of dollars a year off brand name copays and for that you have to go to the source.

So, what's going on here? Where pharmaceutical companies used to discount products to get them placed on the cheaper tiers of formularies, they've now come up with a far more ingenious approach—incentivizing the consumer. When they first started doing this, the companies asked for lots of data about applicants, and they wanted to enroll you in their email SPAM campaign. But fairly quickly, they realized the real value of this program and made it super easy to access, no questions asked. In one fell swoop, the pharmaceutical companies found a way around formularies thereby getting the insurance carriers to cover their much more expensive medications by offering a loss leader direct to the consumer. For once, the consumer won. But so did the stockholders of Shire and other super-pharmas, due to the greatly increased sales these deals generated for new products. And as Yoni Blumberg points out in an article written for CNBC[211], you can bet that any losses sustained from the discount cards are recovered in overall higher drug prices. So, don't cry for the pharmaceutical companies or build a shrine to their generosity, but also don't miss out on an opportunity to save. If you want to learn even more about these schemes—and really who doesn't?—check out C Lee Ventola (2011)[212].

> *For high deductible plans, discount cards won't help much because pharmaceutical companies are banking on gaining access to your insurance benefits.*

For those with high deductible plans, discount cards won't help much because pharmaceutical companies are banking (literally) on gaining access to your insurance benefits by cutting your copay. If there is no benefit to tap into, they aren't willing to give you the loss leader. For example, Shire advertises Vyvanse will cost "no more than $25 a month," but notice the fine print limiting that savings to $75, which just happens to equal the highest copay on the top tier of most drug formularies. That means that on a high deductible plan you'll be charged the full price of about $265 each month minus the $75 from the Shire discount card, leaving you with a price tag of $190 a month. Pretty steep for most consumers.

---

[211] www.cnbc.com/2019/01/10/why-prescription-drugs-in-the-us-cost-so-much.html

[212] www.ncbi.nlm.nih.gov/pmc/articles/PMC3278148/

GoodRx

A different kind of discount card operates at the periphery of the pharmaceutical industry. The most common one is GoodRx. According to Wikipedia, GoodRx is a private startup company founded in 2011 by former Facebook executives Doug Hirsch and Scott Marlette and headquartered in Santa Monica, California. It is described as:

> A free-to-use website and mobile app that tracks prescription drug prices and offers drug coupons in the United States. GoodRx checks more than 75,000 pharmacies in the United States and gets about four million visitors a month… In 2017, GoodRx announced partnerships with major prescription drug companies in the country to negotiate lower prescription drug costs[213].

According to Ellen Sheng, for CNBC[214] Hirsch came up with the idea, as you might, after being told that a single prescription would cost him $450. He set out to do some price comparison and found at the next pharmacy, a price of "just" $300 for the same product. A third store wanted to negotiate with him, offering to match the price at the other pharmacy. Somewhere in here, Hirsch got the idea to search the drug name on Google for other prices, only to learn that this wasn't a thing. Yet. Unlike shopping for plane tickets or shoes, Hirsch learned that drug prices were impossible to attain until you were standing at the pharmacy trying to fill a prescription[215].

As a good capitalist, Hirsch decided that the secret to lowering drug prices was exploiting competition much as gas stations offer comparable or lower costs per gallon of gas. He built GoodRx to allow consumers to find and compare prescription prices close to their home or work. To break into this secretive world, he somehow found a way to partner with all the big pharmacies, CVS, Target, Walgreens, Kroger, and Walmart and with pharmacy benefits managers Express Scripts and Caremark. He even got the pharmaceutical companies themselves on board—sort of. Sounds like a fascinating adventure, and as a result, you can now get real-time prices on medications at 70,000 locations

---

[213] en.wikipedia.org/wiki/GoodRx

[214] www.cnbc.com/2019/05/15/goodrx-app-has-saved-americans-more-than-10-billion-on-prescriptions.html

[215] This was before Walmart started posting its prices online.

nationwide, as I did in Chapter 6. Using this system, the company claims consumers can save up to eighty percent with their free GoodRx pharmacy discount card and coupons. They claim they've saved users some $10 billion in prescriptions costs since launching in 2011. Wow.

And now for the catch. You knew it was coming, didn't you? GoodRx only has access to information on how much patients would pay for their prescriptions without insurance. Buying that way might be a better deal than going with the drug formulary, particularly if you have a high deductible plan, but only for generic medications. But what you pay when using your insurance is governed not by the market place, but by your company's formulary. When it comes to brand name stimulant medication, you'll have to stick with the manufacturer's discount card or, if that won't work because you're on a high deductible plan, the generic extended release versions of Concerta and Adderall XR. Or, you could try our next idea.

Patient Assistance Programs (PAPs)

- Dr. Kelsey -

PAPs were created by pharmaceutical companies to provide free or discounted medicines to people who would otherwise be unable to afford them. A pretty good synopsis of how they work can be found on a website called Needy Meds[216]. In this regard, PAPs violate the loss leader concept discussed above, existing as a way to show the public that big pharma isn't a predatory, money hungry, capitalist enterprise. Except, (catch warning!) the foundations these companies established for this altruistic purpose provide big tax breaks to the manufacturers through charitable contributions that would not have existed had their prices been more affordable in the first place. Moreover, while PAPs work for some folks, they still exclude millions of people who don't meet their income requirements, but who are still so financially strapped that they cannot afford prescriptions. So, I'll leave it to you to decide how well the drug manufacturers are doing on the PR side of things.

Cynicism aside, PAPs may be of great value to you if you have a high medication cost and not enough income to cover it. Most are available directly through their parent drug company's website. To qualify, some

---

[216] www.needymeds.org/pap

require you to have commercial insurance and an income that falls beneath a certain threshold. Others only accept applicants who have a qualifying income but are uninsured. For example, a two-person household making up to $48,720 with a Vyvanse copay of $50 or a deductible greater than $1,000 would qualify for free medication for twelve months. Usually, you can renew your application each year as you continue to meet the criteria.

Yes, this is all pretty confusing, particularly because each PAP operates independently, has its own qualifying criteria, and is highly subject to change. Even with the links listed above, you'll need your prescriber to help you figure it all out, which is one reason many prescribers may not be too interested in mentioning this idea. It's another time-suck. The Needy Meds website can help you search medications of interest and sort out the details before you talk with your prescriber. Or you can use our list in Figure 5, which was current as of March 2020.

Figure 5: Selected Patient Assistance Programs

Vyvanse	www.shire.com/patients/patient-services/shire-cares
Latuda	www.sunovionsupport.com/latuda/index.html
Rexulti	www.otsukapatientassistance.com/check-eligibility
Trintellix	www.takeda.com/siteassets/en-us/home/corporate -responsibility/patient-assistance/hah_application.pdf
Fetzima	allergan-web-cdn-prod.azureedge.net/actavis/actavis/media/pdfdocu- ments/patientassistanceprogram/allergan-us-pap-application.pdf
Clomipramine	www.rxhope.com/pap/pdf/mallinckrodt_pharma_ 0209.pdf

Now you know the best way to get on the right stimulants, how to manage them over the long term, and even how to pay for them using every trick in a very tricky book. With that, let's turn to the dark—or at least the annoying—side of stimulant medication.

Side Effects and Workarounds

There are downsides to everything; there are unintended consequences to everything.

— Steve Jobs

- Dr. Wes -

"We do like what the medication is doing for Trevor." Mrs. Malden shook her head and smiled a tense smile. "But, the side effects are making it hard to want to continue."

"Ugh," I said. "Give me the list, and we'll see what we can come up with to problem-solve."

"First off," she said. "His sleep is worse than it was before medication. We actually watched that closely because, as we discussed in the first session, it wasn't good to begin with. We kind of hoped it would improve, like you said it does with some kids."

"Yeah. I just saw one of those the other day. I'm sorry you're not getting the same benefit, Trevor. What else are you seeing?"

"His weight," Mr. Malden said. "You said that for guys this is sometimes less of a problem, but Trevor doesn't seem to be able to eat unless he's pretty hungry and with the medicine, he usually isn't."

I nodded. "That seems truer for late teens. Trevor is, fourteen, right?" I glanced at my chart. "No. Fifteen. You just had a birthday."

"I did," Trevor said. "And even though mom made my favorite double chocolate fudge cake I didn't even want to eat it."

"That's terrible," I said. "And you were on medication that day?"

"Yes," Mrs. Malden said. "We celebrated on Friday because he had a soccer game on Saturday. I guess the meds hadn't worn off by the time we ate dinner. He picked at his food and blew out the candles and left most of his slice behind."

"How about Saturday?" I asked. "Did you skip medication like we discussed last week?"

"Yeah," Trevor said. "And I definitely played better off of it. Before, when I was taking it on game days, I was like really focused on the ball. I knew where it was every minute of the game, but I just didn't have a lot of spark, you know?"

"Right," I said. "That is kind of the point of this medication. I know people who do better in sports while taking it, but usually it's more about studying than tearing up the soccer field."

"Tell me about it," Trevor said.

"Nice job noticing and reporting back," I said. "That helps us a lot. So, on Saturday evening, did you get to finish the leftover cake?"

"Yes," Mrs. Malden spoke up. "He ate a full dinner and had two pieces, one right after dinner and another before bed."

"How about breakfast?" I glanced toward Trevor.

"Which day?" he asked. "I mean, I don't usually eat much breakfast on or off meds, but I'd say I was a lot hungrier than usual on Saturday. So I had eggs."

I turned to Trevor's dad. "Anything you can add?"

"He's right," Mr. Malden said. "We can't seem to get him to eat much before school. He's always slow waking up, then he has trouble getting around, and he's kind of sleepy and just not with it. But that's not new with meds."

"And besides, it wouldn't be in his system by breakfast time," I said. "Even if he's taking it when he gets up. I'm afraid to ask, but how's lunch going?"

"As bad as you think," Trevor said. "I'm lucky if I can eat a couple chicken nuggets."

"Was your lunch appetite better before medication?" I asked. "I mean the chicken nuggets at my high school were kind of disgusting, so..."

"They still are, but before medicine I could load 'em up with ketchup or barbeque sauce and get by. Now, they just kind of get stuck in my throat, like my body doesn't want to let them in. Like, I'd barf if I pushed them down."

I chuckled. "With such a vivid description, I feel like I'm almost there in the school cafeteria, ready to barf myself."

"Please don't." Trevor laughed. "Sorry. Too much information."

"Which brings us to dinner." I turned to Trevor's parents. "What time do you typically eat?"

"He gets home from practice about five o'clock," Mrs. Malden said. "And the rest of the family gets there over the next hour, and then we like to sit down and have dinner as close to six as we can."

"Like on one of those Hallmark Channel shows," Trevor grinned. "We all sit around the table and pray. It's super weird."

"Hey there," I said. "That's a nice tradition. Some families are always like, grab and go. You might miss that family dinner someday."

"Maybe," Trevor said. "Problem is, there's no way I'm hungry at six, so I just sit there and at like, ten thirty, I come down and eat leftovers."

"We really need to get him over that," Mrs. Malden said. "It's not healthy, and I'm sure that's contributing to him being up at night."

"Maybe," I said. "Here's the deal. These medications were originally intended as diet pills, so they're working their appetite suppression magic on a guy who needs to lose weight like I need a hole in my head."

"So what do we do?" Mr. Malden asked. "I mean if he's going to keep playing soccer, or anything else, he has to eat. He's already lost five or eight pounds this month. We have to do something."

"I'm not saying it isn't a problem." I tapped my keyboard and brought up some links I keep on file for such occasions. "Do we agree that, aside from annoying side effects, the medication is worth continuing?"

"Yes," Mrs. Malden said.

Mr. Malden nodded in agreement. "He's actually doing homework. We haven't had time to see if that translates into grades, but the first emails back from his teachers indicate he's holding it together in class with less clowning and more useful contributions."

"No more clowning," I typed into my computer as I said the words out loud. "That seems like a tragic side effect to have. Almost as bad as not being hungry for cake."

Trevor laughed. "No kidding. But, I have to admit that while I miss my old jackass self, I thought about what you said last time, how there's a time and a place for everything and that school probably wasn't the time or place for replaying the latest *Maximum Fun* podcast."

"Yeah," I said. "I like the hilarity of the McElroy brothers[217], too, but not in the middle of Algebra, yah know? So our goal is to save the medication and try and work around the side effects, because to be honest, we're not going to get rid of them entirely."

Everyone nodded. Then, Mrs. Malden spoke again. "Is it worth trying a different medication?"

"Kelsey and I will discuss that, but you may not see a big difference with these particular side effects. If Trevor's hungry then he's probably not on enough medication or he's built a tolerance to it. The art here is to work with the side effects and not give into them; to sort of integrate them into your life. There are three things I'd like to try. First, we really need to get breakfast into him, and given his weight loss, the more healthy fat he can eat, the better. I'd try and find the most delicious granola you can, or I have some recipes that you can use to make it yourself."

"Okay." Mrs. Malden, started jotting notes into her daily planner. "I think the local natural grocery store has a few good ones. Would you eat something like for breakfast, Trevor?"

"Maybe," he said. "If it tasted good enough to get me hungry."

"Also," I said. "He needs some long acting carbs and vegetable fat at lunch. I'm no chef, but I also have several recipes for oatmeal bars with

---

[217] www.maximumfun.org/shows/my-brother-my-brother-and-me

peanut butter and, if you want, chocolate chips. That will keep his sugars steady and probably taste better than crappy chicken nuggets."

"Why oatmeal?" Trevor asked.

"It breaks down to sugar slowly so you'll have more energy in the afternoon. You said last time that you were really dragging late in the school day. That could be medication washout, but it could just as easily be a drop in blood sugar because you're not eating."

"And the peanut butter is fat," Mr. Malden said. "Do you think you could shove that down at lunch?"

"Yeah, maybe." Trevor lit up at this change in the menu. "If you added the chocolate chips, that would be like, dessert."

"Exactly, except healthy," I said. "But let's just ignore that part and go with the dessert motif. The goal is to override his lack of appetite with something hard to resist."

"Could we just buy those oatmeal bars at the store?" Mrs. Malden asked. "I'm a good accountant but not much of a baker."

"Just be aware that prepackaged foods have more corn syrup than necessary. We want a slow release sugar, not a big rush after lunch. And besides, some of these recipes are no-bake so you can't really screw them up."

"I don't know," Trevor said. "Mom's a pretty terrible cook."

"I'll give it my best shot." She smiled. "And you can help, Trevor." She turned back to me. "You said there were three things to change."

"Trevor, you need to come to the dinner table to do your talking and praying, but don't pick at your food or even get a plate. When my kids and I are on vacation, if they're taking meds, we don't even go out to eat until at least 8:30 p.m. Otherwise, we have a bunch of leftovers to take back to the hotel. Just plan on eating about that time each evening. If you try to eat earlier you'll just tamp down your appetite."

Mrs. Malden sighed. "I don't like it, but I guess I'll have to give in for a higher cause. And what about sleep? Any recipes for that?"

"I'll schedule you with Kelsey for next week. In the meantime, she'll want you to try melatonin. For some people, it helps. For others, no dice or the effect doesn't last. If his sleep isn't improved by next week, we'll need to look at adding something like trazadone or clonidine."

"What about an over-the-counter medication, like Benadryl?" Mr. Malden asked. "Might that be safer than a prescription?"

"Maybe, maybe not," I said. "It can drag one down in the morning, which is the last thing this guy needs, and he'll build tolerance to it, so it will quit working, except for the blah part. Try the melatonin as soon as you can and when you come in to see Kelsey next time, you'll already have data on how it worked."

"Will doing all this straighten everything out?" Mr. Malden asked.

"Nope," I said.

Everyone sat in stunned silence.

"I'm not going to BS you. Most people who need to be on these meds develop a love-hate relationship with them. I've seen stimulants take a B-average student and turn her into a 4.0 graduate student. My daughter is a good example. But most clients fight the side effects every day of the week. They learn to work around them—how to sleep, when to eat, what not to do before bed. The side effects may still be annoying, but in the end, adaptation will get the job done."

- Dr. Wes -

Maximizing the love and minimizing the hate you have with your medication regimen is easier said than done. Above all else it takes (say it with me now!) communicating effectively with your prescriber how you're experiencing your meds. We suggest starting with your therapist and having a trial discussion ahead of time, as Trevor and his parents did with me. We spend at least five or ten minutes discussing meds every time an ADD client comes in for therapy. I even have a check box for that on my notes form so our staff won't forget. If you're getting your meds from a different office, this will usually be a practice round before you go in for a med check. If your therapist and prescriber are in the same clinic, he or she should pass along the information before your next med check to spark discussion.

What is and isn't a stimulant side effect can itself be a complicated question, particularly if you're new to all this. So, here's a point-by-point structure around which to conduct your self-examination and discussion of side effects and some ways to work around each one.

Is This Really Me?

A "side effect" reflected in the title of this book is so common that I've taken to calling it "AIRM syndrome," which stands for "Am I really myself?" As we discussed early on, how you answer that question requires you first to define who you "really are." Are you that off-meds person who can't focus or get anything done? Or is that the person you became, minus the correct brain chemistry?

Remember Josh from Chapter 1 who complained about feeling like a zombie while on stimulants because he just wanted to "sit there reading a book?" One person's liberation is another person's inhibition. If you hate being studious, then you may associate focus and concentration with being disconnected from your impulsive, lively self. Trevor also alluded to this in his comment about losing his class clown status on medication, but he also understood the "time and place" point I'd made the week before. A critical part of being on meds is picking who you mean to be in a given situation or context, not just going with your gut or listening to your heart.

On the other hand, certain stimulants can make certain people feel too serious, drab, or lifeless for the situation at hand. That's not what we're going for. Your job is to try and dig deep and see if the person you are on stimulants is a better version of you and not a zombie substitute. Be sure you consider carefully your viewpoints (and biases) before interpreting your own inner process. It's the very definition of a matter of perspective.

Anastasia was a fascinating high school girl who had just gone on medication for anxiety. Though not treated for ADD, her story illustrates this self-exploration nicely. After about two weeks on Lexapro, her mother was so impressed with her improved mood, reduced irritability, and less anxious behavior that she declared, "This medication has been like a ray of sunshine in our lives!"

Note to parents: never say this. Even in your own head. Just don't.

Anastasia was furious. How dare her mother comment on her mood stability, particularly when assigning its origins to a bottle of pills! It was, for her, an abomination. She might even have used that word. At sixteen, Anastasia was a connoisseur of words who later majored in English. But at our session the week after her mom's "ray of sunshine" comment, Anastasia wasn't sure she even wanted to continue with meds.

"I don't want to not feel anything," she fumed. "I don't want to have my emotions suppressed. That's not who I am."

"Really?" I asked. "So the real Ana is the girl who used to sit in my office every week and sob, even though she couldn't identify anything that was bothering her. That's you?"

"Maybe. Isn't it okay if it is? Why should I be taking medication just to make other people feel comfortable around me?"

"You shouldn't be," I said. "That's a terrible reason to take medication, and if that's why you're taking it, then you need to get with Kelsey, taper off and stop. Medication must never be an agent of social control or a matter of the comfort of others. You're not a Stepford daughter."

"I don't know," she sighed. "I just don't know which girl I am. This one on meds or the other, sad one that felt everything so deeply."

"I'll support whatever you choose," I said. "And I'll make that super clear to your mom. We're not medicating anybody, child, teen, or adult, who is not fully vested in this process. But, before you pull the plug, I'd like you to go home and think about this for a couple weeks until we meet again. Think about both those girls inside you, the emotional one and the one who can choose when and what she wants to let into and out of her heart. Then decide which path you want to go on, because that choice belongs only to you. Your body, your rules."

Anastasia returned in two weeks and announced her decision to remain on medication. She finished high school and went on to graduate from an urban university. We eventually switched her to Effexor, which was an even more effective agent in managing her anxiety with less impact on her personality. Over the course of time, Ana became a true believer not in the "ray of sunshine" illusion, but in the idea that medication could allow her to be more fully who she was.

Low Appetite

Though less existential than AIRM syndrome, appetite suppression causes a lot of people to quit stimulants voluntarily or at the direction of their prescriber. It's especially problematic if you have a low Body Mass Index (BMI) of 17 to 20 to begin with. But even if you can stand to lose thirty pounds, your prescriber won't like it if your stimulant puts you on a crash diet and, believe me, it happens for all the reasons noted in the opening vignette.

Though we don't keep statistics on this, we generally find appetite suppression worse for children and teens of all genders and for young adult women. It's less so for late teen boys and adult men. We hypothesize that this is because children and teens eat mostly in response to cravings with a preference for sugar, salt, and fat instead of behavioral or social cues like, "it's lunch time." When those urges are suppressed with medication, kids have trouble willing themselves to eat.

For women, particularly teens, the societal imperative tends toward calorie restriction. In a worst case scenario, this results in anorexia nervosa. However, many young women are, in the parlance of this book, "anorexic leaners," with subclinical propensities to restrict that go unnoticed in a culture that values such discipline, no matter how unhealthy it may be. Since self-regulation is a problem, most teen girls and young women with ADD cannot will themselves to restrict caloric intake—until you hand them a stimulant that gives them the power to thwart their appetites and to become successful dieters. This is rarely a conscious choice, but an unconscious yielding to opportunity. In short, more women like this side effect, while men tend to eat whether they're hungry or not and can sidestep low appetite more easily.

As illustrated in Trevor's case, the connection between stimulants and appetite is so direct that we can generally gauge a therapeutic dosage and monitor tolerance by recording the point at which appetite is suppressed. The only way to combat this is to engage in consistent, long-term workarounds in which you take in enough food to gain basic nutrients, maintain a healthy blood sugar, and sustain a caloric intake that stabilizes weight over time.

You'll have to shift how you think about eating. You know that old adage, "eat when you're hungry?" It won't work here.

To do this, you'll have to shift how you think about eating. You know that old adage, "eat when you're hungry?" It won't work here. Instead, you have to eat mindfully and in response to time cues, meaning you notice what you're doing and work to make eating into a choice. Imagine eating as something your body needs to do instead of as an instinct you fulfill or a craving you feel. Here's how to make that happen.

Leave Behind "I Can't." One of the most vexing things Kelsey and I hear from people, particularly in the younger crowd, is that they "just can't eat." And yet, when we press the issue, we find many of our ADD kids *are* eating. Late in the day, they head to the pantry and down two bags of chips or eat a chocolate bar from a vending machine instead of lunch. Often, the loss of appetite is really a loss of one's tolerance for foods that aren't super delicious. There are a number of ways around this, but if we start from the concept of "I can't," there's nowhere to go, really.

When You Do Eat, Make It Count. If you're going to eat at the lower limits of your daily caloric requirement, focus not on chips and donuts but on several important nutritional goals. *ADDitude* magazine[218] published some good ideas for an ADD-supportive diet for kids. WebMD has another for both kids and adults.[219] Both emphasize maintaining blood sugar and avoiding spikes by focusing the diet on protein, fiber, and complex carbohydrates, particularly at breakfast and avoiding fast carbs like refined sugar, starchy breads, and fructose. They also recommend some additional supplements like Omega-3s and iron, zinc, and magnesium, which have some preliminary support

---

[218] www.additudemag.com/adhd/article/9136.html

[219] www.webmd.com/add-adhd/guide/adhd-diets

in the research for helping with ADD symptoms. Please note however, that any supplement they suggest is available at your local grocery store, so you don't need to go out and buy expensive "ADD supplements" to follow these plans. While there's little chance that changing diet will impact properly diagnosed ADD (Chapter 11), if you're trying to maintain weight on a stimulant, these plans offer a good way to do so.

I'm not holding myself out as the ADD Baker Man (though that's a really good title for a book), but as a diabetic, I've found some appetizing ways to put into practice the high protein, slow carb, low sugar formula. Those Oatmeal Peanut Butter Energy Bars[220] are great. Just throw the ingredients together and into the fridge. The exact formula is very flexible, so if you or your kids like them better one way or another, mix it up. Samantha, curator of the site I took this recipe from, has a bunch like this, so I'll forgo the cookbook and leave the energy bar field up to her. Writing this made me hungry, so I made a batch. It took me about 30 minutes.

Get on Schedule. Some people take stims and simply forget to eat. As with everything else related to time management, you may need to set reminders. If you're not in a regulated environment, like your mom's kitchen or the school cafeteria, set alarms so you're eating at the same time every day. It takes a while, but doing this will teach your body to use time instead of hunger to regulate eating.

Start with Breakfast. Of all the "I can'ts" that we hear, "I can't eat breakfast" is the most common among kids and young adults. You need to get over this. Breakfast is important for everyone, but it's critical for ADD people; because lunch comes at the peak of the stimulant arc, appetite is always going to be suppressed. If you need to delay taking your meds until you sit down to breakfast, do it. Another good workaround I've recently tried is the fruit and protein smoothie. You can get various smoothie mixers for under $100. Mine cost less than $40[221]. To keep things easy, just buy bags of frozen fruits and vegetables at the store—the variety is immense—mix it with oatmeal, chia seeds, almond milk, Greek yogurt, and maybe some protein powder. In about five minutes, you're good to go. If you really don't like

---

[220] www.fivehearthome.com/no-bake-oatmeal-peanut-butter-energy-bars-recipe/

[221] amazon.com/dp/B003XU3C7M/

oatmeal, this is a great way to hide it, because if you run that mixer long enough, you can't tell it's there. You can also get a fine ground oatmeal intended to be used this way or substitute oat milk, but why pay for something specialized when you can get a whole box of old fashioned oatmeal for a lot less money? And to keep the cleaning time and mess manageable, I just put my pitcher back in the freezer several days in a row before running it through the dishwasher.

If you need more guidance, the Food Network has a list of fifty smoothie recipes[222], though you'll have to add the oatmeal, chia, and other proteins to get the job done. Each suggests that you "sugar to taste," however fruit is sweet as it is, so I'd minimize refined sugar add-ins. I will admit to throwing in a little Splenda (sucralose) now and then.

Since I am a breakfast eater, I eat a high protein, low carb breakfast and save the smoothie for my evening meal. It's like having ice cream for dinner, minus all the refined sugar and fat. If you want to get all Martha Stewart about it, dump the mixture into popsicle molds[223], re-freeze, and really get into the ice cream spirit.

Do Lunch. Mindful eating means seeing lunch as you should see love, something you do and not just something you feel. The goal at noon should be to get just enough energy into your body to prevent the symptoms of undereating from being worse than the symptoms of ADD. This is the best time to deploy the oat and peanut butter bar recipes because they travel easily. Avoid simple carbs like potato chips, crackers, and French fries, which are addictive (literally) but go straight to sugar and have as much nutritional value as a cheap sneaker.

As an alternative to lunch, you can snack on healthy foods from late morning until the end of the day. This effectively stabilizes blood sugar and reduces the effects of washout. If you're in college or the work world, this is easy to do. If you're in middle or high school, you may have to get an accommodation, depending on your school's rules on food in the classroom. I've written a few myself.

---

[222] www.foodnetwork.com/recipes/articles/50-smoothies

[223] amazon.com/dp/B00ZAXMWIA/

If you go to the gym after work or are in a school athletic program, give yourself a high-five. Exercise won't cure ADD, but it sure helps both your physical and mental wellbeing. However, you can't get any kind of a good workout if you aren't eating. Thus, you need to snack before practice or gym time, with enough carbs to manage your blood sugar. People who aren't mindful about this, sometimes end up on the bench, or worse, lying flat out on the track or field. In some cases, we've worked with the pediatrician or primary care doc to deny a student's health release in order to prevent a seriously underweight teen or young adult (<18 BMI) from attending practice. Exercise is only helpful when your body isn't starving.

Stretch Dinner. Like Trevor, if your meds are at a therapeutic dose, you probably won't be very hungry at your traditional dinner time. This is where good nutritional advice and medication management butt heads. Your physician would never suggest you eat dinner later in the evening, nor make it your largest meal, and Mrs. Malden was right to wonder if late eating might contribute to Trevor's insomnia. However, when you're on stimulants, you may have to delay your evening meal until about 8:00 p.m. If you get into that habit, you'll avoid going on a starvation binge at 10:00 p.m., and if you finish eating about 8:30, you'll have just enough time for digestion before you go to sleep.

Use Supplement Shakes. This isn't my favorite solution because there's no more overprocessed food out there than drinks like Ensure; but they will work in a pinch to keep weight on and nutrition flowing. While they taste way better cold, some will keep without refrigeration. Bolthouse Farms makes excellent fruit, vegetable, fiber, and protein drinks in a variety of flavors. Some are even gluten-free. However, their products have to be stored cold, so they're less convenient. A particularly clever approach is to mix prepared nutritional drinks into a small, high quality milk shake. While that's a lot of sugar, it's also a good amount of milk fat which helps maintain weight. When you add in the nutritional drink, you'll be getting more than empty calories. If all else fails, or until you can get a better system going, these shakes can keep a medication regimen on track.

Irritability

This is one of the nastier side effects of stimulant medication, ranging from that problem of being too serious to nonsensical anger to the worst-case scenario, aggression. This kind of irritability looks a lot like amped-up anxiety, ruminating about things that don't warrant such concern. When discussing it with your prescriber or therapist, you must keep track of and describe exactly when irritability is happening, because that will determine if it's a side effect of being on meds or of coming off of them. As we discussed in Chapter 4, severe irritability can be a sign of a co-occurring condition like anxiety or bipolar disorder. Or it may simply mean that you're on the wrong class of stimulants. Or the irritability could be modest, short-lived, and manageable enough that you'll just have to explain it to your people and ask them to be supportive.

As an example of how to get to the bottom of this, let's assume you're on an extended release medication like Vyvanse, Concerta, or Adderall XR. If you're on Daytrana or Mydayis, you'll experience a longer period of effectiveness, so these times won't add up, but the idea remains the same. Let's assume you took the medication before 8:00 a.m. If you're irritable at the top of your medication arc (between 10:00 a.m. and 3:00 p.m.), something's not right with the medication itself. Talk to your prescriber about switching to the opposite class of medication, say from an amphetamine to a methylphenidate product.

If instead, you're only irritable during washout (after about 4:00 or 5:00 p.m.), this is an expected side effect, and you'll need to learn how to practice "quiet time." Take a nap, watch a video, listen to music, anything that doesn't involve interacting with others. And, if I wasn't clear enough about this already, be certain you're eating enough at lunch. If the problem really is washout, you should be over it in the evening after the meds are completely out of your system. If it lasts longer, you may be "hangry" and needing to eat more. If early washout and quiet time won't fly due to a late school or work day, talk with your prescriber about a booster (Chapter 6) or a longer-acting medicine to carry you through 'til bedtime, taking into consideration the next big bugaboo of stimulant medication.

Sleep Disruption

- Dr. Kelsey -

As noted in the vignette, some clients report their sleep improves when they start treatment for ADD. Our theory is that stimulants act like training wheels for your mind to help regulate impulse control and to focus on the task at hand. Perhaps, these changes carry over into bed-time and all the various ways in which sleep requires a focused mind and a quiet body, even when the medication is no longer active. Or perhaps, you're just so worn out from all that focused thinking during the day, that you tumble into bed from mental exhaustion. We've heard clients imagine it both ways and some even report drowsiness while their stimulant medication is at full flourish. So don't operate cars or heavy machinery until you know exactly how your meds affect you.

However, for other clients, stimulants cause sleep disturbance or make an existing sleep problem worse. You'll have to study this issue closely, as Trevor's parents did, to determine if what you're seeing is a stimu-lant problem or ADD-related insomnia (ARI, Chapter 4). Depending on how that turns out, there are roughly three workarounds for this problem, one strategic, one behavioral and the last, psychopharmaceu-tical.

The Strategic Workaround: Shuffle the Meds. If we know that stimulant medication is the culprit because you weren't having sleep problems until you started it, the first order of business is to modify either your medication or the way you're taking it. While a different class of medication could help, it's more likely that you need to modify the release pattern.

To keep things simpler for our discussion than they really are, let's say for a moment that you don't need to do much after 7:00 in the evening. Maybe you're in the workplace and once you get home at 6:00 p.m., your evening is your own or you're a student who somehow gets all your homework done before the meds start running out at about 5:30 or 6:00 p.m. We'll try several strategies to get your meds to fade out earlier. We might try the Daytrana patch and have you take it off just before you leave work or come home from school. We might have you set an alarm every morning at 5:00 a.m. so you can take your Vyvanse extra early, then go back to sleep, and wake at your second alarm at say, 6:30. This has the dual impact of helping you wake up in the morn-ing and setting your meds to fade out earlier in the evening.

A novel approach to this same issue is a newer stimulant called Jor-nayPM. It's given in the evening around 6:30 or 7:00 p.m. which might seem like the dumbest idea ever to come out of a big pharma lab. How-ever, this particular methylphenidate medication lies dormant in your system overnight and only activates twelve hours later, making it the stimulant equivalent of a time-bomb. I've just begun using it, and so far, we've found it works well with clients across the lifespan who are reported to be, shall we say, unpleasant in the morning. You may sacrifice some late day duration on the back end of this medication, but most of the individuals who've tried it are so happy to have a smoother morning, that they're willing to cope with an earlier washout.

- Dr. Wes –

The Behavioral Workaround: Sleep Hygiene. As a rule, Americans have pretty awful sleep habits. That's about tenfold truer for teens, who remain overly connected to their social networks twenty-four-seven. For folks with ADD who have brains that don't like to shut down, it's an even bigger problem. Thus, the first response to any sleep disturbance that isn't a product of some other disorder like apnea or night terror, is to improve your relationship with sleep. Below are some tips for doing so, adapted from the National Sleep Foundation guidelines[224]. Judging from several thousand discussions I've had over the last twenty-seven years, I'm guessing you're not going to like them, because sleep is about the most necessary and boring thing we do.

- **Surrender your cognitive distortions.** Some people are adamant that they "don't need as much sleep" as everyone else. While individual needs vary, they don't vary that much. Research tells us that teenagers need eight to ten hours of sleep and adults need between seven and nine hours. If you think you're "that one person who does fine on six hours of sleep," you are lying to yourself.

- **Spend the right amount of time in bed.** Sleep neither too little nor too much and at about the same amount each night. You can generally determine the number of hours you need to sleep by going to bed on a night you don't have work the next day, not taking your stimulant, and sleeping until you wake up naturally. This only works, however, if you're not already sleep deprived, so run three or four trials and average the results. If the number of hours is super low (four) or super high (eleven), wait on medication and see a sleep specialist. If it's in the seven to ten range, start going to bed at exactly the same time every

---

[224] www.sleepfoundation.org/articles/sleep-hygiene

night while setting an alarm for bedtime plus the number of hours and minutes calculated in your no-alarm sleep test.

- **Keep naps short.** The joy of napping is another cognitive distortion. Napping means inadequate nighttime sleep, and it won't make up a sleep deficit. The exception is a short power nap of twenty to thirty minutes. Research suggests that this can improve mood, alertness, and performance. I take them myself, particularly during allergy season when I'm rundown despite a good night's sleep. Set your alarm for thirty minutes and get up when it rings. If you don't, you'll encroach on your evening sleep routine, which just makes everything worse.

- **Avoid stimulants close to bedtime.** We're talking ancillary stimulants here: caffeine, nicotine, ADD meds, and medicines that contain pseudoephedrine. You might rightly ask, what constitutes "close to bedtime?" The answer depends on you and your metabolism. I personally stop drinking coffee, energy drinks, or my highly caffeinated tea after 2:00 p.m. If I do take a nap, I get that done before 1:00 p.m., and then I have a cup of that tea. And that's it. Your body may respond differently, but watch out for cognitive distortions like, "caffeine doesn't affect me." For some ADD people, that's true. For others, it could be a key reason for poor sleep that you won't realize until you hop on the scientific method and run some low caffeine tests. If you're prescribed a booster dose of short-acting medication, the latest you should take it is 5:00 p.m., presuming you're going to bed by 11:00 or so.

- **Don't use alcohol as a sleep remedy.** Another famous cognitive trick we play on ourselves. While alcohol can make you fall asleep faster, late night drinking actually disrupts your sleep the second half of the night as your body begins to process the alcohol.

- **Exercise.** As little as ten minutes of aerobic exercise can greatly improve nighttime sleep as long as you don't do it too close to bedtime. Starting exercise late riles you up instead of winding you down.

- **Eat very little late in the day.** As noted, very late eating can disrupt sleep, particularly if you're downing a lot of fatty or fried foods, spicy dishes, citrus fruits, and carbonated drinks. I keep my evening fruit smoothies mellow for exactly this reason.

- **Take in natural light during the day.** Exposure to sun-spectrum light during the waking hours, and especially in the morning, helps maintain a healthy sleep-wake cycle. That gets harder in the winter. A great trick that's recently become easier to pull off is to go to your local home improvement store and buy an LED daylight shop light. Get one with a cord[225] unless you are, like me, experienced with wiring to code. If you are electrically skilled or know someone who is, go with 2x4 daylight panels[226]. They're thin and flat and can be easily secured inside your window frame during the winter months when the sun is lazy and refuses to wake you up. Purchase a cord timer[227], plug it in between the panel and the outlet, and set it to your wake up time. It's like having your own private sunrise. There are also alarm clock products that simulate a sunrise. They're not as bright as my light panels, but they get the job done with less work than my project. I bought one on Amazon and so far, so good.

- **Lights out.** It's a lot easier to get rid of light than to produce it, so one of the easiest things you can do to improve your daily sleep ritual is turn off all lighting one and a half to two hours before bedtime. Of course, our friend the sun has something to say about this too, so you might buy some high grade darkening window treatments to keep out early and late sun in the spring and summer months, relying instead on your artificial sunrise system to keep your morning rhythm steady across the seasons. Another solution, favored by my daughter, is to get a sleep mask. I don't like them, but she swears by hers and has no problem getting up with time cues. Nearly all sleep researchers suggest shutting down light-producing computers, phones, and tablets an hour or two before bed. But if you can't bring yourself to click off the TV before hitting the sack, dim the picture and watch in the dark, as you would in a movie

---

[225] homedepot.com/p/206028863

[226] amazon.com/dp/B07BTD1CZP/

[227] amazon.com/dp/B00MVF16JG/

theater. Natural melatonin, come on down. Just be sure that anything you watch before bed adheres to the next rule.

- **Create a calming bedtime ritual.** Another cognitive distortion is that we can just go go go and then fall into bed and slumber restfully. In reality, anything that engages your mind with excitement or intrigue is likely to disrupt your sleep. I had to purposely watch HBO's *Game of Thrones* and Showtime's *Billions* earlier in the evening (lights off) and then finish with something funny like *Veep* as a buffer between big thrills and bedtime. Before I adopted this practice, I found myself riding into battle all night with Jon Snow or figuring out how to get the best of the schemers at Axe Capital, instead of sleeping. Even worse are video games, the point of which is to engage your mind endlessly. I, and just about every other psychologist, recommend shutting them down at least an hour before bed.

- **Get quiet.** Another cognitive distortion prevalent among the ADD crowd is that poor sleepers need background noise to distract from their inner thoughts. This one is based in fact. Certain kinds of noise can interrupt internal dialog, but once you fall asleep, you want any audio of the spoken word to shut off, lest it keep running through your head like my plan to take-over Westeros. I've found certain podcasts and audiobooks good for bedtime as long as they're interesting enough to listen but not interesting enough to keep you on the edge of your bed. Another approach is to listen to music specifically designed for sleep. There's way more of this now than when I wrote *I Always Want to Be Where I'm Not,* but my favorite remains *Delta Sleep*[228] by Jeffery Thompson. Unlike spoken word recordings, this thing can run all night and maybe even improve your sleep by disengaging your mind.

- **Make your sleep space sleepy.** Whenever I stay in a hotel that has a mattress, sheets, or comforter I really like, I take it apart and shoot pictures of the labels, then order them online. I've experimented with a bunch of pillows and finally settled on the double body pillow favored by pregnant women[229]. It's

---

[228] amazon.com/dp/B0011ZYCHA/

[229] amazon.com/dp/B07H3Q8HR6/

not only comfortable, it keeps me sleeping on my side, which is optimal for digestion and this particular U-shaped version allows one to turn over as needed. You may find a different design works best for you, so keep looking until you find something that works. Experiment with different scents to see if one comforts you and ushers you off to dream land. There's no essential oil proven to induce sleep, but anything that's pleasing to you can help you relax for that reason alone.

- **Keep it cold.** Keep your bedroom colder than you think it should be, between 60 and 67 degrees and regulate your temperature with a comforter, while breathing the cooler air. This can be hard on the electric bill in the summer, so you might want to get a small add-on unit just for the bedroom. A fan can also create a similar effect.

Having read through this scolding list of dos and don'ts, I'm guessing you feel pretty irritated right now. That's because Americans are taught not to value sleep, like it's a waste of precious time or something. Then I come along and demand that you follow these approved guidelines or else all hell will break loose in your ADD life. Your natural inclination is to say, "No. I don't want to." Did I mention cognitive distortions? Besides, I'm not the one asking. Your body is, and try as you might you cannot defy its basic design and wiring. This is one area in which there is no skeptic press questioning reality. Nobody is out there saying, "sleep deprivation is overdiagnosed, dagnabbit. People get plenty of sleep already!" Yes, people sit around and privately think that, but nobody dares say it, because it's ridiculous.

While I do not have ADD, I sure have had a long history of sleep problems. In *I Always Want to Be Where I'm Not,* I mentioned having sleep apnea that was, at the time, controlled with a mouthpiece. Or not. Turns out that was a cognitive distortion, too. Eventually, I got smart, did a full sleep study and now enjoy my CPAP every night. Along the way, I became a student of sleep hygiene, and I can assure you that each of these rules is necessary. But they may not be sufficient. That brings us to our final strategy.

The Psychopharmaceutical Workaround: Medication. Despite all my herculean sleep hygiene, advanced training, and love affair with my CPAP, I still have insomnia. It's how I'm wired. It was an issue after graduate school, and got worse in my forties. I don't know when the whole apnea thing came into play, but as best I can figure, it was after primary insomnia was already a problem. Since about 2005, I've taken trazadone, which, along with all the other tricks noted above, gave me seven to eight hours of good sleep more often than not, until I realized it had become an unhelpful workaround for the apnea. Yet, even after conquering that problem, I still had primary insomnia. My children have ARI, and they also take trazadone.

Sleep is about as complicated a problem as you're going to find, even without ADD on the table. For many clients, the solution will require medication.

I share all this to underscore a point made earlier in this book—sleep is about as complicated a problem as you're going to find, even without ADD on the table. For many clients, the solution will require medication. We discussed the pharmacology of insomnia in Chapter 6, and it's no different when poor sleep is triggered by stimulant medication.

For some, the idea of taking A SLEEPING PILL (!!!) is scary, and as we discussed in detail earlier, some sleep aids cause more problems than they're worth. In other cases, including mine and my children, medication comes with no side effects or shortcomings. It just works. At the end of the day, you may have to decide if the value you're getting from stimulants is great enough to accept the need for sleep medication. If all else fails, it may be the best choice.

Tics and Habits

For anyone diagnosed with ADD who also has a personal or family history of tics, your prescriber will want to proceed with caution because stimulants are known to exacerbate existing tics. However, there is no known association between stimulant use and new onset of tics[230].

You may notice the presence of tic-like behaviors even in the absence of previous tics or a family history. Over the years, we've come to realize that if you study these closely, what some people—even

---

[230] Cohen, SC, et al. *J Amer Child Adolesc Psychiatry*. 2015; 54: 728-736. http://bit.ly/iUfjuKi.

physicians—think are tics are actually "small fidgets" which existed before medication, but were much larger. If you're among the hyperkinetic ADHD people, medicine should reduce the tendency to jump around or be "driven as if by a motor," but it may also reorient you to do smaller things like twirl your hair or pull on your eyelashes. Some prescribers will take you off meds if you show up with these quirks, so be sure to consider your before- and after-medication self, to be sure you're not just paying more attention to something that's always been there now that you're on a stimulant.

Having been down this path with my daughter who was, for some time in elementary school, a hair twirler and puller, I can say that the value of stimulants outweighed this annoying side effect, which she eventually outgrew. It took a great deal of cognitive override to look past this small fidget to see the greater good, but everyone agrees it was the right choice. Sometimes, we must consider whether our aversion to something (like pulling hair) is greater than the actual harm done by the tic.

On the other hand, if it is determined that stimulant medication is pushing a tic of neurological concern, you and your prescriber may have to do some major rethinking. If you're getting this side effect and you're not seeing a specialist in psychiatric medication, you need to be.

Physical Side Effects

- Dr. Kelsey -

Some clients report problems with headaches, stomachaches, and dry mouth when taking stimulants, particularly in the first week or two. These usually go away once you're used to the medication, as long as you make sure to stay hydrated. If they continue, but are infrequent (say, once a week) you may treat them with over-the-counter meds, but tell your prescriber if you're regularly chasing stimulants with Advil or Tylenol. That may not be a safe or sustainable solution. As for dry mouth, some clients use Biotene mouthwash to stimulate the production of saliva. Don't confuse it with biotin, a dietary supplement.

Some clients experience teeth grinding at night, but unless they are sleeping with someone who lies awake listening, they may not know it. Ask someone to monitor your sleep before and after you start a stimulant, and always tell your dentist that you're taking one. And go in for a checkup twice a year, so your dentist can keep an eye out for unnatural wear. The workaround here is usually a night guard. Wes wore one for years before getting his CPAP (grinding is yet another symptom of apnea) and he still likes wearing it in tandem with his mask. You can have your dentist make one for you, or you can get some pretty good ones online that you form yourself with water and a microwave. They're much cheaper than the dentist's model, and they seem to last about as long. Wes likes SnoreRx[231], but there are several products on the market. It may take a few trials to see which works best for you.

A very small number of clients have reported problems with breathing, rapid heart rate, and other oddities like a stiff neck. Immediately consult your prescriber if you have any of these side effects. There's no direct work around for this, except to try other classes of medication or delivery systems. Contrary to what you might expect, given the similarities in medications, we are often able to resolve these issues by switching stimulants.

A surprisingly common side effect is laryngopharyngeal reflux, or 'silent reflux', brought on by stimulant usage which can present a cascade of side effects that you may not think to attribute to the medication. Silent reflux is an atypical gastric reflux presentation in which the stomach acid doesn't cause the traditional discomfort behind the breastbone, hence the term "silent." It instead, causes the sensation that there is something caught in the back of your throat, hoarseness, frequent throat clearing, coughing, difficulty swallowing, or a bitter taste at the back of the throat.

The discomfort of this condition is itself a problem, but the frequent swallowing and throat clearing needed to relieve the discomfort can lead to GI disturbances and vocal cord damage. Antihistamines may help those who cough at night. However, the long-term use of medicines like omeprazole to combat acid reflux is controversial, so be sure to discuss any of these side effects with your prescriber so you can weigh the risks and benefits your current stimulant or try a different one.

Mania

As we discussed in Chapter 4, a strong sign of an underlying bipolar disorder (BiD) comes after taking a stimulant and becoming manic. Mania isn't the same as getting a little obsessive for the first few days

---

[231] www.snorerx.com

on medication. That's not unusual and it might even help you organize your room to perfection. Being manic involves uncontrollable, racing thoughts and a lot of energy that makes sense to you, but doesn't make sense to anyone else. It's often accompanied by impulsivity, incessant talking, and several nights without sleeping. In short, it's the stereotypical amphetamine high and definitely not what we want to see.

I probably don't have to tell you this, but if a very small dosage of stimulant makes you even slightly manic, you need to discontinue and call your prescriber at once. Then call your therapist and start looking at co-occurring diagnoses. This isn't really a side effect. It's an indication that ADD may not be the diagnosis for you, and if it is, you won't be able to treat it until you're evaluated and treated for a co-occurring mood disorder (Chapter 6).

Unlike other medications, the obvious solution for a stimulant side effect—quit the medication—is usually the wrong one.

Fortunately, this very rarely happens, and when it does, a good treatment team will react fast. It's one reason we always start the experiment (Chapter 7) with a low dose of stimulant, because the manic episode will be much less pronounced—usually just an acute phase of severe and unusual irritability—and the washout is quick.

Unlike other medications, the obvious solution for a stimulant side effect—quit the medication—is usually the wrong one. If a medication is as effective for you as it was for Trevor, try working closely with your prescriber and therapist to hit all the workarounds we've suggested in this chapter, and any others he or she can think of, then email those to us, so we can try them. Once in a great while, after we've tried every class of medication, and every strategy of administration, we'll give up on conventional approaches and try something else like the new eTNS system (Chapter 11).

Occasionally, a client we think we can help gets impatient with side effects and surrenders. Who can blame anyone who is tired of not sleeping or not being hungry for their favorite double chocolate fudge cake? Thankfully, with most folks, we find a way. Hopefully, with the tips we've provide in this chapter, you'll stay firmly in their ranks and you can declare, "Medication mission accomplished."

And with that, the whole process can switch to autopilot allowing ADD to slide gracefully into your life's rearview mirror, leaving you to focus on what really matters, living life to its fullest with nary a care in the world. Right? If only it were that easy. Instead, just at the point you've ironed out the details and you start feeling optimistic about medication management, your body will begin edging toward a little thing called stimulant tolerance, and henceforth, you and your pre-scriber will be fighting a permanent battle to minimize its impact on your treatment.

Fortunately, we can roll right on to Chapter 9.

Stimulant Tolerance

I propose that an examination of stimulant tolerance and its potential ramifications is important and should be considered in clinical practice.

— Jason Yanofski, MD

The definition of insanity is doing the same thing over and over again, but expecting different results.

— (Probably) Albert Einstein

- Dr. Wes -

"I don't understand how you expect me to get through a break right now, Wes." Lara's lips pursed. "I have to be able to go to work and deal with my cases. I have a trial in three weeks, and I need to prepare."

"Right, I said. "It's hard to be off stimulants for ten to fourteen days, but how long have you been seeing me?""

"You mean in years?" She glanced away. "I don't know. Since I was a sophomore in college, on and off. The end of 2011."

"And for how long have I been recommending you take regular stimulant breaks?"

"Probably, forever." She pulled her phone from her enormous purse and fiddled with it. "I need to return this text. It's from the office."

I didn't mind. If Lara took a text during a session, it was because she was desperately needed at the public defender's office. I couldn't believe it when she took that job straight out of law school. It felt embarrassing now, but at the time I didn't expect her to last three weeks. I thought the job, in one of the roughest counties in the Kansas City metro, would eat her alive, but her second anniversary had just popped up on my LinkedIn. She loved the job, cared about her clients, provided them a vigorous defense, and yet maintained professional boundaries.

"There," she said, dropping her phone back into her purse. "You'd think they couldn't live without me."

"I don't doubt it," I said. "Back in 2011, I couldn't have imagined that flighty sophomore was the best criminal attorney in the county."

"Well thanks." Her expression remained grim, even as I knew she appreciated the compliment. "Which is why we need to put this stimulant break off until, I don't know, the summer or something."

"Because summer is the off-season for criminals?"

"No. It gets hot and crime gets hotter." She emitted a stern breath, like a tigress's chuff. "I just can't handle being off right now."

"Suit yourself. We've wrestled with this since you finished law school. Sometimes you have to find things out the hard way."

"That's a warning, not an invitation, isn't it?" she said. "I know you. You're not going to let me go up any further on meds, even if they aren't working very well any more, which, if I'm being totally honest, they aren't."

"I can't make you do anything." I mimicked an emoji shrug. "You took this job against my recommendation, and you proved me wrong. In the end, it's up to Kelsey. You two can figure it out. But I'll tell you right now that the reason your meds don't feel right any more, despite being maxed out, is because—"

"I went way too long without a break. I know." Lara shifted around on the sofa. "It's just so irritating. Couldn't you tell Kelsey that I need to go up to like maybe 50mg of Adderall, just to get me through this armed robbery trial, and then we can talk about a break later?"

"I could indeed tell her that, but I'm not going to. I respect Kelsey's judgment and she respects mine, and we both agree on the long-term impact of tolerance. You're already on 40mg of Adderall XR and another 10mg booster at 4:00pm. So, it's not whether you can go up or not. You're already at the top of the FDA recommendation for XR. You could go a little farther, at which point you're not going to have any headroom and guess what? You'll still have to take a break, and it will be even harder."

Lara adjusted herself into a cross-examination posture, eyes focused on the witness, watching his every move for a sign of weakness. "You told me one time how you'd seen a girl in here who was on 70mg of Adderall XR and she was in like seventh grade. So, how wouldn't I be eligible to take that much as an adult?"

I shook my head. "You know better. It doesn't have anything to do with age or size. You don't weigh more than what, a hundred and twenty-five pounds?

"Hey, there," she groused. "I've never been over a hundred and twelve."

"Oops. Sorry. But that just makes my point. Your dosage has to do with metabolism and yeah, yours may be high. But, I told you that story about the young girl as a cautionary tale. She'd never taken a break, not even for a day, and the mom refused to let her take one because she couldn't handle her hyperactivity. As I recall, that mom was angry with her pediatrician because he wouldn't go even higher, so she brought her in to see us, thinking we would. That's not an example of the wise limits of Adderall, it's about what happens when you don't take breaks."

"Well, I don't see why there isn't a medication for ADD that doesn't require a break."

"That's not a thing," I said. "Any stimulant is going to have a diminished effect with long-term use, and in your case, long-term isn't very long. I'd like to see you take three breaks a year, like you did in college and if we can't get that, at least two."

"That's a lot harder when you're working for a living." Lara uncrossed her arms and swore her usual blue streak. "There are no spring or winter breaks, and I can't just be down for a week. And that's what it's like for me, d-o-w-n. You know that. I'm flat on the sofa, useless. I'm not like your daughter, who can just pop off meds and be fine or your son, a happy, pleasant guy off of them."

Lara was right. Both my children have taken three or four breaks a year since early elementary school. We work them slowly up from the beginning of the school year until the end with two breaks in between.

"You have paid sick leave," I said. "You've accumulated more than enough days to cover this. I can write an FMLA."[232]

She sighed. "Yeah, but you know better than anyone how hard it is to actually take time off. People need you and—jeez." She paused and pulled her phone up again. "Or they think they do." She answered with a swipe. "What is it? I'm in a meeting. You're not taking that case to trial, John. Are you crazy? You'll die in there. Tell your guy he has to plead it or he's looking at ten years minimum. I don't care. No. Fine. You may just have to learn things the hard way. I'll talk to you later." She swiped off. "Newbies. They're especially needy."

I smiled. "I remember a few rounds of needy with you back in the day."

"Aren't you glad I'm better now?" She scowled, incongruent with her words, like she didn't really feel any better.

"Listen." I leaned in. "You're a very impressive young woman, and all I want to do is keep you that way. Think of the downtime as a way to sharpen your saw, like what Stephen Covey said in his book *Seven Habits of Highly Successful People*[233]."

"We read that in some class I had," she said dismissively. "Or at least I read part of it. He's like, 'take time off and rejuvenate and so on or whatever.' I'm sure he was rich, so he could do that." She paused and answered the next text from work. "John you're a dumbass," she muttered at the phone, then looked up. "Do I look like someone who likes to rest?"

"Nope. Not even at night, which is why we have you set up for a second sleep study. The whole night terrors situation has created too many issues for far too long. Even before stimulants. And it's not getting better in this job."

"Me and sleep just hate each other I guess."

---

[232] Family Medical Leave Act, a law that allows workers to take off time for personal or family disability or illness (www.dol.gov/whd/fmla/).

[233] amazon.com/dp/B01069X4H0/

"The sleep doc is going to take you off the stims anyhow for that study. Besides, that robbery trial will get continued. It always does."

"No. I think it will go this time," Lara said. "Judge is getting impatient. But you're right about the sleep study. They wanted me to have a couple days off before. I guess if you'll write me the FMLA letter, I can ask off for the whole week and we can like, say it has to do with that, because it kind of does."

"I have one in your file." I clicked the document up on my computer. "I can just update it and send it over to the HR department at the courthouse."

"Nothing is ever easy, is it, Wes?" She picked up her purse, glanced at the clock, and headed toward the door. "Sorry I'm salty tonight. Can we talk about boys next time? I'm trying to make some good decisions about that, too."

"We can," I said. "Text me the fax for HR and I'll get the letter set up for the week of the twenty-fifth. And remember, you need to take both weekends on either side of that week."

"Fine. I've done this before," she walked toward the door. "I may not like it, but I know how to do it. I'll get a new swimsuit and just sit by the pool at the apartment complex."

"That might also help with the boy issue." I laughed.

"Right there with you. See you next time." Lara slipped out the door and into the waiting room.

Maxing Out

Each stimulant has an FDA determined maximum recommended dosage. For Vyvanse that is 70mg. For short-acting methylphenidate it's 60mg and for most of its extended release forms, the max is also 60mg.

The exceptions are Concerta, which the FDA extended several years ago to 72mg and Adhansia XR which maxes at 85mg. Dexmethylphenidate, both long acting and short acting, is set at a maximum of 40mg.

However, before you tattoo those figures on your wrist as a reminder of the outer limits of stimulant management, you need to understand that these figures came from the original pharmaceutical trials for a given condition and not from daily clinical practice and the wisdom accumulated therein. This creates some interesting anomalies like Adderall XR being given a higher recommended total daily dose for narcolepsy (60mg) than for ADD (40mg) because that's what showed up in the trials. It's critical to note that most clinical trials for stimulants, and all medications, were short in duration. Among the many questions this might generate is one about how accurate maximum dosages really are in real life practice.

> *The outer limits of stimulant management came from the original pharmaceutical trials not from daily clinical practice and the wisdom accumulated therein.*

In making this point, we're not implying that stimulants are wildly underdosed. We're just saying that the FDA recommended maximums are better than arbitrary but far from precise estimates of how much stimulant you and your brain will need to reach efficacy. Nor do all prescribers adhere to these maximums with any consistency. For example, the maximum FDA-recommended dosage of Adderall XR for children is 30mg, but we routinely seen kids coming in from other prescribers taking far more than that. This often includes a main dose in the morning and short-acting boosters later in the day, a prescribing technique Kelsey explained in Chapter 6. Likewise, Lara's memory was correct in the vignette. I once did an intake on a very small teenage girl who was taking 70mg of Adderall XR prescribed by her pediatrician. She'd never taken the kind of break we describe later in this chapter because her mom said she "couldn't stand her" off medication. Another girl came in on 108mg of Concerta with basically the same story.

Even higher doses are common for adults who've never taken stimulant breaks. The recommended adult dosage for Adderall is 40mg, but the clinical trials for Adderall were tested up to 60mg[234], and it's not uncommon to see clients coming in on that dosage. And if you have occasion to Google "highest dosage of Adderall," you'll find a whole subculture of people claiming that they need to be on 120mg or more to reach a therapeutic response and complaining that their prescribers just won't go there with them.

It is our supposition in this chapter, based on considerable clinical experience, that most of this high-dosing does not reflect a conscious march toward clinical efficacy. It reflects a little-researched and rarely-discussed phenomenon known most commonly as stimulant tolerance, your brain adjusting to stimulant medication such that the impact of the medication decreases over time, leading you to take higher and higher doses to maintain the therapeutic effect. If you keep that up, you'll eventually hit your ceiling, the dose at which you can't safely go higher. For this reason, tolerance will always lie at the heart of the love-hate relationship between you and your ADD medication.

In the short run—the first three to six months—it's possible that you simply aren't yet on a therapeutic dose and you really do need to go up. We saw a high school senior who was a cross-fit fanatic. After testing out as ADD, we started her on the usual entry dose of Concerta. No main effect, no side effect. It was like a drink of water. We tried the next level. Nothing. In just four weeks, she was taking 72mg, the maximum recommended by the FDA[235], before finally getting the effect we were looking for. She took this dose with no side effects and with regular breaks for as long as we worked with her. It's likely this girl metabolized medicine quickly and thus needed a higher dose to get the same effect as her dad who took quite a bit less medication than she did. In contrast to this example, stimulant tolerance emerges more slowly and later in treatment, usually after six months at a therapeutic dose, but even that can vary from person to person.

Yet Another Controversy

We speak of stimulant tolerance in this book as if it were enshrined in the ten commandments of ADD which, in our clinic, it is. In reality, tolerance is a divisive issue among prescribers, with some "believing"

---

[234] www.accessdata.fda.gov/drugsatfda_docs/label/2004/021303s005lbl.pdf

[235] Don't get hung up on this "maximum dose" issue yet. We'll explain what it is and what it means later in the chapter.

Once the idea of tolerance is introduced to our ADD clients, not a single one finds it controversial. They find it obvious.

in it and others "not believing" in it. However, once the idea is introduced to our ADD clients who've been on stimulants for longer than a year or two, not a single one finds it controversial. They find it obvious. Yet, many consumers of stimulants have never been told about tolerance. So, if you want to discuss it with your provider, you may be met with either a big ho hum or a lecture on maintaining consistency in medication management. Feel free to delicately and diplomatically share the following talking points with the person who writes those scripts. They support our case very well.

The FDA Says Tolerance Exists. The FDA notes, quite ominously, that abusing stimulant medication runs the risk of "tolerance, extreme psychological dependence, and severe social disability....There are reports of patients who have increased the dosage to levels many times higher than recommended."[236] Not one of these conditions is unique to the *abuse* of stimulants. Each is also in play with proper and well-regulated clinical use[237]. For this reason you will, without a doubt, need to keep upping your dosage to get a therapeutic effect. Why wouldn't you? And at what point does proper usage become dependence? If you embrace the tolerance potential of stimulants as a key aspect of using them effectively, and act as we recommend in this chapter, you'll never have to find out.

One (Infamous) Prescription Stimulant Acknowledges Tolerance. Desoxyn is the brand name for methamphetamine. Yes, you read that right. It's a little known fact that if you have ADD (or extreme obesity), your prescriber can write you a script for meth. Desoxyn is almost never used, however. We've never written a prescription for it and we never will because far safer alternatives are available. However, what's interesting about Desoxyn's patient information is the very specific warning it gives that tolerance will be achieved within a few weeks and that the stimulant must be discontinued periodically in order to correct it. Some might dismiss this warning as only applying to this

---

[236] www.accessdata.fda.gov/drugsatfda_docs/label/2007/011522s040lbl.pdf

[237] www.oxfordtreatment.com/adderall/tolerance/. This blog post is highly recommended to further explain stimulant tolerance and how it differs from stimulant abuse.

drug, because it is, after all, meth (!). But Desoxyn is in exactly the same controlled substance class as all the other stimulants. It's simply a more powerful agent and thus builds tolerance more quickly. The process itself is exactly the same and the outcome just as predictable.

The MTA Study Demonstrates Tolerance[238]. The Multimodal Treatment of Attention Deficit Hyperactivity Disorder (MTA) study is the largest and longest running ADHD treatment study ever conducted. To give you a sense of what "large" means in this field, the longitudinal (long-term) sample includes just 515 ADD children and 258 neurotypical agemates serving as a normative comparison group. As of 2017, the two groups had been studied for between two and sixteen years after the original baseline assessments were completed.

The most recent MTA update came out in 2017[239] and was widely reported, but is best synopsized by Devon Frye and Stephen Hinshaw in *ADDitude* magazine[240]:

> One of the most publicized follow-up releases was published in August 2007, focusing on 485 of the original 579 children. The researchers were surprised to find that among children who continued to take ADHD medication consistently, the stimulants that had worked so well at first started to lose their effectiveness around three years after treatment started.... Another follow-up, in September 2016, found that more than 60 percent of the children — regardless of their medication use — continued to show ADHD symptoms into adulthood. More than 40 percent still experienced "significant impairment" from their symptoms.

As for the March 2017 data release, the authors note:

> ... in a confounding twist, the two groups (those who took medication consistently and those who didn't) showed no difference in symptom severity — though members of the

---

[238] To be clear, the MTA researchers don't recognize this or discuss it. They just seemed confused by it.

[239] www.ncbi.nlm.nih.gov/pubmed/28295312

[240] www.additudemag.com/latest-mta-results-putting-adhd-treatment-data-in-context/

former had, on average, taken more than 100,000 mg of stimulant medication over the course of their lifetimes.

This is where erroneous conclusions begin to creep into the findings. The authors write:

> The results raised questions about long-standing treatment norms that prioritize stimulants as first-line treatments, leading some parents and adults to worry that taking ADHD medication — especially over the long term — might do more harm than good.

> The 16-year data from the MTA study reveal that, even though an optimal stimulant medication regimen during childhood for children with carefully diagnosed ADHD led to quick and efficacious symptom improvement in the vast majority of cases, when the intensive medication management was stopped after the 14 months of the original randomized clinical trial, medication was used less intensively and systematically over time.

> ... Even when the sample was subgrouped by 'lifetime exposure' to medication, those with relatively high doses across many years fared no better, overall, than those with less consistent medication practices.

The study's authors go on to proffer questions and hypotheses about these supposedly puzzling findings, noting:

> Do the most severe cases continue to receive medicine, or those with the most motivated families, including those with better health coverage...? For ADHD, it could be that if optimal medication practices were maintained for many years, improvement would last. Yet, in the real world, it's increasingly difficult to sustain such practices. It could also be that, for at least some people with ADHD, continuous medication over time leads, ultimately, to some 'burnout' of the dopamine receptors that are the immediate targets of the medication. It could well be the case that measures of ADHD symptom reduction aren't the best measure of medication responsiveness.

We appreciate the authors' attention to this important issue, and their willingness to take a complicated study and bring it to the readers of the key periodical in the ADD community. However, we think they might have wanted to graze a little longer on the "burnout' hypothesis or perhaps call it what it is—stimulant tolerance. In fact, these medication regimens that included 100,000 mg of stimulant were far from optimal. Based on our collective experience, we would predict that if this treatment was continued unabated beyond a few months, or if the dosages were continually increased until the subjects were maxed out, beyond a couple of years, the subjects would be stimulant tolerant well before the point of the last longitudinal measurement.

By our standards, the only optimal medication regimen would be one that included three breaks a year, which the MTA study did not address. Thus, the findings should not be construed as challenging the value of stimulant medication for ADD, but as questioning the uninterrupted use of that medication. And why is that not their conclusion? From our experience, the body of prescribers and researchers have become so immune to the notion of tolerance, that they have ignored the obvious.

A Few Psychiatrists Have Begun to Recognize Tolerance. In 2011 in *Innovations in Clinical Neuroscience*,[241] psychiatrist Jason Yanofski, MD noted that despite the above-cited FDA warnings, "Practice trends suggest that psychiatrists are not concerned about the possibility of paradoxical decompensation…a worsening of [ADHD] symptoms over time." He goes on to note,

> Generally, higher doses of medications and longer durations of use put patients at increased risk of developing dependence and tolerance.… Stimulants' ability to cause tolerance is controversial, but the need for dose increases over time has been recognized in the literature by the American Academy of Child and Adolescent Psychiatry (AACAP). Their treatment guidelines state that 'most' children will 'require dose adjustment upward as treatment progresses.'

Dr. Yanofski adds that despite the clinical evidence that tolerance is worth considering and treating, it is minimized in the literature and

---

[241] www.ncbi.nlm.nih.gov/pmc/articles/PMC3036556/

ignored in the recommended ADD treatment strategy of the American Psychiatric Association. He leaves no doubt as to why.

> There has never been a study designed specifically to examine whether or not stimulants have the potential to worsen ADHD symptoms over time. One review of 166 patients found that 60 percent of children developed dose-dependent tolerance to stimulants. However, because of the lack of other research in this area, the verdict is still out.

Likewise, in a Q&A post on Psych Conference Network[242], a resource for psychiatrists, Rakesh Jain, MD, MPH even acknowledges stimulant tolerance as "a common clinical dilemma faced by many of us." More on that in a moment.

A National Study Is Researching Tolerance. Care to guess why there is such an abject lack of data on this important topic, leaving us only with theory and conjecture? It's pretty simple. Pharmaceutical companies pay for nearly all the research conducted on stimulants. Which one is going to fund a project to prove that ADD consumers should take less of their medication?

And yet a bit of empirical research is starting to leak through. William Pelham and James Swanson, investigators associated with Florida International University, are conducting a study of stimulant tolerance in younger children, which will be reported out in 2020. We'll have a follow up at that time on our blog, familypsychological.com. In their pre-data write up they note:

> While medication can be very effective for improving symptoms of ADHD during the first year of use, it has not been found to significantly improve the long-term course of children with ADHD. For example, in large research studies, groups of children who take medication for ten years do not have consistently better academic grades than groups of children who never used medication (individual results will vary from child to child).

---

[242] www.psychcongress.com/article/treating-patients-who-develop-tolerance-toward-stimulants. The author is Clinical Professor, Department of Psychiatry, Texas Tech Health Sciences Center School of Medicine, Midland, Texas.

In order to help children with ADHD achieve the best possible outcomes, it is important for doctors to study why this happens. One possible reason is development of tolerance to the medication... Some doctors believe that children who take stimulant medication for ADHD develop tolerance to it which would explain why benefits may not persist over time, but no research studies have been done to measure whether this occurs. This study aims to see if children show a tolerance effect to stimulant medication and whether that tolerance can be prevented by taking short breaks from the medication called medication holidays[243].

We heartily support the intent of this study. Unfortunately, it's far too early to see any change in the direction of clinical practice, which is instead based on far too many "beliefs" about stimulants and tolerance, which brings us to...

What Doesn't Work

If they accept that it exists at all, tolerance is often portrayed as insurmountable by prescribers who've written on this topic. In an otherwise excellent article explaining the difference between tolerance and stimulant abuse, Oxford Treatment Centers lament:

Physicians are not likely to reduce the dose of Adderall for a person with ADHD because their body has already developed a tolerance to the stimulant, and the person needs consistent medical treatment to manage their condition. Always follow the prescribing physician's instructions regarding any prescription drug, including Adderall, and let them know if the substance is no longer effective at its current dose.

This paradoxical closing comes from authors who have, in prior paragraphs, cited the seriousness of stimulant tolerance, only to conclude that nothing can be done about it except complaining to the physician who is powerless to respond. No wonder that online subculture of stimulant complainers feels nobody is listening to them.

---

[243] clinicaltrials.gov/ct2/show/NCT02039908

We've seen numerous examples of this: prescribers helplessly speculating on how to handle tolerance without actually addressing its causes. For example, after noting in his Q&A that "development of tolerance to stimulants is a fact of life for many patients," Dr. Jain offers seven strategies for combatting it, none of which involve a stimulant break. Let's review his suggestions to his fellow prescribers, along with our annotations as to why none of them will work. We're not trying to criticize Dr. Jain, who is clearly hip to the concerns we raise in this chapter, but to introduce you to the serious cognitive distortions that exist around tolerance among those writing the scripts. We've heard each one many times and if you're not prepared to be your own expert and advocate, you may get steered down one of these dead-end paths. Here are Dr. Jain's proposals for dealing with tolerance, followed by our perspective:

- Reevaluating the patient. He notes, "I've had poor outcomes when the patient's diagnosis is incorrect." Our view: We're all about accurate diagnosis, but an errant one will have no impact whatsoever on stimulant tolerance. People who have ADD and take stimulants will build tolerance and so will people who don't have ADD and take stimulants. Tolerance is a matter of neurochemistry, not psychodiagnosis.

- Reexamining whether a co-occurring disorder like anxiety, depression, or bipolar might exist, which "if missed, leads to suboptimum response to stimulants." Our view: Of course this is a good idea. We discussed it in Chapter 4, and Lara is a good example. She was also on Effexor for depression and anxiety. But adding a few more diagnoses and treatment protocols won't alter stimulant tolerance. How could it? Tolerance isn't a product of anxiety or depression. It comes from how your neuroreceptor sites naturally respond to an unexpected abundance of dopamine in your synaptic gap.

- Additional treatments. Jain notes, "Even expert psychopharmacologists should never forget to add nonpharmacological treatments to improve the output from stimulants," including school-based interventions, cognitive behavioral therapy, coaching, physical exercise, mindfulness training, etc., which "can all help decrease the need for dose escalation." Our view: Not a chance. Integrative treatment is our stock and trade and we, too, are amazed when prescribers "forget" such key strategies. But, no form of talk therapy or psychosocial intervention can reduce the impact of stimulant tolerance, because tolerance isn't a psychosocial process. It's a neurological one.

- Switching from one class of stimulants to another. Our view: We've heard this one many times, yet it makes no logical sense. A change from say, Adderall XR to Concerta won't alter the long-term impact of dopamine on the neuron because both medications increase dopamine, and stimulant tolerance is your brain's unhelpful adaptation to that very phenomenon.

- Adding "augmentation medication...like clonidine and extended-release guanfacine." Our view: The first problem with this suggestion is that both of these medications work primarily for externalized symptoms of ADHD (hyperkinesis) and little, if at all, for the inattentive symptoms. The second problem is that while these drugs might mask the symptoms of stimulant tolerance in hyperactive clients, they won't address the underlying cause unless they are used instead of a stimulant during a break. However, given their minimal impact on attention and their tendency to subdue clients, that probably won't go well. Strattera would be a better alternative during extended (e.g., summer) medication breaks, but as an ongoing alternative to stimulants, we've found it of limited utility (Chapter 6).

- More stimulant. Jain writes, "When all else fails, I will—if appropriate and safe for that patient—slowly increase the dose of a stimulant to above the label range," adding, "Obviously, one has to be watchful about medication diversion and abuse potential." Our view: Yes, this happens quite often before clients get to our office, and rarely with the caution Dr. Jain proposes. We do it ourselves on occasion, as Lara's case illustrates. In fact, she was eventually on 60mg of Adderall XR and an evening booster before we required her to take a break or get her meds somewhere else. She then changed to Mydayis, but not because that change reduced her tolerance. It simply lasted longer than her Adderall XR. We acknowledge Dr. Jain's strategy, but it only staves off the inevitable and thereby promotes greater tolerance.

- Consultation. When prescribers get stymied by stimulant tolerance, Jain asks them to seek "a medication consultation from an expert colleague" to get "ideas not previously considered... when a complex situation arises." Our view: We wish this happened more often in psychopharmacology and we hope curious physicians will read this book and reconsider how they approach the entire matter of tolerance.

Bottom line: you can put off tolerance, but you cannot avoid it; and those who continue to try will end up in the same spot as Lara, the MTA children, Dr. Jain, Dr. Yanofski, Drs. Pelham and Swanson, and that tiny middle school girl who was on too much Adderall.

Give Yourself A Break

Dr. Yanofski proposes that, "during periods of abstinence from the medication, these phenomena [of tolerance] are reversible." In other words, you have to quit stimulants for a while in order to keep them working. Your prescriber may already have a protocol for doing this. If so, take that ball and run his or her play. If not, here's the protocol we use. It provides two to four breaks per year, lasting at least ten to fourteen days.

- **For students.** Follow the academic calendar. Go off medication over Christmas, spring break, two weeks after spring finals and two weeks just before fall term starts. You'll probably want to break at Thanksgiving, too, particularly if your school takes the whole week off. That will up your appetite for Turkey Day and allow you a little tolerance reduction just before finals. If you don't have much to do over the summer, you *might* consider taking a longer break. Just be very careful. You're on medication for a reason.

- **For working adults.** If your meds are working, your boss and coworkers may not even know you have ADD. Then you suddenly go off meds and all your symptoms jump to the surface. The boss may take that badly. Under the Americans With Disabilities Act (ADA), your employer has to make reasonable accommodations for ADD. Ask your therapist or prescriber to write a nice letter requesting two two-week medication breaks per year, during which the boss should be extra patient, give you no new tasks, and wait to evaluate you until you're back on meds. As long as you're productive the rest of the year, there's rarely a downside. If you can't get by on two working breaks, dip into your vacation pool or holiday time. Just be careful in your first days off meds because...

- **Withdrawal.** Whatever ADD symptoms you had before you took your first stimulant will be worse in the first four or five days after you go off. Sometimes much worse. We call this a period of "withdrawal." It's not like what addicts go through when quitting drugs or alcohol. Clinical stimulant withdrawal is more annoying than scary. If you're hyperactive, you'll be more so. If you have trouble studying or reading, you'd better finish that book before stop day. If you have problems with inattentive driving, *do not drive in those first few days (!!)*. In an attempt to combat withdrawal, your prescriber may suggest tapering down over a few days. We almost never do this, because the longer the tapering goes on, the longer the break must last, and most people, like Lara, really hate long breaks.

- **Weekends?** Dr. Yanofski notes, "Studies have shown that weekend drug holidays reduce stimulant side effects without causing significant symptom increases, likely because the medications were reduced during the days when less focus was required."[244] Maybe, maybe not. You're free to practice this as part of your protocol if your prescriber okays it, but we've rarely found weekend breaks helpful in reducing tolerance. Yes, you're taking about eight fewer doses of medication per month and that might extend the length of the stimulant's effectiveness between breaks, but you're not off it long enough

---

[244] www.ncbi.nlm.nih.gov/pmc/articles/PMC3036556/

over the weekend for your brain to readjust. That gives you maximum withdrawal and minimum gain every single weekend. Besides, when exactly is less focus required?

- **Substitute a helper med.** For some people who have more difficult withdrawal and/or an especially hard time being off stimulants, it's possible to switch to a non-stimulant medication during the off time. The most common one is Strattera, which can provide some limited symptom reduction absent stimulants. However, it's only useful for very long breaks, like in the summer, because it takes many weeks to get to a therapeutic dose and then many weeks to come off of it. We have at times overlapped the phase in and phase out with stimulants to try and maximize the break without clobbering the end or beginning of a high school or college semester. This strategy takes very tight coordination with the prescriber.

- **You might try eTNS.** We discuss this new technology in Chapter 11. Though we haven't tried using it this way, eTNS might theoretically improve the experience of a long-term break, meaning sixteen weeks which is the required treatment run for this product. That's a month longer than a full summer school break, so the timing for students could be risky. It's not meant to be used on top of a stimulant or while phasing in or out, so you have to be all-in for the duration to get any benefit. Let us know if you try it this way and how it works out.

Another strategy that can really help manage (but not eliminate) tolerance is starting on a lower dose right after a break and then working your way up to your maximum dose just before the next break. Our

Doing what we propose in this chapter will change how you take stimulant medication.

true ADD superstars eventually manage their medications so carefully that they start at, say, 50mg of Vyvanse, slowly increase over four months to perhaps 60mg, and occasionally, 70mg just before their winter break.[245] After ten to fourteen days off, they begin again at 50mg and start the process over again. That may seem complicated, but with a collaborative

---

[245] We picked these numbers to illustrate our point. The real dosages depend on where you start and what your ceiling is.

prescriber, it's not difficult at all, and it can lead you toward the Holy Grail of ADD med management: maximum gain and minimum pain.

If you're doing well on your stimulants right now, the last thing you want to think about is taking a break. Who can blame you for relishing your triumph over ADD? But if there's anything we know to be true, it's that long-term stimulant success isn't sustainable without breaks, just as the MTA study indicates. Doing what we propose in this chapter will change how you take stimulant medication, how much you take of it, how well it works over a lifetime, your overall satisfaction with treatment, and your desire to keep taking it.

Just don't tell the pharmaceutical companies any of this. They don't know that they'd actually do more business over a client's lifetime if they did things our way because consumers would be more satisfied with their stimulant experience and more willing to continue over the long haul. Until big pharma revamps its spreadsheet department to imagine all those improved sales and then puts money into researching stimulant tolerance, this will have to be our little secret.

If you or your prescriber aren't, by now, convinced that stimulant tolerance is real and how to address it effectively, consider a final passage from Dr. Yanofski that puts quite a fine point on the subject:

> The potential long-term cost of chasing symptom relief by way of multiple increases in dose size or frequency warrants further study. If paradoxical decompensation [stimulant tolerance] is present, it may be appropriate to view the symptom relief received by stimulants as a 'borrowed benefit.' Much like borrowing money from a bank, these symptoms must be paid back in the future. The payback upon stimulant discontinuation may be a subacute syndrome, during which the patient will function "attention-wise" below their baseline (due to downregulated postsynaptic DA receptors and decreased presynaptic DA release). This subclinical withdrawal would decrease over time, but may be present, to some degree, until the receptors are completely reversed back to their baseline set-point.

To this we say, Amen.

Bad Stimulant Ideas

> That, in my opinion, was the most diabolical aspect of those old-time big brains: They would tell their owners, in effect, "Here is a crazy thing we could actually do, probably, but we would never do it, of course. It's just fun to think about." And then, as though in trances, the people would really do it.
>
> – Kurt Vonnegut, *Galápagos*

- Dr. Wes –

"These guys must be planning to make a big profit off this new drug," I said to Kelsey as I started slicing up my steak.

"No kidding," she said. "This has to be a $60 a plate dinner, but that's how big pharma rolls."

"What's so great about this new stimulant they're hawking?" I asked.

"It's called Alflipanol[246]," Kelsey said. "It's a new formulation that's kind of like Adderall, but supposedly has less side effects."

"Do we need another stim?" I asked. "Vyvanse and Daytrana get the job done. Throw in a little XR and Concerta and we're good."

"I see room for this formulation in our practice. I have people who just don't respond as we'd like them to on the big name meds. This company knows it's moving into a tight market space, so they're

---

[246] I made up a funny pseudonym for this product, but the incident happened just as described.

offering some great incentives for clients who might not be able to afford Vyvanse but need a longer-acting stimulant."

The pharmacy rep and his psychiatrist spokesperson[247] began their slide show, explaining where the new drug fit into the marketplace and how it had performed in clinical trials. When discussion time came, Kelsey and I had a string of questions about the molecular structure and chemical mix of Alflipinol, its release time, when it would be indicated over existing medications, and whether its rate of tolerance had been assessed (hint: "no"). The drug rep and his expert said what they were allowed to say per the FDA and took notes on what they couldn't answer for later follow up.

Finally, a few of the other prescribers, nearly all psychiatrists in their late fifties to early seventies, joined the conversation.

"May, I ask," said Dr. Snow. "What do you do about stimulant abuse? This is such an immense problem now."

The pharma guys looked a little puzzled. "I'm not sure what you're asking," the rep said politely. "These are schedule two medications. Um. So, uh, I mean all stimulants have potential for abuse. We have strict prescribing guidelines—"

"I have a patient who is wanting to take too much stimulant," Dr. Phogg interrupted. "This man went to another psychiatric prescriber—she was a nurse." He glanced sideways at Kelsey. "And she did not know that he was coming also to me and he took medicine from her and also from me. This went on for six months."

The rep and expert stared blankly. "Oh. That's illegal," said the psychiatrist. "Doesn't your state have a tracking system for that?"

"I am from Missouri," Phogg said.

Kelsey jumped in to save the pharmacy reps, a behavior uncommon to her. "We have K-TRACS in Kansas. You just log in if you have concerns and see whether the patient is double or triple dipping or whatever. Unfortunately, Missouri is the only state in the country that doesn't have that kind of system."

---

[247] Companies purchase the time of noted prescribers to serve as expert spokespersons for their medication. The expert isn't supposed to hard sell the product, but simply note the benefits of the drug and suggest ways it could be integrated into practice.

"Oh dear," the expert said, turning to Dr. Phogg. "I think you might want to speak with your state legislature about this."

Before Dr. Phogg could respond, Dr. Storm spoke up, addressing the room and ignoring the reps. "In my practice we have solved this problem."

"How?" several doctors asked in unison.

"We tell our patients that we will only prescribe non-stimulants for attention deficit. We use Strattera and I like to try sometimes, Intuniv. These are medications that cannot be abused."

Several doctors started scribbling notes about two medications that were not the subject of this steak dinner and which had been on the market for many years. One asked how to spell "Intuniv."

The expert seemed at a loss for words. "I appreciate your concern about misuse of stimulants, but there are millions of prescriptions written each year for these products and really there's no indication of widespread abuse among users for whom the drug is indicated. There is a secondary market of people using stimulants as study drugs, and a smaller group that abuses them as amphetamines, but our product is really like Vyvanse in that regard, it's impervious to snorting or injecting. So it's actually safer than say, Adderall."

"That is what they said about opioids," said Dr. Sunny. "I have a woman in our practice who took the Adderall IR and crushed it up and took it by nose, just as you said. We stopped seeing her."

"That's certainly an appropriate response," Kelsey interjected. "We don't tolerate misuse in our practice either, but we do see a lot of young people, so we prefer to curb misuse before it happens by prescribing medications that can't easily be converted to recreational use."

"We have many students come to us and want the study drugs for their college," said Dr. Snow. "And now, even in high school. Things are so competitive now. Children feel such pressures. We just tell them, 'No, that is not something we do.'"

"Are you, um, assessing them for ADD?" asked the rep. "I mean how can you know that they are or aren't diagnosable if you don't do an assessment?"

"We do not," Snow said. "I assume that if they are in high school or college and just now looking for medication, then they do not have the childhood presentation of ADHD necessary to make the diagnosis. Clearly they are just drug seeking."

"This is such an interesting conversation," the expert said. It was clear from his face that he didn't mean it. "But we're really here to talk about Alflipanol and what it could offer your patients. Does anyone have any examples of cases where the client maybe isn't responding to another stimulant as you'd expect? I might have some ideas for that."

"What if I have a patient who has abused Adderall in the past?" Dr. Rain asked. "Would he also be prone to abuse this medication?"

"I have a patient who has been on Vyvanse for five years," Dr. Winter said. "She is always complaining that her medication is not enough, even though I have raised her to 70mg. Would your medication work better for someone like this? Would she feel more satisfied with it?"

"I think it would be worth trying," the expert said. "And the company has a month's free trial offer so your patient could see how it works for her, cost free."

Kelsey stepped in. "Dr. Winter, has your patient ever taken a stimulant break?"

"Not that I'm aware of. Why do you ask?" He didn't wait for an answer. "I just think this patient has become dependent on medication and is seeking a greater high. I see this with many patients. They never get that same high, so they want to go up more."

Kelsey glanced back at me, her lips pursed.

"I'm just eating this steak," I whispered as I leaned in toward her. "You're young. You haven't been through this as many times as I have. Some people have a hammer, so everything looks like a nail."

What Not to Worry About

When it comes to stimulants, the thing people seem to want to talk about most is misuse, abuse, dependency, and addiction. This Greek chorus certainly includes the skeptic press, but as our opening vignette illustrates, many professionals associate stimulant medication with abuse. That's unfortunate for all the good folks with properly diagnosed ADD and those of us who treat them, because it casts aspersions on anyone taking these life changing medications.

Kelsey and I worry that this could, at any point, turn into a mass hysteria. A great example is found in a 2018 WebMD article entitled, "Experts Warn of Emerging 'Stimulant Epidemic'[248]," which compares stimulant prescribing to the opioid crisis. In fact, despite the super click-bait headline, seventy percent of the article is about opioids, twenty percent is about cocaine abuse, and the last three, short paragraphs discuss stimulants. Here they are in full:

> In addition to illegal drugs, legal supplies of stimulants have never been greater. Prescriptions for stimulant medications like Ritalin and Adderall are up for all age groups, according to data from prescription drug monitoring programs. Both are typically prescribed to treat attention deficit disorders.

> In Oregon, for example, the rate of stimulant prescriptions written for every 1,000 adults ages 30 to 44 increased from 159 in 2012 to 238 in 2016, about a 50% increase. The largest percent increase, puzzlingly, was in prescriptions written for people ages 65 to 74.

> [John] Eadie[249] says he doesn't know why prescriptions are up, but he urged people in the audience to start digging into that question.

---

[248] www.webmd.com/mental-health/addiction/news/20180403/experts-warn-of-emerging-stimulant-epidemic

[249] According to the article, John Eadie is the coordinator for something called the National Emerging Threat Initiative, which provides research to the government's High Intensity Drug Trafficking Areas program.

At this point in this book, you should be knowledgeable enough to help John Eadie and his audience "dig into" this not terribly difficult or pressing question. Prescriptions for stimulants are up not because of a conspiracy or epidemic, but because more people are getting diagnosed with ADD. And (repeat after me) some of those people probably shouldn't be diagnosed, most of them probably should be, a bunch more should be but aren't, and we can't ever know how many should and shouldn't because overdiagnosis isn't a thing and good diagnoses and integrative treatments aren't as widely practiced as they should be.

And yet, this article on a popular health website promotes the conflation of clinical stimulant therapy with substance abuse. That, in turn, encourages the virulent myth that taking stimulants, even for correctly diagnosed ADD, raises one's risk of drug or alcohol addiction. The opposite is more likely true, as Timothy Wilens, points out in a 2018 article in *ADDitude* magazine:

> There is considerable evidence to the contrary. Stimulant treatment is well known to improve a child's academic and social functioning. These improvements translate into enhanced self-esteem, less self-medication, and hence, studies show, less substance abuse.

Wilens goes on to note that of ten studies addressing stimulants and long-term substance abuse:

> Six of the studies demonstrate clearly that earlier treatment results in reduced substance abuse. Three studies show no difference [between those treated and their untreated peers]. One study shows higher risk for substance abuse connected to earlier treatment. No study shows any increased risk of substance abuse when the severity of ADHD is factored in.

He closes the article noting:

> Treatment isn't all that matters. So does treatment response. Studies show that adolescents with ADHD who respond well to their medications are at lower risk for

substance abuse compared to those who respond poorly to their medication.

An article on the CHADD website makes the same point[250]. So, if you're agonizing over the threat addiction may pose to you or your ADD loved one, worry just as much about what happens if they don't get treatment. Properly executed, well integrated, stimulant treatment for correctly diagnosed clients is, by every empirical estimation, your friend, not your enemy.

What to Worry About

What about badly executed, fragmented, stimulant treatment for poorly diagnosed clients? Now that's a problem, and we'd be remiss if we didn't give it some ink in a book about fearless medication management for ADD and ADHD. There are several common ways to misuse stimulants. Let's start by discussing the people who shouldn't be on them to begin with, folks who've found a physician or nurse practitioner all too eager to fork over the meds without doing the kind of diligence discussed in Chapter 3 and on nearly every other page of this book.

Study Drugging

By far the most common and best known form of misuse is students taking stimulants to supercharge their academic performance. Practicing in a college town, we hear of this all the time and in fact, we've had our share of young people come in with scant evidence of ADD, hoping to score stims to improve their homework and up test scores. And this isn't just an issue on college campuses any more. As noted in the vignette, stimulants are ubiquitous and affordable enough that high school kids are getting in on the game. Occasionally, we even see parents, faced with the prospect of their child not getting into Yale, come looking for a "little helper" to smooth the way.

In Chapter 2, we discussed this dumb study strategy as part of one ADD myth—that stimulants can help neurotypical people gain an edge over their peers. Because they aren't lacking dopamine in all the right places, non-ADD people are more likely to get a big helping of side effects. Moreover, if they're buying their meds on the secondary

---

[250] chadd.org/for-parents/substance-abuse-and-adhd/

market, there's nobody monitoring them to be sure they're taking regular breaks, managing weight, and getting enough sleep. This leaves them more susceptible to all the stimulant maladies we'll discuss over the rest of this chapter.

Sale and Distribution

Diverting controlled substances for sale is commonplace now[251] [252]. Because so many kids take meds easily purchased from "that guy" in their Western Civ class or borrowed from a roommate, many have become desensitized to the potential danger stims can pose. Add to this their familiarity with party drugs like Ketamine and MDMA[253] and any appropriate fear of stimulant abuse, sale, or distribution drops into the back of their minds. It's just part of the culture.

On the other side of the equation are the suppliers who obtain their wares in several ways. Nobody keeps a spreadsheet on this, but we suspect the most common supply chain comes from people feigning a diagnosis of ADD to a prescriber who isn't doing a thorough assessment and then turning the meds over at a rate of about $20 a pill. Since insurance is covering part of their prescription cost, that leaves one with about a $550 profit each month. If that person can scam up a second prescriber to double dip (see next section) and doesn't get caught on the state database, he or she might clear another $300, since the second script will have to be paid in cash and not turned over to insurance.

Other students, including some with ADD, are less into profit and more into the social value that comes from sharing medication. Perhaps they trade stimulants for opioids. Maybe they just like being seen as generous and helpful to their friends. Many don't realize that even without a money exchange, redistributing controlled substances to friends is both medically unwise and illegal.

---

[251] www.michigandaily.com/section/research/adderall-used-24-university-students

[252] www.center4research.org/study-drug-abuse-college-students/

[253] Known also as Ecstasy or Molly, *3,4-methylenedioxy-methamphetamine* is a synthetic drug that induces hallucinogens and produces feelings of increased energy, pleasure, emotional warmth, and distorted sensory and time perception.

A second supply line we see, comes from stealing the medication of legitimately prescribed peers. Every now and then, an established client comes in claiming that their nearly full bottle of medication was stolen from their locker, car, or purse. Except in the rarest of circumstances, with clients we know like family, Kelsey simply will not replace a lost or stolen script because we're not excited about supporting that supply line. As you can see in the opening vignette, other prescribers are even more suspicious than we are. So dear readers, hang on to your medication, because if you don't, someone else will. It could be your dating partner, your roommate, your BFF, or even (kid you not) your parent. We've seen 'em all, which is why we also suggest you never disclose to anyone that you have ADD or take stimulants, unless it's a matter of accommodation at work or school. We're not trying to create a culture of shame. We're trying to limit your risk.

And if you or a loved one are thinking about getting in on this lucrative trade, just remember that whole felony thing. As suppliers in the opioid trade have been learning the hard way, a business like this can go along great for years and years, until it all falls apart.

Snorting

If one is really into stimulants as party drugs, the top idea on the dumb list is crushing up fast-acting Adderall and blowing it up your nose like cocaine. This delivers the stimulant to your brain faster and with greater intensity, increasing heart rate, blood pressure, and temperature to dangerous levels. The website amphetamines.com[254] notes, that "for many, the euphoria and expected enhancements of snorting Adderall outweigh any perceived risks and they will repeat this behavior multiple times adding to the risk of overdose, health risks, and addiction."

Because of the nature of this particular drug and method of delivery, those health risks will come sooner than you might expect and include cardiovascular and pulmonary problems, hyperthermia and dehydration, withdrawal, tolerance and dependency. Psychologically, stimulant snorting can lead to all manner of emotional instability including extreme anxiety, panic, mania, paranoia, delirium, auditory, visual, or tactile hallucinations, and bizarre or even psychotic perceptions and behavior.

---

[254] amphetamines.com/types/adderall/what-are-the-side effects-of-snorting-adderall/

Here's the good news. Several long-acting stimulants like Vyvanse, Daytrana, and Concerta cannot be misused this way. The patch wouldn't fit up your nose, the ceramic OROS capsule would plug your nostril, and Vyvanse isn't even a stimulant until it gets into your system, so it would just make you sneeze.

Adderall XR, however, can be snorted and because it comes in easy-to-manage small beads inside a capsule, it's even easier to misuse this way than its short-acting cousin. This isn't the only reason we favor newer delivery systems in our practice, but it's one big one. Whenever we have a new client coming in showing a particular fascination with good old Adderall, we get even edgier. The last thing Kelsey or any of our staff are interested in doing, is contributing to this bad idea.

Stimulant Fouls

Sometimes, properly medicated people with ADD start coloring outside the lines, shifting from the standard love-hate relationship with stimulants into one where they become overly attached to their meds and rewrite the playbook without prescriber input. We call these "stimulant fouls." Committing them creates new headaches for clients, their treaters, and everyone caught in between.

We happily fire poseurs who feign symptoms to get drugs or make money. But when legit ADD clients go off the rails, they're usually expressing another facet of the poor judgment, dysregulation, and impulsivity that accompanies this disorder. Kelsey and I hold our clients accountable under the tenets of radical honesty and personal responsibility[255], but we offer more grace to clients who commit fouls than to someone who is deliberately jacking us up. Other prescribers, like those in the opening vignette, make no such distinctions, so stay on the right side of the line. With that in mind, let's look at the most common bad ideas that show up among the genuine ADD crowd.

Exceeding Dosage

Even properly treated ADD clients may try to get in on the study drug craze by secretly hording pills and then taking two (or more) capsules over the course of a treatment day, maybe one at 8:00 a.m. and another at noon. Occasionally, a client may even take two pills at once, perhaps

---

[255] See Chapters 8 and 9 of *I Always Want to Be Where I'm Not.*

as an unwise preparation for a big test. Sometimes, this comes in response to stimulant tolerance that the client feels isn't being adequately addressed. More often, it results from the cognitive distortion that they can supercharge their performance to keep up with their classmates, some of whom are also misusing stimulants.

We work with this population often. We understand the drive to compete. We're excited when our ADD clients get it together and blow out the competition. But, doubling or tripling a stimulant without a direct order from a prescriber is a terrible idea. At best, you may get yourself so screwed up on stimulants that you have to take a two to four week break and then start over from scratch. Or you may find yourself fired by your prescriber after blowing up a carefully developed treatment plan for a single night or two of academic indulgence. And good luck finding another one once you've been terminated for misuse.

At worst, you could incite some low-grade versions of the health problems we discussed under the "Snorting" section. Taking a bit too much medication isn't usually as dangerous as blowing it up your nose, but too much stimulant is too much stimulant, and at some point your body is going to retaliate. Dosing limits exist for a reason.

We're good at discerning the difference between someone who's trying to work the program and someone who's trying to work us. If you're battling tolerance or simply not on enough medication, don't take matters into your own hands. In our office we're good at discerning the difference between someone who's trying to work the program and someone who's trying to work us. Have an honest conversation with your provider, explain tolerance, and see if you can come up with a reasonable arrangement. If you don't commit any stimulant fouls, you're more likely to be taken seriously, and your prescriber may be open to exceeding the limits in between regular breaks.

Staying Up

Though it often overlaps with other bad ideas in this chapter, using stimulants to extend or eliminate your bedtime[256] is particularly lame. Whether you're doing it to party, clean, pull an all-nighter, drive cross-

---

[256] In the stimulant abuse world, this is colloquially referred to as "staying up."

country, talk all night online to your lover, or play video games 'til 6:00 a.m., stimulant induced insomnia will lead to a huge crash[257].

Over the years, we've found this foul to be about the fastest way to let stimulants destroy your life without really meaning to. Most people who snort Adderall don't need anyone to advise them to stop. It's self-evident. But taking stimulants late in the evening so you can work all night and get important stuff done? That seems so productive and goal oriented. Even a bit noble. Except, it's just another cognitive distortion, one in which you become that one person who can pop a pill, skip bed, and churn out an award winning product, and then pop another one and head off to school or work, free of a massive sleep debt that you can never repay because, as noted in Chapter 4, paying back sleep isn't a real thing.

Double Dipping

There's an obvious and immediate consequence to overusing prescription medication: you run out. And when it comes to controlled substances, it's not easy to re-up your supply. The study-druggers and partiers can horde all those pills they don't really need and then take more than they should whenever the urge strikes. But ADD clients who misuse their meds will eventually need more supply than one prescriber can provide, particularly if they're out chasing tolerance. Even if they overstate their need, that tolerance only grows, eventually eating up the overage. This leads some people to seek a second prescriber, repeating the same intake they've already done at the first office, and ending up with a second prescription for a drug they often claim to have "been on in the past" without mentioning that "the past" was nine o'clock that morning. Such folks will go to great lengths and take great risks to acquire a bunch of stimulants.

If a client is written a prescription for something affordable like say, immediate-release Adderall, from several different prescribers, then he or she can go to several different pharmacies and fill them without challenge. This actually works as long as the client is paying cash at one office, is good at lying and deception, doesn't show any obvious signs of overuse, and is going to a prescriber who does ten minute appointments and doesn't require patients to also see a therapist. Otherwise,

---

[257] Another fine tweaker term that means what it sound like it means.

it takes almost no effort on the part of the prescriber to catch double dippers. We just log onto our state database, as Kelsey described in the vignette, key in the client's name and birth date and we can see every controlled substance script he or she has filled in the last five years. These systems are in place to protect and educate the public and not to be punitive. We're not pulling an "I Gotcha!"

Eventually all double dippers get caught.

In addition to putting you on the bad side of any prescriber, these stimulant fouls have, in our experience, ended marriages, blown up good jobs, flunked students out of college, imploded families, and ruined promising lives. They also give juice to the skeptic press by exaggerating the extent of such behavior among legitimately diagnosed people with ADD.

Addiction
- Dr. Kelsey -

Just because addiction is comparatively rare among properly diagnosed and treated ADD clients doesn't mean it's nonexistent. Stimulants are DEA controlled substances for a reason. Their potential for misuse can, in extreme cases, lead to addiction. Unfortunately, that term gets thrown around a lot and interchanged with terms like "misuse" and "abuse" when in fact, each word has a different meaning.

Chemical addiction is a persistent condition that affects the brain's reward system such that one is unable to abstain from a given substance (or behavior) despite obvious negative consequences to the person's life[258]. This generally requires one to feel something very desirable when taking the substance which in turn, leads one to crave its use. Rarely does a person who has uncomplicated ADD feel that kind of a jolt after the first few days or weeks on a stimulant. This is why stimulant addiction is more often found in neurotypical people who are taking stimulants to get high or as a study drug. Or, as former meth addict Robert commented at intake after being released from rehab, "I've had ADD for years, and then I tried meth and it wasn't like it was for

---

[258] National Institute on Drug Abuse: www.drugabuse.gov/publications/media-guide/science-drug-use-addiction-basics

everyone else on our construction crew. They were tweaking and I was like, 'Wow, I can think so clearly now.' I was never high on meth. I was always on my game."

For Robert and other ADD clients prone to addiction, we take great care to manage expectations and modify cognitive distortions. The goal should never be to feel energized but to more adequately function. In fact, we discourage any hint of tweaking. If you find yourself craving more medication to feel high, you may be at risk for addiction. If committing stimulant fouls becomes a habit or if you're fighting an urge to snort, talk at once to your therapist and/or prescriber.

Treatment for Stimulant Addiction. Given the gravity of this situation, you may be astonished to learn that having a tendency toward stimulant addiction does not immediately disqualify you from using them in a well-organized treatment plan. We're incredibly cautious about who we're willing to see under these circumstances and even more careful about how we see them. Robert was a successful case because he followed every one of these rules for walking the fine line between stimulant consumer and stimulant addict. They're nonnegotiable.

- **Involve the family.** Under no circumstances will we see anyone at risk of stimulant abuse as an individual therapy case. We need all the help we can get, and regardless of your age, you'll need to bring in an accountability partner who is not at risk of misuse to help manage your meds. That person must take responsibility for obtaining your prescription from the pharmacy, locking it down, and handing it out to you at the agreed upon time. They're allowed to make no changes without my written consent as documented on paper or in an email. Robert's wife happened to be a nurse, which made all the difference in how his case came out.

- **Use technology.** There are several excellent secure pill boxes that can take some of the load off your meds partner. Your accountability partner loads the box on a weekly basis and sets its clock. The little door for each pill only opens at a preset time each day, so unless you go on the street and buy more medication, you'll only have access to the prescribed amount. Anyone in this situation who commits that street drug foul, will have one less prescriber to deal with. And how might we find out about such sneaky conduct...?

- **Submit to drug testing.** I can order urine tests at any point I want to on any client I deem at risk of a foul. It's in our informed consent package and anyone who wants to be on stimulants with us—whether or not they have a history of drug abuse—must sign on. For those on our stimulant abuse risk program, I order these tests with some frequency. They reveal with great precision how much amphetamine is in your system. If it's more than it should be, I blow the whistle.

Crossing Stimulants and Other Substances

Our clients are always surprised to learn that when combined with alcohol, marijuana, benzodiazepines, or nicotine, the lingering physiological effects of stimulants can create real short- and long-term health risks. Perhaps they imagined stimulants to pose little concern because they don't "build up" in the system. Compared to say, antidepressants, that's true because of the "here today, gone tomorrow" nature of stimulants. It just seems reasonable that a stim you took this morning would be gone from your body by the time you took a drink or lit a cigarette after school or work. That's just not how it works.

Regardless of whether you're taking short-acting or extended-release, the medication actually sticks around well after the noticeable effect has ended. Even short-acting stimulants have a half-life of around eleven hours[259]. This means a 20mg dose is only reduced to 10mg at hour eleven, to 5mg at hour twenty-two, and 2.5mg at hour thirty-three. While that will slip beneath your therapeutic dose threshold by 5:00 p.m. so you no longer get any effect, it doesn't mean the medication is gone. With that in mind, let's review the most common substances likely to crash into your stimulant.

Alcohol

You'd think combining a depressant like alcohol with a stimulant would cancel out the effect of both, right? Unfortunately, the answer is "yes" with heavy emphasis on "unfortunately." Drinking while

---

[259] This is how we measure the rate of disposal of medication in your body. Every eleven hours the amount of stimulant in your body is reduced by half. Other medications have a different half-life.

stimulants are still active in your system is a recipe for alcohol poisoning. Stims can mask the symptoms of alcohol intoxication by increasing alertness, awareness of one's surroundings, and memory, giving you the impression of being less drunk than you are. If you continue to consume alcohol thereafter, you can more easily drink past your individual safe threshold before sensing the danger. Alcohol also raises the threat of stimulant overdose by muting the physical and emotional signs that a lethal or near-lethal dose has been consumed. Moreover, drinking alcohol during any twenty-four hour period in which stimulants were taken raises the risk of elevated blood pressure, seizures, anxiety, and even psychosis.

You don't have to become a teetotaler in order to be treated for ADD. Many of our clients drink. You just need to take into consideration the way in which your stimulant could impact how and how much you drink and respond accordingly. We talked earlier about mindful eating. This is mindful drinking. If that seems like an oxymoron, you may need to try the teetotaler plan.

Marijuana

Marijuana is more popular today than ever, especially if you live in one of the growing number of states that has legalized it for medicinal or recreational use. This poses several concerns for people taking stimulants. Most notably, clinically significant levels of THC, the psychoactive ingredient in marijuana, may remain in the body for up to seventy-two hours. While the idea of a "weed hangover" remains controversial, THC-induced brain fog, headache, and fatigue are possible within that elimination period. Regular pot use, particularly if it is heavy, can make it difficult for you and your prescriber to differentiate between the residual symptoms of weed, clinically significant depression unrelated to marijuana use, and waning efficacy of the prescribed stimulant. This makes it next to impossible to determine how well your stimulant is working and how much more (or less) to prescribe.

While some teens and young adults claim pot improves their focus and reduces their hyperactivity, our experience working in a big Midwestern college town suggests a far more likely result: lethargy. While the effects vary from one strain to another, a principal use of marijuana is to mellow out. For ADD folks taking medication and modifying behavior to better function in school and work, being chill is not a recipe for success. That's why we mentioned in Chapter 2 that taking medication for anxiety may worsen ADD symptoms by making you care too little. The same is often true for marijuana. And when combined with stimulants, weed can mask certain behavioral expressions of stimulant misuse, particularly heightened agitation and aggression.

For this reason, we often ask our pot-friendly clients, particularly heavy users, to abstain for a period of time until we can get their meds right. That causes some to drop out of treatment or seek a prescription elsewhere, which is unfortunate for many reasons, including the fact that a behavioral addiction is defined as not being able to stop doing something that is causing problems or which limits pursuit of your own best interests.

We both know people with ADD who smoke marijuana and also take stimulants and are successful in work, family, and school. But most of them use it on a strictly recreational basis and with a careful eye toward their daily stimulant cycle and task schedule. We've come across many others who've been unable to wisely manage their use of marijuana and between that and their ADD symptoms, find themselves accomplishing less than they're capable of. Some of them, far less.

Benzodiazepines

From a behavioral standpoint, the misuse of benzodiazepines (e.g. Xanax, Valium, Ativan) will counteract any positive impact stimulants might have on focus, motivation, concentration, and performance. While a small number of clients with co-occurring disorders may occasionally use these as rescue meds for panic attacks or severe anxiety, chronic use in clients who also use stimulants can create a pinball effect between overstimulation and rescue, particularly when the meds are taken outside a carefully controlled regimen.

Like alcohol and marijuana, benzodiazepines can also mask signs of stimulant overdose and the amount taken to come down from a high can well exceed the daily recommended dose. Worse, misuse can also set you up for abrupt discontinuation due to a shortage of supply, which can, in severe cases, lead to seizures or, occasionally, death.

Other Stimulants

Nicotine. Rates of smoking in adults with ADD have gone largely unstudied, probably because people who use nicotine are intentionally excluded from experimental groups because they are not stimulant na-ïve. This is because all stimulants, including nicotine, enhance dopamine levels and activity in the brain, which may increase attention and awareness. In fact, nicotine given via a transdermal patch, has been shown to improve symptoms in adults with ADHD, but has not gained acceptance as a treatment because of its many negative side effects.

For many years, and following national trends, the rate of smoking in populations we serve had decreased significantly. Now, with vaping on the rise, we've begun again to caution clients about the impact of doubling up their stimulants through nicotine use. The risks include not only agitation and excess focus, but cardiovascular concerns like high blood pressure and even stroke.

Caffeine. Many a person with ADD has, prior to seeking treatment, found a savior in caffeine. Unfortunately, if that worked over the long haul, someone would have packaged it as a treatment for ADD. Instead, "therapeutic" doses of caffeine provide less focus and more side effect than actual medication. Yet, we still see some clients at the point of intake so overusing this stimulant that we've required them to do a period of detox before we'll even discuss medication. And after they're in treatment, we caution them to consider all caffeine use—energy drinks, coffee, tea, soda, pre-workout supplements—as if it were an additional dose of medication. For most teens and adults, the implications of a slightly elevated blood pressure and heart rate are negligible side effects of proper stimulant use. However, those symptoms become incrementally more dangerous when combined with caffeine, particularly coffees and teas that have widely varying and poorly described dosing.

Pseudoephedrine. We caution clients to be careful with this drug, which you should recognize as both a popular decongestant and the core element of illegal methamphetamine. Even in its over-the-counter formulation, pseudoephedrine can add to your overall stimulant load on a given day. Clients who are using stimulant medication should move to a non-stimulant guaifenesin (branded as Mucinex) which contains no stimulant at all.

Now you know how much attention prescribers give to misuse and abuse of substances in tandem with stimulants. This might well discourage you from being truthful with a prescriber as to your drug and alcohol proclivities. Trust me when I say that keeping substance use quiet is a terrible idea when working closely with the person handing out mind-altering substances via a prescription pad. Yes, we do know prescribers who won't touch your case if you drink a shot on a weekend or smoke a bowl twice a month with friends. If you run into that, ask yourself if you really want to work with a mental health professional with whom you cannot be honest? It's better to discuss your bad ideas and fouls openly as a part of treatment than to hide them and hope things turn out okay, which they probably won't.

Honesty is the foundation of any team effort, even when that's hard. Without it in abundance, you'll end up less satisfied, less successful, and less fearless in your long-term management of ADD and ADHD.

Alternatives to Medication?

If you look for truth, you may find comfort in the end; if you
look for comfort you will not get either comfort or truth only
soft soap and wishful thinking to begin, and in the end, despair.

— C. S. Lewis

- Dr. Wes -

"Before we get to medication, I'd like to try some alternatives," Janelle said. A single mom to a rambunctious sixth-grade girl, she'd come to see me for a consultation[260] after her daughter, Sarah, had run afoul of her teachers. "I just feel so pressured by the school to get her behavior under control, and I just don't know what to do."

"I went over the evaluation they did at the University Psychological Center. While it doesn't have quite the level of interviewing around ADD that we'd do here, the testing itself is pretty sound. They used you as an observer, her biological father, and two teachers. That's pretty thorough and all the profiles converge. Are you still doubting the diagnosis?"

"Not really," Janelle said. "I can accept that Sarah has ADD. Her dad sure did. It's one of the reasons that relationship never went anywhere.

---

[260] A consultation is different than therapy. It's when someone meets with one or both of us live or on video and seeks our professional input on a case that we're not seeing for treatment.

I was always having to make up for his lack of attention to details, or to me, for that matter."

"What alternatives are you looking for, because we're pretty well known for doing boring conventional treatments with our own spin. They've worked well for us."

"I know. I read your book about the thirteen principals for living with ADD. I thought it was spot on. But I just don't want Sarah to have to deal with all the consequences of medication, and all those side effects."

"That can be hard," I said. "We spend a lot of time alongside our clients, trying to beat a path through that jungle."

She smiled. "It sounds like it from the examples you gave in the book. What if there's a situation where you can't do medication, what do you do instead?"

"You can buy fifty books to get fifty different approaches, but Sarah will be twenty-two by the time you've tried them and to be honest, you're already pretty late in the game. A lot of her personality and style of learning is developed, so if it were me—and I've been in your shoes—I'd try the medication route first, not last. And if it doesn't work out, then start considering alternatives."

"I was talking to my doctor about an elimination diet. What do you think about that?"

"There's an analysis or two that suggests a very restricted diet could be helpful, but only for people who have certain allergies. Our experience is that it's hard to get kids to eat anything healthy to begin with, and when you restrict that down to the tiny number of foods on those diets, you're going to have a hard time keeping them fed. It's not unreasonable to experiment with that approach, but I'd set a time frame and if the symptoms aren't better, change course. If it works, I'd give up on the ADD diagnosis altogether."

"What about something like Brain Balance?" Janelle asked.

"There's a reason why most of the clinics that use that approach carry a disclaimer that it's not meant to treat any mental disorder. The FDA hasn't approved it, and there's no legitimate research to back it up. If you have $12,000 laying around and don't know what to do with it, feel free to spend it that way, but I don't and I wouldn't."

"Nope." Janelle sighed. "No money in the cookie jar. I was thinking of asking my parents to chip in and maybe running a GoFundMe."

"You can get a lot of what they do in that program for free and the rest of it for not much money. It's up to you. Just watch out because companies market programs like that as if they were quite revolutionary, when they aren't based on any accepted science."

"I saw a news article about an electrical stimulator I could put on Sarah's forehead. Is that sketchy?" Janelle wanted to know.

"No," I said. "eTNS is FDA approved, and we've used it here for a few cases like Sarah's, where parents didn't want to do meds or when we just couldn't make them work. We consider eTNS experimental right now because the research is still thin. The cost is about $1,000, so it's probably a less expensive way to spend your parents' money. It's a sixteen week treatment. You could try it, see how it goes for Sarah, and if she's not showing improvement, then it might be time for a medication evaluation."

"Is that what you think I should do?" Janelle asked.

"No. I think you should try conventional treatment first. Her dad apparently has ADD, so it's that much more likely she has it, so diet isn't likely to help. If meds don't work or you don't like the side effects, you could switch up and go for eTNS later."

"What about behavioral interventions? I read that you can teach your child through reinforcement to be more on task and that if you pair that with cognitive therapy, they'll eventually gain the tools they need to be more successful in classroom settings and at home."

"Have you tried anything like that already?"

"Yeah, but it's hard to get her motivated to do anything that isn't the most interesting thing in the world, like a video or something online. I try to redirect her and give her incentives, but I think maybe I'm just not doing it right. Like I'm not a good parent or something."

"Don't beat yourself up," I said. "This is a neurological problem. We strongly believe in cognitive and behavioral interventions and a lot of parent training, but if you don't pair that with stimulant medication, you're probably just going to frustrate youself and Sarah because she may want to respond to those interventions really badly and her brain will just keep taking her off on the next adventure—productive or not."

"It's just so hard to know what's right. I think I'll do some more research and then make a decision. Could we meet again to discuss it?"

"Sure. Just be super careful in your research. There are a lot of treatments out there claiming to be 'evidence-based,' when they're basically snake oil. Use trusted sources. I have some I can send you."

"That would be great," Janelle said. "I promise to read anything you send over."

The skeptic press gets one thing right about ADD, it's created a huge market of consumers and a lot of enterprising individuals trying to monetize a chunk of it. There's nothing wrong with making a living by helping people. Kelsey and I do it. But in this era of fake news, it's easy to be led down a false, and at times, nonsensical garden path by folks who purport alternatives to the medical-industrial complex. I don't know about you or your loved one, but I've no time for illusions.

What Makes a Treatment Conventional?

No matter what we're talking about—food, music, sex—the word "conventional" sounds super boring and "alternative" sounds pretty adventurous. But when it comes to psychiatric care, sounding great and working great are often very different. When considering what is known to be helpful for ADD, you generally want to seek treatments that are "evidence based" or "empirically validated," meaning they've been subjected to research not once, but a number of times. In the scientific community this is referred to as a study being replicated.

Before we start, I'll warn you that there's a lot to critique in the empirical basis for conventional ADD treatments. Since we want you to be thinking and not just believing, let's get that out front and center. Evidence means research and research means money. Money for research in this business mostly comes from two sources, government agencies and pharmaceutical companies, so it's both reasonable and wise to question how good that research really is.

In the case of government funding, most money relevant to our discussion is funneled through university departments of psychology and psychiatry to test various treatment protocols, mostly of the non-pharmaceutical variety. Getting your hands on that cash is a competitive process and it always favors treatments that are easily manualized, meaning they can be easily divided into rigidly controlled sets of steps and procedures and deployed again and again. This eliminates variance that could throw off the experiment allowing the studies to be easily replicated.

Behavioral and cognitive-behavioral programs are ideally suited for this kind of research because they come pre-manualized and fit neatly into the university research setting. Models of treatment like family therapy, person-centered therapy, psychoanalysis, gestalt therapy, and most others, do not. They're more free flowing and inter-

A good question, which is rarely asked is how treatments work in the real world of clinical practice with diverse populations and competing needs.

personal approaches and thus harder to manualize. For this reason, behavioral and CBT approaches are easier to pitch for grants. A good question, which is rarely, if ever, asked or answered is how these programs actually work in the real world of clinical practice with diverse populations and competing needs. We could write a whole book arguing both sides of this issue, but it is my experience that, with a few top-shelf exceptions, most manualized treatments do not translate well to the client-therapist relationship. Clinicians don't live in the sterile world of a college lab, nor are our clients well represented by the carefully selected subjects necessary for a university-based study.

When it comes to evidenced based medication, the science is supposedly stronger because we're measuring the impact a drug has on a sample group, a procedure that can be easily manualized by type, timing, and dosage and precisely deployed again and again. You give the subject a pill and they take it, no variance. The problem is that nearly every psychopharmaceutical study is funded by the company that owns the experimental drug and is conducted with the primary goal of getting the FDA to approve it. For stimulant medication, the grand exception is the Multimodal Treatment of Attention Deficit Hyperactivity Disorder Study (MTA) discussed in Chapter 9. It was paid for by the National Institute of Mental Health (NIMH), a governmental agency. As noted, the long-term findings for stimulant medication weren't great. We proposed this as proof of stimulant tolerance, but the study's authors made no such attribution. They just left it at "not great."

So, with that in mind, we must ask ourselves whether evidenced-based interventions for ADD are so well proven in clinical practice that they outshine the popular alternatives discussed in this chapter. As one who essentially minored in multivariate statistics and research design in graduate school[261], if I had to sum up the answer in one sentence, I'd say: Not as proven as they need to be, but leaps and bounds ahead of the treatments we'll discuss next.

Evidenced Based: More, Less, and Snake Oil

In a book intended to get you on a successful medication management path, we don't have enough space to debunk every gimmick that has little or no support in the treatment of ADD, but we can list the most popular ones to get you started doing your own research.

Special Diets. We're all for a good diet and there's growing evidence that anti-inflammatory meal plans may stave off health problems. Some people may have allergies to certain foods, like gluten, that could mimic ADD, particularly if there's no history of it in the nuclear or extended family. For these folks, a change in diet could help.

Absent a clearly defined food sensitivity however, there's little evidence that gluten, dairy, refined sugar, or any color of dye underlies

---

[261] You can't really minor in grad school, but I did take every available class at both the master's and doctoral level, meaning about eighteen hours, and I was a dissertation consultant and research assistant.

ADD, as noted in a 2009 article in the Harvard Mental Health newsletter[262]. However, a more recent 2018 meta-analysis[263] of fourteen previous studies[264] did find some efficacy for the "few foods diet" in reducing symptoms in children. The catch here is that the diet is exactly what its name implies, eliminating every item that has an allergenic potential. You can read about it online and consider whether you or your loved one can adhere to it. Just be aware that it should only be implemented under the supervision of a doctor.[265] There's no way to know how many people might benefit from something like this, because the diet is so far removed from most families' daily style of eating.

What little experience we've had in a town with lots of people who love such diets[266] points to a nearly zero hit rate with ADD. Admittedly, this non-scientific pool comes from clients having tried this approach with their kids or other loved ones—often diligently—failing, and then coming in to try our model. So, there might be a bunch of folks we don't know out there doing just fine. All in all, however, we cannot promote dietary restriction as the substantial equivalent of a conventional approach, especially if there's a clear family history of ADD.

Brain Balance. In 2018, NPR's Chris Benderev reported a story for *All Things Considered* on Brain Balance, a supposedly "cutting edge, non-medical and drug-free program" for autism and ADHD. The headline noted it was based on "razor-thin evidence," and in that observation, the author was being kind. The first clue comes when the article notes that in the dozen years it's been in business, Brain Balance now has 113 franchises across the U.S. Yes, the company has trademarked and franchised the name Brain Balance Program. Like McDonalds.

Reporting the story of Natalie and Stephanie, two moms with an autistic child, Benderev goes on to note:

> Brain Balance says, it has helped roughly 25,000 children [and] is currently taking in over $50 million in annual

---

[262] www.health.harvard.edu/newsletter_article/Diet-and-attention-deficit-hyperactivity-disorder

[263] A scientific composite of many different studies on a given topic.

[264] www.ncbi.nlm.nih.gov/pmc/articles/PMC5266211/

[265] www.ncbi.nlm.nih.gov/pmc/articles/PMC4322780/

[266] We have three natural groceries stores in a county of 110,000 people.

revenue. Although Brain Balance isn't the only purveyor of alternative approaches for developmental disorders in the U.S., the scale of the enterprise sets it apart. The company's approach is still relatively new and not widely known, meaning many experts in the field of childhood develop-ment have not vetted its effectiveness.

He adds that Brain Balance has "overstated the scientific evidence in its messaging to families, who can easily spend over $10,000 in six months, a common length of enrollment." The company claims that as these families shell out their cash they're loving everything about the program, giving it an 8.5 satisfaction rating on a scale of 10.

The problem is, feeling satisfied and believing your child is doing better does not an evidenced-based treatment make. People who've spent that kind of money on a treatment are likely to look more favorably upon it simply because they're so vested. In fact, thirty-six of the Brain Balance centers were started by happy customers who presumably saw this as a profitable endeavor, having just dropped $10,000 themselves. A real empirical study of this, or any approach, would include only subjects who had no investment in the treatment and who would then be compared with subjects taking an alternative program with no known benefit. In research we call that a "placebo group" which con-trols for the belief that one is getting better from treatment[267] and not from the illusion of just being in treatment. None of that occurred in any study of Brain Balance.

For those of us used to accompanying clients on the tough road to a better life, the sales pitch on Brain Balance is incredible. Literally. NPR cites a television commercial (yes, they have those) beginning with "a montage of formerly frustrated mothers," who are frustrated no more because Brain Balance has put an end to their kids' challenges. One woman insists "It will completely, absolutely, one hundred percent change your life." No, really. One hundred percent. Change. Your life.

Kelsey and I have found that conventional therapy can change lives, too, and there's research beyond our clinical experience to support

---

[267] Lest readers think I'm holding Brain Balance to an impossible standard, please note that I'm taking these techniques from undergraduate Research Methods 101. This is literally an introductory lesson on a somewhat rigorous research design.

that, including recent findings in the *Journal of Adolescent Health*[268] that indicate stimulant medication is a protective factor for children and teens from academic failure, conduct and oppositional disorders, problems with anxiety and depression, substance abuse, car wrecks, cigarette smoking, and even bipolar disorder. That's pretty life changing. But at no point are we going to propose that our treatment is the great panacea. That's the language of *Madmen* not of science; the kind of thing pharmaceutical companies are prohibited from saying in ads for medication. But in the world of Brain Balance, we're just getting started.

Robert Melillo, a doctor of chiropractic, not only came up with this program, but an entirely new concept of brain functioning to explain it. He calls this "functional disconnection syndrome" and claims in his book *Disconnected Kids* that it underlies every brain disorder from autism to ADHD to dyslexia. Under his model, the two hemispheres of the brain are thought not to be "electrically balanced or synchronized." And that's about all he's going to tell you, except for a series of metaphors about concert orchestras with bad timing or tuning. Melillo claims a "weak right hemisphere" leads to autism while a "weak left hemisphere" causes learning disorders like dyslexia.

Here's the problem. Real neuroscientists do nothing but sit around and study the brain with the most cutting edge technology known to humanity, and nobody has ever come up with this idea except Melillo, who simply envisioned it himself, no science required.

So what happens in Brain Balance? Is there a large machine that zaps your brain with magnetic energy? Nope. That actually exists, by the way. It's called Transcranial Magnetic Stimulation (TMS)[269], and it has an evidence base for treating serious mood disorders. But it has nothing to do with balancing your brain hemispheres, because that's not actually a thing.

Benderev follows Natalie's and Stephanie's son through the program. First, a Brain Balance staff member runs the child through a series of tests to do "a baseline assessment," which generates an eight page report indicating the child has a "weak right hemisphere" and lacks

---

[268] www.psychcongress.com/article/stimulants-may-protect-against-negative-outcomes-adhd

[269] www.mayoclinic.org/tests-procedures/transcranial-magnetic-stimulation/about/pac-20384625

"frontal lobe acquisition." You might want to Google this latter term in order to learn that it doesn't exist. The report also says his "primitive reflexes" are somehow impaired. Primitive reflexes do exist[270], but problems with them are only found in people who have severe conditions like Cerebral Palsy, Parkinson's Disease, or brain injuries. Benderev notes this in his report, citing New York developmental pediatrician Andrew Adesman who opines, "Typically, by one year of age these primitive reflexes have disappeared." Predictably, Dr. Melillo disagrees. When asked, he instead claims:

> "I think they're completely wrong. Pediatricians rarely look at primitive reflexes after infancy, but if they did, they will find that, in many cases, they are still there."

If this isn't making much sense to you, that's because it doesn't make much sense. Saying something about "primitive reflexes," sounds very sciencey, when in fact it's neurological doubletalk. Asked, Melillo also takes issue with the uncontested medical fact that autism, ADHD, and dyslexia have nothing to do with hemispheric differences, but offers no evidence to support his dissent.

The Brain Balance shop recommended a six month treatment to Stephanie and Natalie consisting of one-hour sessions three times a week. The sessions include three areas of focus: academic exercises, nutrition, and "sensory-motor training."

The academic component focuses on the same areas many tutoring programs like Sylvan Learning Centers address. The nutritional component decreases gluten, dairy, and refined sugar and provides optional nutritional supplements and blood tests that can add hundreds of dollars to the cost of the program. When pressed on the lack of evidence for any of this, Melillo claims:

> "I can show you a lot of papers that actually say that there is a relationship between food sensitivities, gluten sensitivity and different types of issues and conditions. So again, it depends on the expert."

He's certainly right about that. Quite a few papers claim this, but few have any scientific basis and none recommend diets that cost $10,000.

---

[270] en.wikipedia.org/wiki/Primitive_reflexes

Brain Balance's third prong is the proprietary part, "sensory-motor training." Parents and former employees describe these as including walking across balance beams, syncing actions with a computerized metronome and being spun in swivel chairs. Benderev describes other interventions:

> For instance, with a "right brain weak" child, like Stephanie and Natalie's son, Brain Balance may have him wear a vibrating armband on his left biceps or eyeglasses that allow light only onto the left visual field. Or they may simply have him stand on his left leg.

The overall cost for this program sounds incredible, but when you compare it to a lifetime on Vyvanse and many sessions of therapy, it wouldn't be a bad deal if it, you know, worked. That's not obvious at first because conventional treatment costs are stretched out over many months and, presuming you have mental health benefits, are covered in part by insurance.

Brain Balance isn't covered by any insurance. That isn't because insurance companies don't care enough about their covered lives to pay for an expensive innovation. NeuroStar has effectively sold their TMS technology to insurance companies based on the long-term cost savings of a treated patient being on less or no medication for some very expensive conditions like bipolar disorder. That's because there's actual empirical evidence that TMS does what it claims. If Brain Balance could prove the same in valid clinical trials, it could save insurance companies billions over conventional approaches. Except they can't.

Melillo disputes this, noting that his centers can "correct these problems completely. We've proved that in research," and that "We use really cutting-edge brain science to address the issue." Except they don't. Benderev reports:

> A dozen experts in autism spectrum disorder, ADHD, dyslexia and childhood psychiatry interviewed by NPR all identified flaws in Brain Balance's approach. They said the company's idea of imbalanced hemispheres was too simplistic and built upon the popular, discredited myth of the logical left brain and the intuitive right brain.
>
> "It doesn't make sense," says Mark Mahone, a pediatric neuropsychologist at the Kennedy Krieger Institute in

Baltimore. "In virtually every activity that one does...both hemispheres of the brain are very, very active. ...It's not as simple as just being a left- or a right-hemisphere problem. Nothing is that simple."

Melillo claims there exist two published studies of Brain Balance, which show that eighty-one percent of children with ADHD no longer displayed symptoms after three months in the program. He has elsewhere claimed this to mean that Brain Balance is evidence-based.

Not surprisingly, Melillo, the guy making the most money on this project, coauthored the first study. He used parents, not independent observers, to rate their own children's improvement in ADHD. He also didn't compare the Brain Balance kids with any control or placebo group. As any undergraduate psych major could tell you, such a study would be unpublishable in a respectable journal, because we cannot know whether the experimental treatment caused the improvement or whether the parents just think their kids are better because they paid $10,000 to make them so.

The second study (kind of) featured a control group of children with ADHD who didn't do Brain Balance, but it compared that group with the same children from the first study published years earlier instead of randomly assigning children into treatment and control groups and testing them at the same time. Worse, Benderev reports that the kids in the treatment and control groups differed in several important ways, most notably that the entire treatment group was medicated while only sixty percent of the controls were. Even worse, at baseline the controls were scored as more severe on an ADHD rating scale than the treatment group. This means the experimental and control groups were wholly incomparable. And yet, even stranger, Benderev adds:

> Though the second study reused the treatment group data from the first study published years earlier, it reported different improvements on those same kids' test scores. The lead author on both studies, Gerry Leisman, a professor of neuro and rehabilitation sciences at the University of Haifa in Israel, explained one of the test score differences as a "reviewer correction" but did not provide explanations for any of the six remaining discrepancies.

This makes the studies not only unpublishable, but laughable. As Dr. James McGough, a professor of clinical psychiatry at UCLA notes, the study "means absolutely nothing. What we have here, in my view, is a marketing piece."

Asked by NPR why Brain Balance hadn't been tested more thoroughly, Melillo claims to have faced a "dilemma," in which he felt obligated to validate his approach, but because he was so certain that Brain Balance worked, he didn't want to deprive his potential clients of such rich benefits while waiting for some silly old clinical trials. He notes, "Families are out there struggling and suffering, and they don't really give a crap about the data or the research, to be quite honest. When they go through it and they see the difference in their child…that's what matters to them." Uh huh. That's how many gallons of snake oil were sold before science and government regulation got involved. Some of it led sick people away from treatments that might have done them some good. And, like snake oil, Brain Balance remains unapproved and uncleared by the FDA to treat any brain disorder, leaving it to exist on faith alone.

Or as Eric Rossen of the National Association of School Psychologists puts it, "Most parents will say they would die for their children. So to say, 'I want to provide some therapy and pay a few thousand dollars' is quite short of dying for them and it's totally reasonable. The problem is [such parents] are easy prey for certain providers that can make promises that cannot necessarily be kept or are not necessarily backed by scientific data." Dr. Susan Hyman, professor of pediatrics at the University of Rochester adds, "If you were to come to a traditional provider who said, 'You know I'm going to have you work really, really, really hard. I might have some drugs. Drugs have side effects. And ninety percent of the time, as an adult, he is still going to have autism,' that's a far less attractive message than 'I can help you.'" Benderev closes his report by noting that Brain Balance's program may not pose physical or developmental harm to children, but it could eat up precious time and money better spent on empirically validated treatments.

Bloomberg did a similar study of Brain Balance in 2018, overlapping and extending this reporting[271]. If you're not convinced, check out

---

[271] www.bloomberg.com/news/features/2018-02-05/how-much-would-you-pay-to-cure-your-kid-s-learning-disability

Science-Based Medicine[272] which thoroughly skewers the entire theory and method.

Neurofeedback. There's been a lot of legitimate science conducted on this one. The most accessible, recent, and balanced article for consumers is by Zawn Villines in the British online publication *Medical News Today*[273]. Villines explains the theory and treatment:

> In a person with ADHD, the brain may display characteristic patterns of behavior, particularly in the frontal lobe. This area is linked with personality, behavior, and learning… Changes in behavior can change the brain, and changes in the brain can change behavior. Neurofeedback aims to change a person's behavior by changing their brain. A practitioner of neurofeedback measures [brain] waves, usually with a device called an electroencephalograph (EEG). There are five types of brain wave: alpha, beta, gamma, delta, and theta. Each has a different frequency, which an EEG can measure. Some research suggests that people with ADHD have more theta waves and fewer beta waves than people without the disorder. In theory, neurofeedback aims to correct this difference.

In clinical treatment, the practitioner attaches a set of EEG electrodes to the client's head allowing a live scan of the client's brain waves to show up on a screen. Before and during treatment, the practitioner and client discuss in depth the target symptoms. The practitioner instructs the client to perform a series of tasks that encourage the brain to process information in different ways. As the brain responds to the stimuli, the feedback on the EEG shows how the stimuli interrupt, change, or increase brain activity. Based on established neurological science, this process is said to slowly alter the brain's waves, impacting a person's behavior and related symptoms of ADHD.

But does it work? As Villines points out, the findings are mixed and confusing. A 2016 meta-analysis on neurofeedback for ADHD concludes:

---

[272] sciencebasedmedicine.org/brain-balance/

[273] www.medicalnewstoday.com/articles/315261.php

Evidence from well-controlled trials with probably blinded outcomes currently fails to support neurofeedback as an effective treatment for ADHD. Future efforts should focus on implementing standard neurofeedback protocols, ensuring learning, and optimizing clinically relevant transfer[274].

I suspect the jury is still out because the literature keeps seesawing back and forth, but for now, the best answer on neurofeedback is, "No, don't pursue this as an alternative treatment for ADD." If you're just itching to give it a try, read the entire Villines article first and do a little more research. Just know you won't find this procedure at our office.

The eTNS System. Let's take a look at the one and only alternative treatment gadget that has FDA approval for treating correctly diagnosed ADD. Manufactured by NeuroSigma, it's called (deep breath) the Monarch external Trigeminal Nerve Stimulation (eTNS) System. It came on the market just as we were writing the first draft of this chapter.

According to an April 2019 press release from Carlos Peña, Ph.D., director of the Division of Neurological and Physical Medicine Devices in the FDA's Center for Devices and Radiological Health, the new device is considered:

A safe, non-drug option for treatment of ADHD in pediatric patients through the use of mild nerve stimulation, a first of its kind. Today's [FDA approval] action reflects our deep commitment to working with device manufacturers to advance the development of pediatric medical devices so that children have access to innovative, safe and effective medical devices that meet their unique needs[275].

At the time of this writing, eTNS was intended for use in children ages seven to twelve who were not, at initiation of treatment, taking stimulants. It's not clear where the FDA came up with that age range, but it's reasonable to guess it reflects the clinical trials performed by

---

[274] www.ncbi.nlm.nih.gov/pubmed/27238063

[275] www.fda.gov/news-events/press-announcements/fda-permits-marketing-first-medical-device-treatment-adhd

NeuroSigma. It's also reasonable to wonder whether it might be effective for older teens and adults. And if it is not, why not?

The cell phone-sized device requires a prescription and is shipped directly to the prescriber's office. The family takes the device home and each evening at bedtime attaches it via a small patch and wire to the child's forehead just above the eyebrows. The child wears this for sixteen weeks, every night of the week. You can imagine how my sixteen-year-old son reacted when I proposed we give this thing a trial run. I had to explain that after the device is switched on, he would not light up like our downtown's Christmas celebration. He would feel only a tingling sensation on his skin. And yet, he remained unimpressed.

The manufacturer explains how eTNS works without resorting to alternative theories of brain functioning or sketchy metaphors. It simply delivers low-level electrical stimulation to the branches of the trigeminal nerve, which send therapeutic signals to the parts of the brain understood by neurologists to be involved in ADD. NeuroSigma and the FDA admit that "the exact mechanism of eTNS is not yet known," but that neuroimaging studies indicate this stimulation increases activity in the brain regions that regulate attention, emotion, and behavior.

While the FDA found enough early evidence to approve the device, that all comes from a single clinical trial conducted over three years using sixty-two children diagnosed with moderate to severe ADD and ADHD. The researchers compared eTNS to a placebo device that wasn't putting out any therapeutic current. The children were randomly assigned to each group and then given either eTNS or the placebo for four weeks. The study was double-blind, meaning that neither researchers nor participants knew who had the real treatment or who had the placebo. Both groups were given norm-referenced ADHD scales to monitor the severity and frequency of symptoms. Subjects who used the eTNS device showed statistically significant improvements in symptoms when compared with the placebo group[276].

So, great! Everyone rush out and give this thing a try. Or not. While the single study that lead to FDA approval was based on gold-standard research procedures (especially compared to the junk science reviewed earlier), it has four serious shortcomings:

---

[276] clinicaltrials.gov/ct2/show/NCT02155608

- **Small sample:** When researchers only include sixty-two children, half in the experiment and half in the control group, the results may be "statistically significant" and still not be meaningful in the clinical population. To enhance confidence in eTNS technology, there needs to be replications of this study and then a meta-analysis to gauge effect size. We hope that will happen, but until it does, families who want to give this a try are essentially joining an experiment.

- **Duration:** The study didn't run very long and well short of the eTNS sixteen week treatment protocol. In fairness, you'd be horrified to learn how short most drug trials are, so this isn't an unusual situation, but it's still worth noting, particularly when testing a completely new technology.

- **Conflict of interest:** NeuroSigma has ties to two of the study's coauthors, one of whom is the company's chief medical officer. As with Brain Balance, when people have a huge financial interest in something they're researching, there's a tendency to find a path to success. NeuroSigma would do well to get eTNS out to some unattached researchers.

- **Researchers didn't compare eTNS to stimulant.** Another key reason why eTNS isn't creating more earth-shattering headlines on the ADD Nightly News is because, so far, they've only proven that it's better than nothing after four weeks. Yawn. At $1,000 a pop, eTNS will only be a game changer if it is easier, safer, more efficient, has fewer side effects, and/or is more effective than conventional approaches.

eTNS isn't cheap, but you do own the unit once it's paid for. Because it's FDA approved, it's also possible that insurance might cover the cost, but at the time of this writing we're still sorting that out[277]. If it's proven to work well enough to reduce or eliminate the need for medication, eTNS could save insurance companies money within a year. But that's a very tall order, and until the device is better proven in real clinical treatment, those insurers may stick with what they know.

With those limitations in mind, we are working with families to try out eTNS. In fact, I wasn't kidding when I suggested my son give it a try, even if he's past the age parameter in the trial group. For now, and

---

[277] As a prescribed, durable medical device, we believe HSA and FSA cards will pay for it.

until better research arrives, we're considering eTNS experimental and recommending it in only three circumstances:

- **When all else fails.** We're trying eTNS in a handful of cases that have proven stimulant resistant. Perhaps the client had a negative reaction to several medications in both classes of stimulant. Maybe there was improvement but also problem side effects, like weight loss no matter how we changed the diet and eating times, or intolerable mood changes.

- **Clients refuse medication.** If, like Janelle, you're bent on an alternative to stimulant treatment, at least stick with something that has preliminary evidence. By that standard, eTNS isn't just the best alternative, it's the only one.

- **On a summer break.** For kids and college-aged adults, summer is the best time to do a stimulant break. However, few clients are ready to just lay around all summer and accomplish nothing. Theoretically, eTNS might be a perfect summer alternative and in fact, we're most likely to try it with my son under that rubric. There are a couple catches, however. First, we have no idea if or how it will work under that condition because it hasn't been tested that way. So, if you try it, you really are, in the vernacular of this book, a guinea pig. Second, summer is at best, twelve weeks long. If one stopped medication and started eTNS after finals in May, the student wouldn't be finished with the treatment until mid-September, well into the school year. If it didn't work, that could spell disaster for the semester.

At the time of this writing, eTNS is an emerging story. We'll keep it updated, along with the rest of this book, on our blog familypsychological.com. Presuming my son is amenable, we'll give you an update on his experience over summer 2020 along with others who are willing to give informed consent to this alternative treatment.

Mindfulness Meditation. We're big fans of this one and not because we're groovy and Zen. Neither Kelsey nor I are really the kind of people who have Buddhist bells on our shelves and take retreats to Esalen. We like mindfulness meditation because the research on the practice, when combined with cognitive therapy, is solid. Two therapies we've referenced elsewhere in this book—Dialectical Behavior Therapy

(DBT) and Acceptance and Commitment Therapy (ACT)—include mindfulness meditation as core components of treatment.

Given the way in which ADD impacts focus, concentration, awareness, intentionality, and decision making, a lot of research has been done on how mindfulness could be used to treat it. Though not a meta-analysis, a 2015 article by Mitchell, Zylowska, & Kollins[278] has a good list of past studies on the topic as well as original research findings. The authors conclude:

> Overall, current empirical studies support the rationale for application of mindfulness to ADHD, show that mindfulness is a feasible and well-accepted intervention in ADHD samples, and provide promising preliminary support for its efficacy. However, more methodologically rigorous trials are needed, particularly larger randomized controlled trials and assessment of long-term effects with ecologically valid measures. In addition to being a standalone treatment, mindfulness can be integrated with CBT for adults diagnosed with ADHD, which is an area that warrants future treatment development.

Unfortunately, a newer meta-analysis published in 2018[279] countered this position by pointing out the poor quality of existing research, noting:

> Despite statistically significant effects on ADHD combined core symptoms, due to paucity of [randomly controlled trials], heterogeneity across studies and lack of studies at low risk of [research] bias, there is insufficient methodologically sound evidence to support meditation-based therapies for ADHD.

We think mindfulness is essential for people with ADD. I spoke of it in *I Always Want to Be Where I'm Not*, and with more experience and training, I'll double down on that in the next revision of that book. So, please, go out and do it. But don't consider it an alternative treatment in and of itself. There's no reliable evidence that meditation will allow

---

[278] www.ncbi.nlm.nih.gov/pmc/articles/PMC4403871/

[279] www.ncbi.nlm.nih.gov/pubmed/29991532

you or your loved one to manage ADD medicine-free. It's just one component in the larger treatment.

Cognitive Behavioral Therapy (CBT). Cognitive behavioral therapy has been a boon to folks with ADD. Acceptance and Commitment Therapy (ACT), the third wave of this approach, is particularly well suited to helping clients with ADD cope better with daily demands. As I stressed in *I Always Want to Be Where I'm Not*, taking medication without out therapy is like filling your car up with gas and driving around and around the parking lot all day.

While the validity of CBT is, as I noted at the beginning of this chapter, stuck in a chasm between university research and real world practice, there's no doubt that cognitive methods offer a rich foundation upon which to build a good therapy for ADD and ADHD. Your therapist just has to make the delivery more interesting and engaging than the manual it comes from. ACT, with its lively metaphors and engaging synthesis of theories, makes that a lot easier to do.

That said, some of my brothers and sisters in psychology and the related mental health disciplines have at times pitched CBT as a standalone alternative to integrated treatment for ADD. This makes little sense. As a neurological condition, ADD is impervious to behavioral or cognitive change unless you can change the brain functioning itself to take advantage of those therapeutic influences.

Even the American Psychological Association, superhero of CBT, agrees that therapy alone isn't very effective for treating ADD without medication[280]. The footnoted article cites Russell Ramsay, PhD, associate professor of psychology and co-director of the Adult ADHD Treatment and Research Program at the University of Pennsylvania School of Medicine. Ramsay actually wrote the book *Nonmedication Treatments for Adult ADHD,* yet in that article, he cites the case of Brody, a thirty-nine-year-old father with two young children who found he needed medication as well as therapy. Ramsay notes:

> "Brody's experience is common for adults with ADHD who try cognitive-behavioral therapy without medication. Therapy can be very helpful in teaching time management and organization skills, but ADHD symptoms can lead to

---

[280] www.apa.org/monitor/2012/03/adult-adhd.aspx

late or missed appointments, failure to complete home-work, and little progress on a treatment plan. Medication in conjunction with therapy can help bring ADHD symp-toms under control through life coaching skills and coun-seling for underlying negative thoughts that can lead to procrastination and frustration."

Remarkably, there hasn't been a lot of research comparing stimulants with CBT alone versus in integrative treatment for ADD. The most recent meta-analysis comments on this lack of research, before con-cluding:

> Clinical differences may exist between the pharmacological and non-pharmacological treatment used for the manage-ment of ADHD. Uncertainties about therapies and the bal-ance between benefits, costs and potential harms should be considered before starting treatment. There is an urgent need for high-quality randomized trials of the multiple treatments for ADHD in children and adolescents[281].

A short synopsis of this study was reported by Devon Frye for *ADDi-tude* magazine.[282] Our position continues to be that for maximum ben-efit, one should do both.

If you and your people find any of these alternatives are working for you, don't quit them on our account. We didn't write this book to talk anyone out of any form of treatment. We wrote it to teach how we work with cases ranging from easy and straight forward to difficult and perplexing by integrating methods that are widely accepted but can be hard to bring together under one roof. If conventional isn't your style, you're free to walk the road less traveled. But, having finished this chapter, you can no longer say you weren't warned about the good, bad, and ugly of alternative approaches to ADD. Conventional ways may be boring, but when it comes to brain science, boring can be a pretty cool deal.

---

281 www.ncbi.nlm.nih.gov/pubmed/28700715

282 www.additudemag.com/study-behavior-therapy-medication-effective-adhd-treatment/

Keep the Faith

When I first took ADHD medications it was just like the first time I got glasses…the world came into focus. I just wish I could have had them forty years ago. My life would be very different.

– Anonymous[283]

- Dr. Wes -

I just finished texting with Tressa (Chapter 4). She aired her lamentation of the daily ups and downs of ADD, autism, mood dysregulation, and anxiety. When asked, she said I could share those thoughts with our readers. Tressa:

I don't know how to explain my mental health to other people. I can't read the text for science class because it's too dense. Too many words shoved onto a white screen, and I can't comprehend that. I can't seem to explain my anxiety towards the smallest things. I'm unable to communicate why a spider can stress me out to the point of a panic attack. There might be spiders in my bed, and other bugs too. Socially, I can't seem to connect the same way as others. I feel like I'm missing some piece of a conversation. That piece seems to hold me back, but nothing's there. But I can't seem to identify that piece of nothing. I see there's a lot of can'ts written in here, but that's what my brain seems to do. If I could explain it better, I would.

---

[283] www.adhdawarenessmonth.org/survey-quotes/

She remains in the middle of a storm Kelsey and I have encountered many times before, and we know that even when success seems distant and failure preordained, the world keeps spinning, and if you stay the course and keep running the experiment, things really can turn out okay in the end. Of course, Tressa doesn't know that yet, because when you're in the eye of the hurricane, it's hard to imagine the sun ever shining.

Reading her text got me to thinking. Perhaps the best way to close out this book would be to allow those with ADD, who've weathered that same storm, have their say. We sent out a request to clients for anonymous comment and got back more material than we could possibly use, so I apologize to those who contributed and weren't included.

Don't look at these comments as testimonials to our practice. We aren't guaranteeing anything will "absolutely one hundred percent change your life, absolutely." See them as reflecting a success that comes not from our special secret sauce, but from optimizing in clinical practice what the scientific literature tells us will work. Yes, it helps to have a clinic set up the way ours is, but there's not much in this book that you, a willing prescriber, and a trained therapist can't piece together on your own. We've given you the map. You just have to go out and work your way through it. Let these short essays serve as inspiration to find a thousand better tomorrows waiting ahead.

Lori: I first realized that maybe I needed to start doing something to improve my focus while I was in graduate school. I was fortunate enough to have never struggled in school until then because I never had to study or try and I had always really liked learning. Suddenly, I had to try, and I found I couldn't get anything done. My grades were suffering, my anxiety was through the roof, and I couldn't get myself to sit down and complete any of my school work. Initially, I thought it was anxiety and depression and began seeking treatment for that, but it just wasn't helping. One day, I talked to my brother who'd been diagnosed with ADD as a child. He told me how much better his life was on stimulants, and that's when it kind of clicked for me.

I started thinking about incidents in my past, how I had to take a coloring book to my high school classes so I wouldn't interrupt my teachers. How I never did my assignment until the last second because I "performed better under stress." How I self-medicated with caffeine to the point that my friends joked, "We're going to bring a twelve-pack of Mountain Dew and Monster Energy Drinks to your funeral," because I obviously couldn't be without them, even in death. So, I took one of those online surveys to see if I might have ADD/ADHD and I checked almost every single box for signs of ADHD.

I was terrified to go to the doctor, convinced she would suspect me of being just another college student trying to get legal speed to study. Finally I went in. I started seeing results within the next few days. I still had bad studying habits, but I could actually focus long enough in class and while reading to get my assignments done. I started sleeping better because my brain could focus during the day and then shut off at night and I started to feel awake the next day. My anxiety dropped to a manageable level because I wasn't in a constant state of "I need to do this but I can't get it done." I finished my master's degree and started my career. I can focus at work, while driving, when talking to others, and best of all, I can process my own thoughts.

Life isn't perfect now. I still have difficulties with ADHD even on medication. I still procrastinate. I still struggle to remain undistracted in some situations. I still have to keep my hands busy when I sit for long periods of time. But, now that I can manage my ADHD, I function so much better.

Amanda: As an adult, dealing with ADD is a constant and evolving process. Successful and fulfilling interactions professionally and personally rely on the social currencies of consistency, reliability, and thoughtfulness. These are areas of weakness when you can't channel your focus where you'd prefer it to be. Before treatment, I didn't recognize ADD as the root of many of my biggest frustrations. I couldn't understand or predict when I would fail to meet expectations in relationships. Communicating was a frustrating process full of misunderstandings and, as a result, there were a lot of bewildering and heartbreaking interactions and consequences. With treatment, it's like having an interpreter to navigate these situations. The act of meeting social and professional expectations may not come naturally to me, but I can at least predict and understand them.

Jordan: When I first reached out to get help, it was for anxiety. Therapy helped me understand the kind of situations that caused me the most anxiety. In those conversations, it became pretty obvious that focusing in school, work, or any normal environment was very hard for me. I knew I had ADD but I didn't realize it played such a big role in my stress and anxiousness. My mom was very skeptical at first about me getting on medication. She didn't like the idea at all. But I made the decision myself and after seeing such a great difference, she now understands that meds help with so many aspects of my life. They've allowed me to focus and prioritize homework and everyday activities so I don't feel so distracted and anxious with everything around me. I always thought I was going to struggle in college, playing a sport and going to class, but here I am and for the first time, I see myself really succeeding.

Trey: Although I was not officially diagnosed until age thirty-seven, I long suspected ADHD played a role in my life. However, thinking I may have it and learning from a professional that it is in fact true are two completely different things. It was such a relief, honestly, because it helped explain my erratic behavior that was, at times, deeply upsetting to me and those around me. But what I have learned is that while it's not my fault I have ADHD, it's up to me to accept it, learn about it, and instead of using it as a crutch to blame my behavior on, discover how it affects me in every setting I am in and not let it control my life and the lives of those around me.

Susan: Since beginning my ADD medication one year ago, along with monthly check ins, my life is much more balanced. Prior to my diagnosis, I assumed that my condition was chronic depression as it had been a constant in my life. Turns out, it was my inability to focus and deal with stimuli from the outside world that had me feeling those daily negative emotions. Since being treated, the range in my days is as close to normal as I can imagine. Some days are great, some are not, but in most, I'm just a busy single working mother trying to figure it all out. With treatment, I'm just more capable of doing so.

Soraya. I've had ADD and terrible anxiety for as long as I can remember. I felt like my ADD and anxiety were always at odds with each other. I was never a very good student, and I knew I could do so much more. But when I was first diagnosed, I was only given a prescription and left to my own devices.

After starting college, I knew I needed to try harder. I did the best I could on my own before seeking treatment to learning how to work with my ADD. From day one of therapy, I was coaxed (maybe shoved) outside my comfort zone, which my therapist warned me about, but which is always hard for me. But all that pushing, along with better medication management, allowed me to be more successful in school and work. Today, I'm more organized and less nervous about doing all those things that come easy to others and never did to me. With greater confidence in myself, I've also met so many new people. It's very satisfying to see how much I've accomplished.

Carter: After much speculation, I've concluded that the best way to relay the value of having guidance on navigating life with ADHD is through a zombie apocalypse metaphor in which I imagine that I never had therapy or took medication for ADHD. If all world order suddenly came crashing down and we were to fight for our lives or die, I would (sans therapy and meds) quickly be killed through post-apocalyptic natural selection. By design, I am not a strategist; I feel like a slug all the time, both physically and mentally; my self-awareness is perpetually five seconds late, and I lack the energy and wit to execute all my brilliant ideas.

Now let's alter the scenario and say that I haven't gone to therapy, but I did get a prescription for Vyvanse, that medication that gave rise to my razor-sharp mind and unfailing stamina. That would solve everything in the zombie apocalypse until an enemy caravan comes along and steals my stimulant stash. Game over. Too bad I never went to therapy and never learned to manage any of my symptoms.

Thankfully, in the real world, I have gone to therapy, and if the apocalypse suddenly presented itself, I would probably kick ass. I've learned to be strategic because I've worked with a professional to analyze all the dumb stuff I've done so I can look ahead and not do it again, making me a seasoned veteran of foreseeing disastrous chain reactions and curbing fallouts before they escalate. I know various conditions that eventually result in self-destruction, like irregular sleep and following reasonable expectations. Ultimately, therapy with an ADHD-specialist has been the best training program for survival in any sort of cataclysmic undoing, whether in an imaginary future or the one waiting for me tomorrow.

Emily: I was put on stimulant medication at a very pivotal point in my life, as a rising senior in college and battling insidious depression and anxiety. What was missing however, was the treatment of my underlying ADD. Once on medication and in therapy, I became a more purposeful person who can participate at a higher level of functioning in work, school, and life in general. I was less haphazard in my way of going about things, and I could better hone-in and focus my efforts instead of running in circles chasing my own tail. It helped me become more organized in my thoughts and actions, allowing me to start and complete nursing school and pass nursing boards with relative ease. It wasn't stims alone that got me through school, but also my support system, frequent medication monitoring and teaching, and therapy. I had to learn how to utilize my meds so I could perform at my highest level and become successful. With ADD medicine comes great power and that requires great responsibility.

Linda: I first sought help as a sophomore in college when I started struggling academically. I was having a really difficult time waking up for class and when I did make it to campus, I'd often doze during lectures. I had always been good at school and maintained a near perfect GPA. I took medication for depression as a child and continued med management until I moved away for college, so I figured I just needed to get back on antidepressants. Seeking treatment as an adult, I realized that my failures in college were really symptoms of combined ADD and anxiety. At the direction of my therapist, I was additionally tested for and diagnosed with narcolepsy and night terrors, so stimulants become doubly vital to my functioning. Having to take breaks from them is especially hard. However, I know that's necessary because I start regressing back to old patterns when my body has built up some resistance to them.

My biggest "tell" that it was time to take a break was when I was in school trying to write papers. I would spend hours in front of the computer but my thoughts didn't seem to make sense or want to come out as coherent words on the page. Consequently, I would fib to professors, claiming I submitted the paper by the due date and was just as perplexed as they were, wondering why it never arrived in an email I never really sent. Medication treatment and therapy have made a remarkable difference in my life. I have no doubt that without it, I would not have survived the demands of my undergraduate program let alone achieved a master's degree.

Ashlyn: In the relatively short time I've been learning to navigate the world of being medicated for ADD, I have learned how to be proud of myself and how to be horrified of the person I once was prior to treatment. You lose a lot of opportunities in life when dates, dead-lines, and meeting times aren't acknowledged as hard-and-fast rules but merely things to later punish yourself for missing or messing up. My ability to simultaneously be present in what I am doing but to also see value in forward, future-thinking is new and welcome, but I am realizing this does not happen inherently with my brain. Thus, the basis for the love/hate relationship with medication. Every morning I want to *believe* that my brain can perform just as well unmedicated, and sometimes I pause before I take my medication. "Maybe today will be different," I whisper. But while I know I have the best intentions to be that person who is dependable, efficient, and consistently motivated, I know that just isn't the genetic hand I was dealt. So, I do the right thing and I take my medication, even if begrudgingly, every day. I am a better person, employee, and partner for it.

Don: Therapy was the only way I became able to understand that most of my "anxiety" symptoms were adult ADHD. This lead me to a path of research, reflection, and patience with myself. With courage I trusted my prescriber's suggestion of medication and it became my "lightbulb" moment. It was only then when my thoughts were clear enough to make this distinction, that I felt like my best self, and a sense of contentment came over me like I had never felt in my entire life. I was educated, I'd done well in life, I knew what I was *supposed* to be thinking, but I just couldn't get there without that constant brain loop and self-doubt of ADHD. I realized that these waves of intolerable, uncomfortable emotions and emotional avoidance were lasting too long. With medication the intolerable was now tolerable. My vibrant personality was still present. I am forever grateful for the diagnosis that changed my life and the lives of people closest to me.

Look for updates to this book at:

www.familypsychological.com

Index

American Academy of Pediatrics, 49, 93

American Psychiatric Association, 49, 51, 93, 129, 135, 153-54, 286

American Psychological Association (APA), 99, 116, 332

Americans with Disabilities Act (ADA), 76, 291

amphetamine(s), 174-75, 179-84, 187, 193, 208, 228, 263, 273, 296, 302, 308

anorexia nervosa, 258

anticonvulsants, 201, 210

antidepressants, 111, 152, 178, 191, 204, 308, 339

antipsychotics, 153, 210
    atypical, 210-13

Antisocial Personality Disorder (ASPD), 126-31, 144

anxiety, 52, 54, 62-5, 105-110, 117-18, 173, 201-8, 288

anxiety disorder, 51, 64, 192

Anxious-ADD, 64-5, 106-7

Aptensio XR, 189

aripiprazole, 201, 212

Ativan, 100, 201-3, 310

autism, 40, 53-4, 56, 110, 319, 321-22, 325, 334

Autism Spectrum Disorder (ASD), 54, 118-22, 125, 136-38, 143, 145, 323

Barkley Scales, 82-3

behavioral activation, 100

behavioral dependency, 203

bell curve, 55, 62

Benadryl, 214, 255

Benderev, Chris, 319, 321-25

benzodiazepines, 202-05, 214, 216, 233, 308, 310

Big Pharma, 43, 236, 248, 264, 293, 294

Bipolar Disorder (BiD), 40-1, 86-88, 97-8, 104, 113-18, 122, 132, 138-9, 143-45, 152, 170, 195, 209-13, 263, 272, 321, 323

Bipolar II Disorder, 54, 86, 103

blood peak level, 188

blood pressure medications, 210, 211

Body Mass Index (BMI), 258, 262

Borderline Personality Disorder, 98, 126-42

Brain Balance, 314, 319-26, 329

About The Authors

Wes Crenshaw, PhD is a licensed psychologist and board-certified in Couple and Family Psychology by the American Board of Professional Psychology. He specializes in working with adolescents, young adults, and their families from his private practice, Family Psychological Services, LLC in Lawrence, Kansas. In addition to this book, he is the author of *Treating Families and Children in the Child Protective System* (Brunner-Routledge, 2004), and *I Always Want to Be Where I'm Not: Successful Living with ADD and ADHD* (Family Psychological Press). He also appears occasionally on public radio stations across the  nation and regularly in the Kansas City and St. Louis metros both on radio and TV. He writes regularly for *ADDitude* magazine. You can learn more about his work at www.dr-wes.com, follow his tweets of pithy wisdom about ADD, teens, parenting, dating, divorce, marriage, and young adulthood at @wescrenshawphd, or read his blog at familypsychological.com.

Kelsey Daugherty, DNP PMHNP is a board-certified nurse practitioner specializing in psychiatric medication management. She works with Dr. Wes and nine other therapists at Family Psychological Services, LLC in Lawrence, Kansas prescribing psychopharmaceuticals including stimulant medication on protocol. She did her doctoral research project on stimulant tolerance and has coauthored several articles in *ADDitude* magazine. She consults worldwide via video on complex cases of ADD, ADHD, and co-occurring mental health disorders.

CPSIA information can be obtained
at www.ICGtesting.com
Printed in the USA
BVHW011808181121
621977BV00002B/73